BOTH FLESH AND NOT

ALSO BY DAVID FOSTER WALLACE

The Broom of the System

Girl with Curious Hair

Infinite Jest

A Supposedly Fun Thing I'll Never Do Again

Brief Interviews with Hideous Men

Everything and More

Oblivion

Consider the Lobster

McCain's Promise

This Is Water

The Pale King

BOTH FLESH AND NOT

Essays

David Foster Wallace

175 LB YEARS

Little, Brown and Company

New York Boston London

Little, Brown and Company
Hachette Book Group
237 Park Avenue, New York, NY 10017
www.hachettebookgroup.com

First Edition: November 2012

Little, Brown and Company is a division of Hachette Book Group, Inc., and is celebrating its 175th anniversary in 2012. The Little, Brown name and logo are trademarks of Hachette Book Group, Inc.

The publisher is not responsible for websites (or their content) that are not owned by the publisher.

Copyright acknowledgments appear on pages 326–327.

Library of Congress Cataloging-in-Publication Data

Wallace, David Foster.
Both flesh and not : essays / David Foster Wallace.—1st ed.
p. cm.
ISBN 978-0-316-18237-9 (hc) / 978-0-316-22411-6 (large print) /
978-0-316-22514-4 (international)
I. Title.
PS3573.A425635B58 2012
814'.54—dc23 2012020794

10 9 8 7 6 5 4 3 2 1

RRD-C

Book design by Marie Mundaca
Printed in the United States of America

CONTENTS

PUBLISHER'S NOTE

Readers familiar with David Foster Wallace's work know that he possessed an insatiable love for words and their meanings. On his computer he constantly updated a list of words that he wanted to learn, culling from numerous sources and writing brief definitions and usage notes. A selection from this vocabulary list appears before each essay of *Both Flesh and Not.*

It was one of the great thrills of Wallace's life to be invited to serve on the Usage Panel of *The American Heritage Dictionary.* The definitions in his vocabulary list reprinted here are quoted or paraphrased from that excellent reference work.

BOTH FLESH AND NOT

abattoir—slaughterhouse or slaughterhousish **abrogate** (adj.)—abol
ding leaves and stems **accoutre** (v.)—to outfit and equip, especially for
egary **Achates**—a loyal friend; faithful companion to Aeneas in *The Ae*
e.g., ovaries & uterus **adumbrate** (v.)—to give a sketchy outline of; to
adj.)—word that expresses opposition or antithesis: the adversative con
tool **aerobe**—organism requiring oxygen to live **affined** (adj.)—linked
afterclap—unexpected, often unpleasant sequel to a matter that had I
tor—avenging deity or spirit **albescent** (adj.)—becoming white or pale
dosteronism—disorder that causes weakness, cardiac irregularities, etc.
liquids **alible**—having nutrients, nourishing **aliform** (adj.)—shaped like
"a [huge] pipe that looked like an alpenhorn" **altricial**—helpless, naked,
contains the tooth sockets **amalgam**—alloy of mercury with silver or tin
amandine **amaurosis**—loss of vision w/o damage to eye; (adj.) amaurotic
amentia—insufficient mental development **amontillado**—pale dry sherry
and Romans to carry wine and oil **anabatic**—relating to rising wind cur
on others; "anaclitic" **anchorite**—religious hermit **androgyne**—an androg
of twists and turns; tortuous **anlage**—axiom, fundamental principle, foun
heat...via process for tempering glass **anosmia**—loss of sense of smell
opposite sides of world **antipode**—direct or diametrical opposite **an**
dai—traditional Vietnamese woman's dress: long tunic that's split along
tive **apocarpous**—flower with two or more distinct pistils, like roses **apoc**
phal rumors" **apophasis**—allusion to something by denying that it will

ished or annulled by authority **abscission**—act of cutting off plants' shed-
military duty **acerose**—needlelike, as in pine needles, etc. **acetous**—vin-
neid **adnexal** (adj. of adnexa)—accessory or adjoining anatomical parts;
disclose vaguely or partly; q.v. "adumbration" **adversative** (both n. and
junction "but"; "he put out a string of adversatives" **adz**—axlike carpentry
by very close relationship; q.v. "affinity" **affray**—noisy quarrel or brawl
been considered closed **akimbo**—hands on hips and elbows out **alas-**
aldosterone—hormone that regulates salt-v.-water balance of body **al-**
alembic—chemist's device w/ two vessels connected by tube for distilling
a wing **alpenhorn**—horn so huge you have to lay the front on the ground;
and blind when hatched; "altricial birds" **alveolar**—part of the jaw that
amandine—means there's almonds in a dish or as garnish for dish: trout
ambeer—saliva w/ tobacco juice **ambeer**—spittle colored w/ tobacco
from Spain **amphora**—two-handled jug w/ slender neck used by Greeks
rents (speed, or direction upward?) **anaclisis**—psychological dependence
ynous person **anent**—regarding, concerning, w/r/t **anfractuous**—full
dation for further development **anneal**—to strengthen or toughen via
antimacassar—doily for head/arms on armchair **antipodal**—situated on
trorse—directed forward and upward, as in the hairs on certain plants **ao**
sides and worn over loose trousers **aperient** (adj.)—acting as gentle laxa-
ryphal—of dubious authorship or reliability; fictitious; "wildly apocry-
be mentioned: "I will not bring up my opponent's shady financial history"

FEDERER BOTH FLESH AND NOT

Almost anyone who loves tennis and follows the men's tour on television has, over the last few years, had what might be termed Federer Moments. These are times, watching the young Swiss at play, when the jaw drops and eyes protrude and sounds are made that bring spouses in from other rooms to see if you're OK. The Moments are more intense if you've played enough tennis to understand the impossibility of what you just saw him do. We've all got our examples. Here is one. It's the finals of the 2005 U.S. Open, Federer serving to Andre Agassi early in the fourth set. There's a medium-long exchange of groundstrokes, one with the distinctive butterfly shape of today's power-baseline game, Federer and Agassi yanking each other from side to side, each trying to set up the baseline winner... until suddenly Agassi hits a hard heavy cross-court back hand that pulls Federer way out wide to his ad (= his left) side, and Federer gets to it but slices the stretch backhand short, a couple feet past the service line, which of course is the sort of thing Agassi dines out on, and as Federer's scrambling to reverse and get back to center, Agassi's moving in to take the short ball on the rise, and he smacks it hard right back into the same ad corner, trying to wrong-foot Federer, which in fact he does—Federer's still near the corner but running toward the centerline, and the ball's heading to a point behind him now, where he just was, and there's no time to turn his body around, and Agassi's following the shot in to the net at an angle from the backhand side...and what Federer now does is somehow instantly reverse thrust and sort of skip backward three or four steps, impossibly fast, to hit a forehand out of his backhand corner, all his weight moving backward, and the forehand is a topspin screamer down the line past Agassi at net, who lunges for it but the ball's past him, and it flies straight down the sideline and lands exactly in the deuce corner of Agassi's side, a winner—Federer's still dancing backward as it lands. And there's that familiar little second of shocked silence from the New York crowd before it erupts, and John McEnroe with his color man's headset on TV says (mostly to himself, it sounds like), "How do you hit a winner from that position?" And he's right: given Agassi's position and world-class quickness, Federer had to send that ball down a two-inch pipe of space in order to pass him, which he did, moving backward, with no setup time and none of his weight behind the shot. It was impossible. It was like something out of *The Matrix*. I don't know what-all sounds were involved, but my spouse says she hurried in and there was popcorn all over the couch and I was down on one knee and my eyeballs looked like novelty-shop eyeballs.

Anyway, that's one example of a Federer Moment, and that

was merely on TV—and the truth is that TV tennis is to live tennis pretty much as video porn is to the felt reality of human love.

Journalistically speaking, there is no hot news to offer you about Roger Federer. He is, at twenty-five, the best tennis player currently alive. Maybe the best ever. Bios and profiles abound. *60 Minutes* did a feature on him just last year. Anything you want to know about Mr. Roger N.M.I. Federer—his background, his hometown of Basel, his parents' sane and unexploitative support of his talent, his junior tennis career, his early problems with fragility and temper, his beloved junior coach, how that coach's accidental death in 2002 both shattered and annealed Federer and helped make him what he now is, Federer's thirty-nine career singles titles, his eight Grand Slams, his unusually steady and mature commitment to the girlfriend who travels with him (which on the men's tour is rare) and handles his affairs (which on the men's tour is unheard-of), his old-school stoicism and mental toughness and good sportsmanship and evident overall decency and thoughtfulness and charitable largesse—it's all just a Google search away. Knock yourself out.

This present article is more about a spectator's experience of Federer, and its context. The specific thesis here is that if you've never seen the young man play live, and then do, in person, on the sacred grass of Wimbledon, through the literally withering heat and then wind and rain of the '06 fortnight, then you are apt to have what one of the tournament's press bus drivers describes as a "bloody near-religious experience." It may be tempting, at first, to hear a phrase like this as just one more of the overheated tropes that people resort to as they try to describe the feeling of Federer Moments. But the driver's phrase turns out to be true—literally, for an instant ecstatically—though it takes some time and serious watching to see this truth emerge.

Beauty is not the goal of competitive sports, but high-level sports are a prime venue for the expression of human beauty. The relation is roughly that of courage to war.

The human beauty we're talking about here is beauty of a particular type; it might be called kinetic beauty. Its power and appeal are universal. It has nothing to do with sex or cultural norms. What it seems to have to do with, really, is human beings' reconciliation with the fact of having a body.[1]

Of course, in men's sports no one ever talks about beauty, or grace, or the body. Men may profess their "love" of sports, but that love must always be cast and enacted in the symbology

[1] There's a great deal that's bad about having a body. If this is not so obviously true that no one needs examples, we can just quickly mention pain, sores, odors, nausea, aging, gravity, sepsis, clumsiness, illness, limits—every last schism between our physical wills and our actual capacities. Can anyone doubt we need help being reconciled? Crave it? It's your body that dies, after all.

There are wonderful things about having a body, too, obviously—it's just that these things are much harder to feel and appreciate in real time. Rather like certain kinds of rare, peak-type sensuous epiphanies ("I'm so glad I have eyes to see this sunrise!," etc.), great athletes seem to catalyze our awareness of how glorious it is to touch and perceive, move through space, interact with matter. Granted, what great athletes can do with their bodies are things that the rest of us can only dream of. But these dreams are important—they make up for a lot.

of war: elimination vs. advance, hierarchy of rank and standing, obsessive stats and technical analysis, tribal and/or nationalist fervor, uniforms, mass noise, banners, chest-thumping, face-painting, etc. For reasons that are not well understood, war's codes are safer for most of us than love's. You too may find them so, in which case Spain's mesomorphic and totally martial Rafael Nadal is the man's man for you—he of the unsleeved biceps and Kabuki self-exhortations. Plus Nadal is also Federer's nemesis, and the big surprise of this year's Wimbledon, since he's a clay-court specialist and no one expected him to make it past the first few rounds here. Whereas Federer, through the semifinals, has provided no surprise or competitive drama at all. He's outplayed each opponent so completely that the TV and print press are worried his matches are dull and can't compete effectively with the nationalist fervor of the World Cup.[2]

July 9's men's final, though, is everyone's dream. Nadal vs. Federer is a replay of last month's French Open final, which Nadal won. Federer has so far lost only four matches all year, but they've all been to Nadal. Still, most of these matches have been on slow clay, Nadal's best surface. Grass is Federer's best. On the other hand, the first week's heat has baked out some of the Wimbledon courts' slickness and made them slower. There's

[2] The U.S. media here are especially worried because no Americans of either sex survived into even the quarterfinals this year. (If you're into obscure statistics, it's the first time this has happened at Wimbledon since 1911.)

also the fact that Nadal has adjusted his clay-based game to grass—moving in closer to the baseline on his groundstrokes, amping up his serve, overcoming his allergy to the net. He beat the absolute shit out of Agassi in the third round. The networks are in ecstasies. Before the match, on Centre Court, behind the glass slits above the south backstop, as the linesmen are coming out on court in their new Ralph Lauren uniforms that look so much like children's navalwear, the broadcast commentators can be seen practically bouncing up and down in their chairs. This Wimbledon final's got the revenge narrative, the king-vs.-regicide dynamic, the stark character contrasts. It's the passionate machismo of southern Europe versus the intricate clinical artistry of the north. Dionysus and Apollo. Cleaver and scalpel. Southpaw and righty. Numbers 2 and 1 in the world. Nadal, the man who's taken the modern power-baseline game just as far as it goes...versus a man who's transfigured that modern game, whose precision and variety are as big a deal as his pace and foot-speed, but who may be peculiarly vulnerable to, or psyched out by, that first man. A British sportswriter, exulting with his mates in the press section, says, twice, "It's going to be a war."

Plus it's in the cathedral of Centre Court. And the men's final is always on the fortnight's second Sunday, the symbolism of which Wimbledon emphasizes by always omitting play on the first Sunday. And the spattery gale that has knocked over parking signs and everted umbrellas all morning suddenly quits an hour before match time, the sun emerging just as Centre Court's tarp is rolled back and the net posts are driven home.

Federer and Nadal come out to applause, make their ritual bows to the nobles' box. The Swiss is in the buttermilk-colored sport coat that Nike's gotten him to wear for Wimbledon this year. On Federer, and perhaps on him alone, it doesn't look absurd with shorts and sneakers. The Spaniard eschews all warm-up clothing, so you have to look at his muscles right away. He and the Swiss are both in all-Nike, up to the very same kind of tied white Nike hankie with the swoosh positioned right above the third eye. Nadal tucks his hair under his hankie, but Federer doesn't, and smoothing and fussing with the bits of hair that fall over the hankie is the main Federer tic TV viewers get to see; likewise Nadal's obsessive retreat to the ballboy's towel between points. There happen to be other tics and habits, though, tiny perks of live viewing. There's the great care Roger Federer takes to hang the sport coat over his spare courtside chair's back, just so, to keep it from wrinkling—he's done this before each match here, and something about it seems childlike and weirdly sweet. Or the way he inevitably changes out his racket sometime in the second set, the new one always in the same clear plastic bag closed with blue tape, which he takes off carefully and always hands to a ballboy to dispose of. There's Nadal's habit of constantly picking his long shorts out of his bottom as he bounces the ball before serving, his way of always cutting his eyes warily from side to side as he walks the baseline, like a convict expecting to be shanked. And something odd on the Swiss's serve, if you look very closely. Holding ball and racket out in front, just before starting the motion, Federer always places the ball precisely in the V-shaped gap of the racket's throat, just below the head, just for an instant. If the fit isn't perfect, he adjusts the ball until it is. It happens very fast, but also every time, on both first serves and second.

Nadal and Federer now warm each other up for precisely ten minutes; the umpire keeps time. There's a very definite order and etiquette to these pro warm-ups, which is something that television has decided you're not interested in seeing. Centre Court holds thirteen thousand and change. Another several thousand have done what people here do willingly every year, which is to pay a stiff General Admission at the gate and then gather, with hampers and mosquito spray, to watch the match on an enormous TV screen outside Court 1. Your guess here is probably as good as anyone's.

Right before play, up at the net, there's a ceremonial coin-toss to see who'll serve first. It's another Wimbledon ritual. The honorary coin-tosser this year is William Caines, assisted by the umpire and tournament referee. William Caines is a seven-year-old from Kent who contracted liver cancer at age two and somehow survived after surgery and horrific chemo. He's here representing Cancer Research UK. He's blond and pink-cheeked and comes up to about Federer's waist. The crowd roars its approval of the honorary toss. Federer smiles distantly the whole time. Nadal, just across the net, keeps dancing in place like a boxer, swinging his arms from side to side. I'm not sure whether the U.S. networks show the coin-toss or not, whether this ceremony's part of their contractual obligation or whether they get to cut to commercial. As William Caines is ushered off, there's more cheering, but it's scattered and disorganized; most of the crowd can't quite tell what to do. It's like once the ritual's over, the reality of why this child was part of it sinks in. There's a feeling of something important, something both uncomfortable and not, about a child with cancer tossing this dream-final's coin. The feeling, what-all it might mean, has a tip-of-the-tongue-type quality that remains elusive for at least the first two sets.[3]

[3] Actually, this is not the only Federer-and-sick-child incident of Wimbledon's second week. Three days prior to the men's final, a Special One-on-One Interview with Mr. Roger Federer* takes place in a small, crowded International Tennis Federation office just off the third floor of the Press Center. Right afterward, as the ATP player-rep is ushering Federer out the back door for his next scheduled obligation, one of the ITF guys (who's been talking loudly on the telephone through the whole Special Interview) now comes up and asks for a moment of Roger's time. The man, who has the same slight, generically foreign accent as all ITF guys, says: "Listen, I hate doing this. I don't do this, normally. It's for my neighbor. His kid has a disease. They will do a fund-raiser, it's planned, and I'm asking can you sign a shirt or something, you know—something." He looks mortified. The ATP rep is glaring at him. Federer, though, just nods, shrugs: "No problem. I'll bring it tomorrow." Tomorrow's the men's semifinal. Evidently the ITF guy has meant one of Federer's own shirts, maybe from the match, with Federer's actual sweat on it. (Federer throws his used wristbands into the crowd after matches, and the people they land on seem pleased rather than grossed out.) The ITF guy, after thanking Federer three times very fast, shakes his head: "I hate doing this." Federer, still halfway out the door: "It's no problem." And it isn't. Like all pros, Federer changes his shirt a few times during matches, and he can just have somebody save one, and then he'll sign it. It's not like Federer's being Gandhi here—he doesn't stop and ask for details about the kid or his illness. He doesn't pretend to care more than he does. The request is just one more small, mildly distracting obligation he has to deal with. But he does say yes, and he will remember—you can tell. And it won't distract him; he won't permit it. He's good at this kind of stuff, too.

* (Only considerations of space and basic believability prevent a full description of the hassles involved in securing such a One-on-One. In brief, it's rather like the old story of someone climbing an enormous mountain to talk to the man seated lotus on top, except in this case the mountain is composed entirely of sports-bureaucrats.)

A top athlete's beauty is next to impossible to describe directly. Or to evoke. Federer's forehand is a great liquid whip, his backhand a one-hander that he can drive flat, load with topspin, or slice—the slice with such snap that the ball turns shapes in the air and skids on the grass to maybe ankle height. His serve has world-class pace and a degree of placement and variety no one else comes close to; the service motion is lithe and uneccentric, distinctive (on TV) only in a certain eel-like all-body snap at the moment of impact. His anticipation and court sense are otherworldly, and his footwork is the best in the game—as a child, he was also a soccer prodigy. All this is true, and yet none of it really explains anything or evokes the experience of watching this man play. Of witnessing, firsthand, the beauty and genius of his game. You more have to come at the aesthetic stuff obliquely, to talk around it, or—as Aquinas did with his own ineffable subject—to try to define it in terms of what it is not.

One thing it is not is televisable. At least not entirely. TV tennis has its advantages, but these advantages have disadvantages, and chief among them is a certain illusion of intimacy. Television's slow-mo replays, its close-ups and graphics, all so privilege viewers that we're not even aware of how much is lost in broadcast. And a large part of what's lost is the sheer physicality of top tennis, a sense of the speeds at which the ball is moving and the players are reacting. This loss is simple to explain. TV's priority, during a point, is coverage of the whole court, a comprehensive view, so that viewers can see both players and the overall geometry of the exchange. TV therefore chooses a specular vantage that is overhead and behind one baseline. You, the viewer, are above and looking down from behind the court. This perspective, as any art student will tell you, "foreshortens" that court. Real tennis, after all, is three-dimensional, but a TV screen's image is only 2-D. The dimension that's lost (or rather distorted) on the screen is the real court's length, the seventy-eight feet between baselines; and the speed with which the ball traverses this length is a shot's pace, which on TV is obscured, and in person is fearsome to behold. That may sound abstract or overblown, in which case by all means go in person to some professional tournament—especially to the outer courts in early rounds, where you can sit twenty feet from the sideline—and sample the difference for yourself. If you've watched tennis only on television, you simply have no idea how hard these pros are hitting the ball, how fast the ball is moving,[4] how little time the players have to get to it, and how quickly they're able to move and rotate and strike and recover. And none are faster, or more deceptively effortless about it, than Roger Federer.

[4] Top men's serves often reach speeds of 125–135 m.p.h., true, but what all the radar signs and graphics neglect to tell you is that male power-baseliners' groundstrokes themselves are often traveling at over 90 m.p.h., which is the speed of a big-league fastball. If you get down close enough to a pro court, you can hear an actual *sound* coming off the ball in flight, a kind of liquid hiss, from the combination of pace and spin. Close up and live, you'll also understand better the "open stance" that's become such an emblem of the power-baseline game. The term, after all, just means not turning one's side all the way to the net before hitting a groundstroke, and one reason why so many power-baseliners hit from the open stance is that the ball now is coming too fast for them to get turned all the way.

Interestingly, what is less obscured in TV coverage is Federer's intelligence, since this intelligence often manifests as angle. Federer is able to see, or create, gaps and angles for winners that no one else can envision, and television's perspective is perfect for viewing and reviewing these Federer Moments. What's harder to appreciate on TV is that these spectacular-looking angles and winners are not coming from nowhere—they're often set up several shots ahead, and depend as much on Federer's manipulation of opponents' positions as they do on the pace or placement of the coup de grâce. And understanding how and why Federer is able to move other world-class athletes around this way requires, in turn, a better technical understanding of the modern power-baseline game than TV—again—is set up to provide.

Wimbledon is strange. Verily it is the game's Mecca, the cathedral of tennis; but it would be easier to sustain the appropriate level of on-site veneration if the tournament weren't so intent on reminding you over and over that it's the cathedral of tennis. There's a peculiar mix of stodgy self-satisfaction and relentless self-promotion and -branding. It's a bit like the sort of authority figure whose office wall has every last plaque, diploma, and award he's ever gotten, and every time you come into the office you're forced to look at the wall and say something to indicate that you're impressed. Wimbledon's own walls, along nearly every significant corridor and passage, are lined with posters and signs featuring shots of past champions, lists of Wimbledon facts and trivia, historic lore, and so on. Some of this stuff is interesting; some is just odd. The Wimbledon Lawn Tennis Museum, for instance, has a collection of all the various kinds of rackets used here through the decades, and one of the many signs along the Level 2 passage of the Millennium Building[5] promotes this exhibit with both photos and didactic text, a kind of History of the Racket. Here, *sic,* is the climactic end of this text:

> Today's lightweight frames made of space-age materials like graphite, boron, titanium and ceramics, with larger heads—mid-size (90–95 square inches) and over-size (110 square inches)—have totally transformed the character of the game. Nowadays it is the powerful hitters who dominate with heavy topspin. Serve-and-volley players and those who rely on subtlety and touch have virtually disappeared.

It seems odd, to say the least, that such a diagnosis continues to hang here so prominently in the fourth year of Federer's reign over Wimbledon, since the Swiss has brought to men's tennis degrees of touch and subtlety unseen since (at least) the days of McEnroe's prime. But the sign's really just a testament to the power of dogma. For almost two decades, the party line's been that certain advances in racket technology, conditioning, and weight training have transformed pro tennis from a game of quickness and finesse into one of athleticism and brute

[5] This is the large (and presumably six-year-old) structure where Wimbledon's administration, players, and media all have their respective areas and HQs.

power. And, as an etiology of today's power-baseline game, this party line is broadly accurate. Today's pros truly are measurably bigger, stronger, and better conditioned,[6] and high-tech composite rackets really have increased their capacities for pace and spin. How, then, someone of Roger Federer's consummate finesse has come to dominate the men's tour is a source of wide and dogmatic confusion.

There are three kinds of valid explanation for Federer's ascendancy. One kind involves mystery and metaphysics and is, I think, closest to the real truth. The others are more technical and make for better journalism.

The metaphysical explanation is that Roger Federer is one of those rare, preternatural athletes who appear to be exempt, at least in part, from certain physical laws. Good analogs here include Michael Jordan,[7] who could not only jump inhumanly

[6] (Some, like Nadal or Serena Williams, look more like cartoon superheroes than people.)

[7] When asked, during the aforementioned Special One-on-One Interview, for examples of other athletes whose performances might seem beautiful to him, Federer mentions Jordan first, then Kobe Bryant, then "a soccer player like—guys who play very relaxed, like a Zinédine Zidane or something: he does great effort, but he seems like he doesn't need to try hard to get the results."

Federer's response to the subsequent question, which is what-all he makes of it when pundits and other players describe his own game as "beautiful," is interesting mainly because the response is pleasant, intelligent, and cooperative—as is Federer himself—without ever really saying anything (because, in fairness, what could one say about others' descriptions of him as beautiful? What would you say? It's ultimately a stupid question):

high but actually hang there a beat or two longer than gravity allows, and Muhammad Ali, who really could "float" across the canvas and land two or three jabs in the clock-time required for one. There are probably a half-dozen other examples since 1960. And Roger Federer is of this type—a type that one could call genius, or mutant, or avatar. He is never hurried or off-balance. The approaching ball hangs, for

"It's always what people see first—for them, that's what you are 'best at.' When you used to watch John McEnroe, you know, the first time, what would you see? You would see a guy with incredible talent, because the way he played, nobody played like this. The way he played the ball, it was just all about *feel*. And then you go over to Boris Becker, and right away you saw a *powerful* player, you know?* When you see me play, you see a 'beautiful' player—and maybe after that you maybe see that he's fast, maybe you see that he's got a good forehand, maybe then you see that he has a good serve. First, you know, you have a base, and to me, I think it's great, you know, and I'm very lucky to be called basically 'beautiful,' you know, for style of play. Other ones have the 'grinder' [quality] first, [some] other ones are the 'power player,' [still] other ones are 'the quick guy.' With me it's, like, 'the beautiful player,' and that's really cool."

* (N.B. Federer's big conversational tics are "maybe" and "you know." Ultimately, these tics are helpful because they serve as reminders of how appallingly young he really is. If you're interested, the world's best tennis player is wearing white warm-up pants and a long-sleeved white microfiber shirt, possibly Nike. No sport coat, though. His handshake is only moderately firm, though the hand itself is like a carpentry rasp (for obvious reasons, tennis players tend to be very callusy). He's a bit bigger than TV makes him seem—broader-shouldered, deeper in the chest. He's next to a table that's covered with visors and headbands, which he's been autographing with a Sharpie. He sits with his legs crossed and smiles pleasantly and seems very relaxed; he never fidgets with the Sharpie. One's overall impression is that Roger Federer is either a very nice guy or a guy who's very good at dealing with the media—or [most likely] both.)

him, a split-second longer than it ought to. His movements are lithe rather than athletic. Like Ali, Jordan, Maradona, and Gretzky, he seems both less and more substantial than the men he faces. Particularly in the all-white that Wimbledon enjoys getting away with still requiring, he looks like what he may well (I think) be: a creature whose body is both flesh and, somehow, light.

This thing about the ball cooperatively hanging there, slowing down, as if susceptible to the Swiss's will—there's real metaphysical truth here. And in the following anecdote. After a July 7 semifinal in which Federer destroyed Jonas Bjorkman—not just beat him, *destroyed* him—and just before a requisite post-match news conference in which Bjorkman, who's friendly with Federer, says he was pleased to "have the best seat in the house" to watch the Swiss "play the nearest to perfection you can play tennis," Federer and Bjorkman are evidently chatting and joking around, and Bjorkman asks him just how unnaturally big the ball was looking to him out there, and Federer confirms that it was "like a bowling ball or basketball." He means it just as a bantery, modest way to make Bjorkman feel better, to confirm that he's surprised by how unusually well he played today; but he's also revealing something about what tennis is like for him. Imagine that you're a person with preternaturally good reflexes and coordination and speed, and that you're playing high-level tennis. Your experience, in play, will not be that you possess phenomenal reflexes and speed; rather, it will seem to you that the tennis ball is quite large and slow-moving, and that you always have plenty of time to hit it. That is, you won't experience anything like the (empirically real) quickness and skill that the live audience, watching tennis balls move so fast they hiss and blur, will attribute to you.[8]

Velocity's just one part of it. Now we're getting technical. Tennis is often called a game of inches, but the cliché is mostly referring to where a shot lands. In terms of a player's hitting an incoming ball, tennis is actually more a game of micrometers: vanishingly tiny changes around the moment of impact will have large effects on how and where the ball travels. The same principle explains why even the smallest imprecision in aiming a rifle will still cause a miss if the target's far enough away.

By way of illustration, let's slow things way down. Imagine that you, a tennis player, are standing just behind your deuce corner's baseline. A ball is served to your forehand—you pivot (or rotate) so that your side is to the ball's incoming path and start to take your racket back for the forehand return. Keep

[8] Special One-on-One support from the man himself for this claim: "It's interesting, because this week, actually, Ancic [comma Mario, the towering Top-Ten Croatian whom Federer beat in Wednesday's quarterfinal] played on Centre Court against my friend, you know, the Swiss player Wawrinka [comma Stanislas, Federer's Davis Cup teammate], and I went to see it out where, you know, my girlfriend Mirka [Vavrinec, a former Top 100 female player, knocked out by injury, who now basically functions as Federer's Alice B. Toklas] usually sits, and I went to see—for the first time since I have come here to Wimbledon, I went to see a match on Centre Court, and I was also surprised, actually, how fast, you know, the serve is and how fast you have to react to be able to get the ball back, especially when a guy like Mario [Ancic, who's known for his vicious serve] serves, you know? But then once you're on the court yourself, it's totally different, you know, because all you see is the ball, really, and you don't see the speed of the ball. . . ."

visualizing up to where you're about halfway into the stroke's forward motion; the incoming ball is now just off your front hip, maybe six inches from point of impact. Consider some of the variables involved here. On the vertical plane, angling your racket face just a couple degrees forward or back will create topspin or slice, respectively; keeping it perpendicular will produce a flat, spinless drive. Horizontally, adjusting the racket face ever so slightly to the left or right, and hitting the ball maybe a millisecond early or late, will result in a cross-court versus down-the-line return. Further slight changes in the curves of your groundstroke's motion and follow-through will help determine how high your return passes over the net, which, together with the speed at which you're swinging (along with certain characteristics of the spin you impart), will affect how deep or shallow in the opponent's court your return lands, how high it bounces, etc. These are just the broadest distinctions, of course—like, there's heavy topspin vs. light topspin, sharply cross-court vs. only slightly cross-court, etc. There are also the issues of how close you're allowing the ball to get to your body, what grip you're using, the extent to which your knees are bent and/or weight's moving forward, and whether you're able simultaneously to watch the ball and to see what your opponent's doing after he serves. These all matter, too. Plus there's the fact that you're not putting a static object into motion here but rather reversing the flight and (to a varying extent) spin of a projectile coming toward you—coming, in the case of pro tennis, at speeds that make conscious thought impossible. Mario Ancic's first serve, for instance, often comes in around 130 m.p.h. Since it's seventy-eight feet from Ancic's baseline to yours, that means it takes 0.41 seconds for his serve to reach you.[9] This is less than the time it takes to blink quickly, twice.

The upshot is that pro tennis involves intervals of time too brief for deliberate action. Temporally, we're more in the operative range of reflexes, purely physical reactions that bypass conscious thought. And yet an effective return of serve depends on a large set of decisions and physical adjustments that are a whole lot more involved and intentional than blinking, jumping when startled, etc.

Successfully returning a hard-served tennis ball requires what's sometimes called "the kinesthetic sense," meaning the ability to control the body and its artificial extensions through complex and very quick systems of tasks. English has a whole cloud of terms for various parts of this ability: feel, touch, form, proprioception, coordination, hand-eye coordination, kinesthesia, grace, control, reflexes, and so on. For promising junior players, refining the kinesthetic sense is the main goal of the extreme daily practice regimens we often hear about.[10] The

[9] We're doing the math here with the ball traveling as the crow flies, for simplicity. Please do not write in with corrections. If you want to factor in the serve's bounce and so compute the total distance traveled by the ball as the sum of an oblique triangle's* two shorter legs, then by all means go ahead—you'll end up with between two and five additional hundredths of a second, which is not significant.

* (The slower a tennis court's surface, the closer to a right triangle you're going to have. On fast grass, the bounce's angle is always oblique.)

[10] Conditioning is also important, but this is mainly because the first thing that physical fatigue attacks is the kinesthetic sense. (Other antagonists are fear,

training here is both muscular and neurological. Hitting thousands of strokes, day after day, develops the ability to do by "feel" what cannot be done by regular conscious thought. Repetitive practice like this often looks tedious or even cruel to an outsider, but the outsider can't feel what's going on inside the player—tiny adjustments, over and over, and a sense of each change's effects that gets more and more acute even as it recedes from normal consciousness.[11]

The time and discipline required for serious kinesthetic training are one reason why top pros are usually people who've devoted most of their waking lives to tennis, starting (at the very latest) in their early teens. It was, for example, at age thirteen that Roger Federer finally gave up soccer, and a recognizable childhood, and entered Switzerland's national tennis training center in Ecublens. At sixteen, he dropped out of classroom studies and started serious international competition.

It was only weeks after quitting school that Federer won Junior Wimbledon. Obviously, this is something that not every junior who devotes himself to tennis can do. Just as obviously, then, there is more than time and training involved—there is

self-consciousness, and extreme upset—which is why fragile psyches are rare in pro tennis.)

[11] The best lay analogy is probably to the way an experienced driver can make all of good driving's myriad little decisions and adjustments without having to pay real attention to them.

also sheer talent, and degrees of it. Extraordinary kinesthetic ability must be present (and measurable) in a kid just to make the years of practice and training worthwhile... but from there, over time, the cream starts to rise and separate. So one type of technical explanation for Federer's dominion is that he's just a bit more kinesthetically talented than the other male pros. Only a little bit, since everyone in the Top 100 is himself kinesthetically gifted—but, then, tennis is a game of inches.

This answer is plausible but incomplete. It would probably not have been incomplete in 1980. In 2006, though, it's fair to ask why this kind of talent still matters so much. Recall what is true about dogma and Wimbledon's sign. Kinesthetic virtuoso or no, Roger Federer is now dominating the largest, strongest, fittest, best-trained and -coached field of male pros who've ever existed, with everyone using a kind of nuclear racket that's said to have made the finer calibrations of kinesthetic sense irrelevant, like trying to whistle Mozart during a Metallica concert.

According to reliable sources, honorary coin-tosser William Caines's backstory is that one day, when he was two and a half, his mother found a lump in his tummy, and took him to the doctor, and the lump was diagnosed as a malignant liver tumor. At which point one cannot, of course, imagine... a tiny child undergoing chemo, serious chemo, his mother having to watch, carry him home, nurse him, then bring him back to that place for more chemo. How did she answer her child's question—the big one, the obvious one? And who could answer hers? What could any priest or pastor say that wouldn't be grotesque?

It's 2-1 Nadal in the final's second set, and he's serving. Federer won the first set at love but then flagged a bit, as he sometimes does, and is quickly down a break. Now, on Nadal's ad, there's a sixteen-stroke point. Nadal is serving twenty m.p.h. faster than he did in Paris, and this one's down the center. Federer floats a soft forehand high over the net, which he can get away with because Nadal never comes in behind his serve. The Spaniard now hits a characteristically heavy topspin forehand deep to Federer's backhand; Federer comes back with an even heavier topspin backhand, almost a clay-court shot. It's unexpected and backs Nadal up, slightly, and his response is a low hard short ball that lands just past the service line's T on Federer's forehand side. Against most other opponents, Federer could simply end the point on a ball like this, but one reason Nadal gives him trouble is that he's faster than the others, can get to stuff they can't; and so Federer here just hits a flat, medium-hard cross-court forehand, going not for a winner but for a low, shallowly angled ball that forces Nadal up and out to the deuce side, his backhand. Nadal, on the run, backhands it hard down the line to Federer's backhand; Federer slices it right back down the same line, slow and floaty with backspin, making Nadal return to the same spot. Nadal slices the ball right back—three shots now all down the same line—and Federer slices the ball to the same spot yet again, this one even slower and floatier, and Nadal gets planted and hits a big two-hander down the same line—it's like Nadal's camped out now on his deuce side; he's no longer moving all the way back to the baseline's center between shots; Federer's hypnotized him a little. Federer now hits a very hard, deep topspin backhand, the kind that hisses, to a point just slightly on the ad side of Nadal's baseline, which Nadal gets to and forehands cross-court; and Federer responds with an even harder, heavier cross-court backhand, baseline-deep and moving so fast that Nadal has to hit the forehand off his back foot and then scramble to get to center as the shot lands maybe two feet short on Federer's backhand side again. Roger Federer steps to this ball and now hits a totally different cross-court backhand, this one much shorter and sharper-angled, an angle no one would anticipate, and so heavy and blurred with topspin that it lands shallow and just inside the sideline and takes off hard after the bounce, and Nadal can't move in to cut it off and can't get to it laterally along the baseline, because of all the angle and topspin—end of point. It's a spectacular winner, a Federer Moment; but, watching it live, you can see that it's also a winner that Federer started setting up four or even five shots earlier. Everything after that first down-the-line slice was designed by the Swiss to maneuver Nadal and lull him and disrupt his rhythm and balance and open up that last, unimaginable angle—an angle that would have been impossible without extreme topspin.

Extreme topspin is the hallmark of today's power-baseline game. This is something that Wimbledon's sign gets right.[12]

[12] (...assuming, that is, that the sign's "with heavy topspin" is modifying "dominate" rather than "powerful hitters," which actually it might or might not—British grammar is a bit dodgy)

Why topspin is so key, though, is not commonly understood. What's commonly understood is that high-tech composite rackets impart much more pace to the ball, rather like aluminum baseball bats as opposed to good old lumber. But that dogma is false. The truth is that, at the same tensile strength, carbon-based composites are lighter than wood, and this allows modern rackets to be a couple ounces lighter and at least an inch wider across the face than the vintage Kramer and Maxply. It's the width of the face that's vital. A wider face means there's more total string area, which means the sweet spot's bigger. With a composite racket, you don't have to meet the ball in the precise geometric center of the strings in order to generate good pace. Nor must you be spot-on to generate topspin, a spin that (recall) requires a tilted face and upwardly curved stroke, brushing over the ball rather than hitting flat through it—this was quite hard to do with wood rackets, because of their smaller face and niggardly sweet spot. Composites' lighter, wider heads and more generous centers let players swing faster and put way more topspin on the ball... and, in turn, the more topspin you put on the ball, the harder you can hit it, because there's more margin for error. Topspin causes the ball to pass high over the net, describe a sharp arc, and come down fast into the opponent's court (instead of maybe soaring out).

So the basic formula here is that composite rackets enable topspin, which in turn enables groundstrokes vastly faster and harder than twenty years ago—it's common now to see male pros pulled up off the ground and halfway around in the air by the force of their strokes, which in the old days was something one saw only in Jimmy Connors.

Connors was not, by the way, the father of the power-baseline game. He whaled mightily from the baseline, true, but his groundstrokes were flat and spinless and had to pass very low over the net. Nor was Björn Borg a true power-baseliner. Both Borg and Connors played specialized versions of the classic baseline game, which had evolved as a counterforce to the even more classic serve-and-volley game, which was itself the dominant form of men's power tennis for decades, and of which John McEnroe was the greatest modern exponent. You probably know all this, and may also know that McEnroe toppled Borg and then more or less ruled the men's game until the appearance, around the early mid-1980s, of (a) modern composite rackets[13] and (b) Ivan Lendl, who played with an early form of composite and was the true progenitor of power-baseline tennis.[14]

Ivan Lendl was the first top pro whose strokes and tactics appeared to be designed around the special capacities of the

[13] (which neither Connors nor McEnroe could switch to with much success—their games were fixed around pre-modern rackets)

[14] Formwise, with his whippy forehand, lethal one-hander, and merciless treatment of short balls, Lendl somewhat anticipated Federer. But the Czech was also stiff, cold, and brutal; his game was awesome but not beautiful. (My college doubles partner used to describe watching Lendl as like getting to see *Triumph of the Will* in 3-D.)

composite racket. His goal was to win points from the baseline, via either passing shots or outright winners. His weapon was his groundstrokes, especially his forehand, which he could hit with overwhelming pace because of the amount of topspin he put on the ball. The blend of pace and topspin also allowed Lendl to do something that proved crucial to the advent of the power-baseline game. He could pull off radical, extraordinary angles on hard-hit groundstrokes, mainly because of the speed with which heavy topspin makes the ball dip and land without going wide. In retrospect, this changed the whole physics of aggressive tennis. For decades, it had been angle that made the serve-and-volley game so lethal. The closer one is to the net, the more of the opponent's court is open—the classic advantage of volleying was that you could hit angles that would go way wide if attempted from the baseline or midcourt. But topspin on a groundstroke, if it's really extreme, can bring the ball down fast and shallow enough to exploit many of these same angles. Especially if the groundstroke you're hitting is off a somewhat short ball—the shorter the ball, the more angles are possible. Pace, topspin, and aggressive baseline angles: and lo, it's the power-baseline game.

It wasn't that Ivan Lendl was an immortally great tennis player. He was simply the first top pro to demonstrate what heavy topspin and raw power could achieve from the baseline. And, most important, the achievement was replicable, just like the composite racket. Past a certain threshold of physical talent and training, the main requirements were athleticism, aggression, and superior strength and conditioning. The result (omitting various complications and subspecialties[15]) has been men's pro tennis for the last twenty years: ever bigger, stronger, fitter players generating unprecedented pace and topspin off the ground, trying to force the short or weak ball that they can put away.

Illustrative stat: When Lleyton Hewitt defeated David Nalbandian in the 2002 Wimbledon men's final, there was not one single serve-and-volley point.[16]

The generic power-baseline game is not boring—certainly not compared with the two-second points of old-time serve-and-volley or the moon-ball tedium of classic baseline attrition. But it is somewhat static and limited; it is not, as pundits have publicly feared for years, the evolutionary endpoint of tennis. The player who's shown this to be true is Roger Federer. And he's shown it from *within* the modern game.

This *within* is what's important here; this is what a purely neural account leaves out. And it is why sexy attributions like touch and subtlety must not be misunderstood. With Federer, it's not either/or. The Swiss has every bit of Lendl's and Agassi's pace on his groundstrokes, and leaves the ground when he

[15] See, for one example, the continued effectiveness of some serve-and-volley (mainly in the adapted, heavily ace- and quickness-dependent form of a Sampras or Rafter) on fast courts through the 1990s.

[16] It's also illustrative that 2002 was Wimbledon's last pre-Federer final.

swings, and can out-hit even Nadal from the backcourt.[17] What's strange and wrong about Wimbledon's sign, really, is its overall dolorous tone. Subtlety, touch, and finesse are not dead

[17] In the '06 final's third set, at three games all and 30-15, Nadal kicks his second serve high to Federer's backhand. Nadal's clearly been coached to go high and heavy to Federer's backhand, and that's what he does, point after point. Federer slices the return back to Nadal's center and two feet short—not short enough to let the Spaniard hit a winner, but short enough to draw him slightly into the court, whence Nadal winds up and puts all his forehand's strength into a hard heavy shot to (again) Federer's backhand. The pace he's put on the ball means that Nadal is still backpedaling to his baseline as Federer leaves his feet and cranks a very hard topspin backhand down the line to Nadal's deuce side, which Nadal—out of position but world-class fast—reaches and manages to one-hand back deep to (again) Federer's backhand side, but this ball's floaty and slow, and Federer has time to step around and hit an inside-out forehand, a forehand as hard as anyone's hit all tournament, with just enough topspin to bring it down in Nadal's ad corner, and the Spaniard gets there but can't return it. Big ovation. Again, what looks like an overwhelming baseline winner was actually set up by that first clever semi-short slice and Nadal's own predictability about where and how hard he'll hit every ball. Federer surely whaled that last forehand, though. People are looking at each other and applauding. The thing with Federer is that he's Mozart and Metallica at the same time, and the harmony's somehow exquisite.

By the way, it's right around here, or the next game, watching, that three separate inner-type things come together and mesh. One is a feeling of deep personal privilege at being alive to get to see this; another is the thought that William Caines is probably somewhere here in the Centre Court crowd, too, watching, maybe with his mum. The third thing is a sudden memory of the earnest way the press bus driver promised just this experience. Because there is one. It's hard to describe—it's like a thought that's also a feeling. One wouldn't want to make too much of it, or to pretend that it's any sort of equitable balance; that would be grotesque. But the truth is that whatever deity, entity, energy, or random genetic flux produces sick children also produced Roger Federer, and just look at him down there. Look at that.

in the power-baseline era. For it is, still, in 2006, very much the power-baseline era: Roger Federer is a first-rate, kick-ass power-baseliner. It's just that that's not all he is. There's also his intelligence, his occult anticipation, his court sense, his ability to read and manipulate opponents, to mix spins and speeds, to misdirect and disguise, to use tactical foresight and peripheral vision and kinesthetic range instead of just rote pace—all this has exposed the limits, and possibilities, of men's tennis as it's now played.

...Which sounds very high-flown and nice, of course, but please understand that with this guy it's not high-flown or abstract. Or nice. In the same emphatic, empirical, dominating way that Lendl drove home his own lesson, Roger Federer is showing that the speed and strength of today's pro game are merely its skeleton, not its flesh. He has, figuratively and literally, re-embodied men's tennis, and for the first time in years the game's future is unpredictable. You should have seen, on the grounds' outside courts, the variegated ballet that was this year's Junior Wimbledon. Drop volleys and mixed spins, off-speed serves, gambits planned three shots ahead—all as well as the standard-issue grunts and booming balls. Whether anything like a nascent Federer was here among these juniors can't be known, of course. Genius is not replicable. Inspiration, though, is contagious, and multiform—and even just to see, close up, power and aggression made vulnerable to beauty is to feel inspired and (in a fleeting, mortal way) reconciled.

—2006

appoggiatura—embellishment note that's one note up or down from something; "his hair appressed from hours in a cap" **aquarelle**—draw bling clay **arrant** (adj.)—completely such, thoroughgoing: "an ar and flowers in flowing sinuous lines, like on vases, columns, etc. **ash** building stone **Asmodeus**—demon in Tobit book of Bi ble; "Asmo fas to steeple of church, highest point in city, and all the roofs of all one's house. A kind of voyeurism-of-the-gods. From Brewer, p. 55 water **athanasian**—defender of Christianity; see Athanasius, Greek pa **atony**—lack of normal muscle tone **atopic**—relating to inherited oversen for sterilizing surgical instruments, some kinds of cooking **autophagy**—forcible tearing away of a body part by trauma or surgery; (v.) avulse **awl** part, like the hollow under a bird's wing **axiology**—philosophy: the study **bacchante**—femalereveler/orgier(priestessatBaccanal) **baculiform**—rod band for the hair **bandoleer**—chest-crossing belt w/ pockets for cartridges sidewalk in east Texas and southern LA; long upholstered bench against or over the parapet **barbican**—tower or other fortification on the approach array **belvedere**—open, roofed structure built to command a view, like a **benefice**—sinecure, church post w/ secure income **benignity**—niceness, butter & scallion sauce served w/ seafood **bezel**—a slanting sur fin **bifacial**—having two faces or (of a bldg.) facades **bifid**—forked part of an extended rope or cable (phone lines have bights in the

precedent note **appressed**—lying flat or pressed closely against

ing in transparent watercolor **argillaceous**—containing or resem-

rant idiot" **art nouveau**—decorative style of early 20th c. using leaves

cake—Southern/rural for johnnycake **ashlar**—a square block of

deus flight" in Lesage's *Le Diable boiteux,* Asmodeus takes Don Cléo-

the houses open and they can see private stuff going on in every-

aspergillum—Catholic perforated container for sprinkling holy

triarch of Alexandria **atomy**—a very skinny person; (adj.) atomical

sitivity like allergies, hay fever **autoclave**—strong pressurized steam-heater

self-digestion (of a cell via cell's own enzymes) **avulsion** (medical n.)—the

—pointed tool for making holes **axilla**—armpit or similar hollow in a body

of values and value judgments **Baals**—fertility gods of ancient Semitics

shaped **baize**—green felty stuff used for pool tables **bandeau**—narrow

or bullets **banquette**—platform lining trench where soldiers can fire from;

built into wall **barbette**—raised mound inside fort from which guns are fired

to a castle or town **beadle**—usher at church service **bedight**—to dress or

press box **bema**—platform from which services are conducted in synagogue

gentleness **berm**—narrow ledge or shelf on cliff or slope **beurre blanc**—

face or bevel on a cutting tool like a chisel **bier**—stand for a cof-

or split into two parts; botany **bight**—loop in a rope; middle or slack

middle, etc.) **birl**—cause to spin rapidly with feet (as with logrolling)

FICTIONAL FUTURES AND THE CONSPICUOUSLY YOUNG

THE METRONOME OF LITERARY fashion looks to be set on *presto.* Beginning with the high-profile appearances of David Leavitt's *Family Dancing,* Jay McInerney's *Bright Lights, Big City,* and Bret Ellis's *Less Than Zero,* the last three-odd years saw a veritable explosion of good-willed critical and commercial interest in literary fiction by Conspicuously Young[1] writers. During this interval, certain honored traditions of starvation and apprenticeship were inverted: writers' proximity to their own puberties seemed now an asset; rumors had agents haunting prestigious writing workshops like pro scouts at Bowl games; publishers and critics jockeyed for position to proclaim their own beardless favorite "the first voice of a new generation." Too, the upscale urban young quickly established themselves

[1] Hereafter abbreviated "C.Y."

as a bona fide audience (and market) for C.Y. fiction: Ellis and McInerney, Janowitz and Leavitt, Simpson and Minot enjoy a popularity with their peers unknown since the relative popular disappearance of the sixties' hip black humor squad.

As of this writing, late 1987, the backlash has been swift and severe, if not wholly unjustified. Many of the same trendy reviewers who in the mid-eighties were hailing the precocity of a New Generation now bemoan the proliferation of a literary Brat Pack. The *Village Voice,* which in 1985 formalized the apotheosis of McInerney in a gushy cover story, this autumn uses a scathing review of some McInerney disciples as occasion to headline the news that THE BRAT PACK SPITS UP, with crudely cut-out faces of Janowitz, McInerney, Ellis, et al. pasted on photos of diaper models. Nineteen eighty-seven saw the staff and guests of the *New York Times Book Review* suddenly complaining of a trend toward "world-weary creative writing projects," a spate of "Y.A.W.N.S. (Young Anomic White Novelists)," an endless succession of flash-in-the-pan "short-story starlets." In its October 11 issue, no less an éminence grise than William Gass administers "A Failing Grade for the Present Tense":

> You may have noticed the plague of school-styled [writers] with which our pages have been afflicted, and taken some account of the no-account magazines that exist in order to publish them. Thousands of short-story readers and writers have been released like fingerlings into the thin mainstream of serious prose.... Well, young people are young people, aren't

> they.... Adolescents consume more of their psyches than soda, and more local feelings than junk food. Is no indulgence denied them?... I read [a recent Leavitt-edited anthology of C.Y. fiction] as a part of my researches. It is like walking through a cemetery before they've put in any graves.

What's caused this quick reversal in mood? Is it capricious and unfair, or overdue? Most interesting: what does it imply?

In my own opinion, the honeymoon's end between the literary Establishment and the C.Y. writer was an inevitable and foreseeable consequence of the same shameless hype that led to many journeyman writers' premature elevation in the first place: condescending critical indulgence and condescending critical dismissal inhabit the same coin. It's true that some cringingly bad fiction gets written by C.Y.s. But this is hardly an explanation for anything, since the same is true of lots of older artists, many of whom have clearly shot their bolts and now hang by name and fashion alone.

More germane is the frequent charge of a certain numbing *sameness* about much contemporary young writing. To a certain extent anyone who reads widely must agree with it. The vast bulk of the vast amount of recently published C.Y. fiction reinforces the stereotype that has all young literary enterprises falling into one or more of the following three dreary camps:

(1) Neiman-Marcus Nihilism, declaimed via six-figure Uppies and their salon-tanned, morally vacant offspring, none of whom seem to be able to make it

from limo door to analyst's couch without several grams of chemical encouragement;

(2) Catatonic Realism, a.k.a. Ultraminimalism, a.k.a. Bad Carver, in which suburbs are wastelands, adults automata, and narrators blank perceptual engines, intoning in run-on monosyllables the artificial ingredients of breakfast cereal and the new human non-soul;

(3) Workshop Hermeticism, fiction for which the highest praise involves the words "competent," "finished," "problem-free," fiction over which Writing-Program pre- and proscriptions loom with the enclosing force of horizons: no character without Freudian trauma in accessible past, without near-diagnostic physical description; no image undissolved into regulation Updikean metaphor; no overture without a dramatized scene to "show" what's "told"; no denouement prior to an epiphany whose approach can be charted by any Freitag on any Macintosh.

Mean, but unfortunately fair—except for the fact that, like most generalizations, these apply validly only to the inferior examples of the work at hand. Ironically for the critic who wants both to bemoan invasions and pigeonhole the invaders, the very proliferation of C.Y. fiction, with its attendant variety, raises the generation's cream above stereotype. The preternatural smarts with which a Simpson or Leavitt can render complex parental machinations through the eyes of thoroughly believable children; the gritty white-trash lyricism of Pinckney Benedict's *Town Smokes;* the wry, bitchy humor of a good Lorrie Moore or Amy Hempel or Debra Spark story; the political vision of William Vollmann's *You Bright and Risen Angels;* the conscientious exploration of *motive* behind Yuppie dissolution in McInerney's *Bright Lights*—these transcend Camp-following and, more important, merit neither head-patting nor sneers. See for yourself. Among the C.Y. writers who do, yes, seem to crowd the last half of this decade, there are some unique and worthy talents. Yes, all are raw, some more or less mature, some more or less apt at transcending the hype the hype-mills crank out daily. But more than a couple are originals.

But it's weird: all we C.Y. writers get consistently lumped together. Both lauds and pans invariably invoke a Generation that is both New and, in some odd way, One. Unfamiliar with the critical fashions of past decades, I don't know whether this perception has precedent, but I do think in certain ways it's not inappropriate. As of now, C.Y. writers, the good and the lousy, are in my opinion A Generation, conjoined less by chronology (Benedict is twenty-three, Janowitz over thirty) than by the new and singular environment in and about which we try to write fiction. This, that we are agnate, also goes a long way toward explaining the violent and conflicting critical reactions New Voices are provoking.

The argument, then, is that certain key things having to do with literary production are radically different for young American writers now; and that, fashion-flux aside, the fact that these key things affect our aesthetic values and literary choices serves at once to bind us together and to distance us from much of an Establishment—literary, intellectual, political—that reads and judges our stuff from their side of a...well, generation gap. There are, of course, uncountable differences between the formative experiences of consecutive generations, and to exhaust and explain all the ones relevant here would require both objective distance and a battalion of social historians. Having neither at hand, I propose to invite consideration of just three specific contemporary American phenomena, viz. the impacts of television, of academic Creative Writing Programs, and of a revolution in the way educated people understand the function and possibility of literary narrative. These three because they seem at once powerfully affective and normatively complex. Great and grim, tonic and insidious, they are (I claim) undeniable and cohesive influences on this country's "New Voices."

Stats on the percentage of the average American day spent before small screens are well known. But the American generation born after, say, 1955 is the first for whom television is something to be *lived with,* not just looked at. Our parents regard the set rather as the Flapper did the automobile: a curiosity turned treat turned seduction. For us, their children, TV's as much a part of reality as Toyotas and gridlock. We quite literally cannot "imagine" life without it. As it does for so much of today's developed world, it presents and so defines our common experience; but we, unlike any elders, have no memory of a world without such electronic definition. It's built in. In my own childhood, late sixties, rural downstate Illinois, miles and megahertz from any center of entertainment production, familiarity with the latest developments on *Batman* or *The Wild Wild West* was the medium of social exchange. Much of our original play was a simple reenactment of what we'd witnessed the night before, and verisimilitude was taken very seriously. The ability to do a passable Howard Cosell, Barney Rubble, Cocoa Puffs bird, or Gomer Pyle was a measure of status, a determination of stature.

Surely television-as-lifestyle influences the modes by which C.Y. writers understand and represent lived life. A recent issue of *Arrival* saw critic Bruce Bawer lampoon many Brat-Packers' habit of delineating characters according to the commercial slogans that appear on their T-shirts. He had a scary number of examples. It's true that there's something sad in the fact that Leavitt's sole description of some characters in, say, "Danny in Transit" consists of the fact that their shirts say "Coca-Cola" in a foreign language—yet maybe more sad is that, for most of his reading contemporaries, this description *does the job.* Bawer's distaste seems to me misplaced: it's more properly directed at a young culture so willingly bombarded with messages equating what one consumes with who one is that brand loyalty is now an acceptable synecdoche of identity, of character.

This schism between young writers and their older critics probably extends to the whole issue of strategic reference to "popular culture" in literary fiction. The artistic deployment of pop icons—brand names, television programs, celebrities, commercial film and music—strikes those intellectuals whose consciousness was formed before the genuine Television Age as at best frivolous tics and at worst dangerous vapidities that compromise fiction's "seriousness" by dating it out of the

Platonic Always where it properly resides. A fine and conscientious writing professor once proclaimed to our class that a serious story or novel always eschews "any feature that serves to date it," to fix it in history, because "literary fiction is always timeless." When we protested that, in his own well-known work, characters moved about in electrically lit rooms, propelled themselves in autos, spoke not Anglo-Saxon but post-WWII English, inhabited a North America already separated from Africa by continental drift, he amended his ruling's application to those explicit references that would date a story in the transient Now. Pressed by further quibbling into real precision, his interdiction turned out really to be against what he called the "mass-commercial-media" reference. At this point, I think, trans-generational discourse breaks down. For this gentleman's automobiled Timeless and our F.C.C.'d own were different. Time had changed Always.

Nor, please, is this stuff a matter of mere taste or idiosyncrasy. Most good fiction writers, even young ones, are intellectuals. So are most critics and teachers (and a surprising number of editors). And television, its advertising, and the popular culture they both reflect and define have fundamentally altered what intellectuals get to regard as the proper objects of their attention. Those cognoscenti whose values were formed before TV and advertising became psychologically pandemic are still anxious to draw a sharp distinction, à la Barbara Tuchman, between those sorts of things that have genuine "quality" and are produced and demanded by people with refined tastes, on one hand, and those sorts of things that have only "popularity" or "mass appeal" and are demanded by the Great Unwashed and cheerfully supplied by those whom egalitarian capitalism has whored to the lowest of denominators, the democratic market, on the other. The enlightened older aesthete, erudite and liberal, weaned let's say between 1940 and 1960, is able to operate from a center of contradiction between genuine refinement and genuine liberalism that advertising scholars like Martin Mayer had already begun to deride by the fifties' end:

> The great bulk of advertising is culturally repulsive to anyone with any developed sensitivity. So are most movies and television shows, most popular music, and a surprisingly high proportion of published books.... But a sensitive person can easily avoid cheap movies, cheap books, and cheap art, while there is scarcely anyone outside the jails who can avoid contact with advertising. By presenting the intellectual with a more or less accurate image of the popular culture, advertising earns his enmity and calumny. It hits him where it hurts worst: in his politically liberal and socially generous outlook—partly nourished on his avoidance of actual contact with popular taste.

I claim that intellectuals of the New Generation for whom C.Y. writers are supposed to be voices can no longer even wrap their minds around this kind of hypocrisy, much less suffer from it. Not that this "enlightenment" is earned, or even necessarily a good thing. Because it's not as though television and advertising and popular entertainments have ceased to be mostly bad art or cheap art, but just that they've imposed themselves on our generation's psyches for so long and with such power that they have entered into complicated relations with our very ideas of the world and the self. We simply cannot "relate to" the older aesthete's distanced distaste for mass entertainment and popular appeal: the distaste may well remain, but the distance does not.

And, as the pop informs our generation's ways of experiencing and reading the world, so too will it naturally affect our artistic values and expectations. Young fiction writers may spend hours each day at the writing table, performing; but we're also, each and every day, part of the great Audience. We're conditioned accordingly. We have an innate predilection for visual stimulation, colored movement, a frenetic variety, a beat you can dance to. It may be that, through hyper- and atrophy, our mental capacities themselves are different: the breadth of our attentions greater as attention spans themselves shorten. Raised on an activity at least partly passive, we experience a degree of manipulation as neutral, a fact of life. However, wooed artfully as we are for not just our loyalty but our very *attention,* we reserve for that attention the status of a commodity, a measure of power; and our choices to bestow or withhold it carry for us great weight. So does what we regard as our God-given right to be entertained—or, if not entertained, at least stimulated: the unpleasant is perfectly OK, just so long as it *rivets.*

As one can see popular icons seriously used in much C.Y. fiction as touchstones for the world we live in and try to make into art, so one might trace some of the techniques favored by many young writers to roots in our experience as consummate watchers. E.g., events often refracted through the sensibilities of more than one character; short, dense paragraphs in which coherence is often sacrificed for straight evocation; abrupt transitions in scene, setting, point of view, temporal and causal orders; a surfacy, objective, "cinematic" third-person narrative eye. Above all, though, a comparative indifference to the imperative of mimesis, combined with an absolute passion for narrative choices that conduce to what might be called "mood." For no writer can help assuming that the reader is on some level like him: already having seen, ad nauseum, what life *looks like,* he's far more interested in how it *feels* as a signpost toward what it means.

The technical coin, too, has a tails. For instance, it's not hard to see that the trendy Ultraminimalism favored by too many C.Y. writers is deeply influenced by the aesthetic norms of mass entertainment. Indeed, this fiction depends on what's little more than a crude inversion of these norms. Where television, especially its advertising, presents everything in hyperbole, Ultraminimalism is deliberately flat, understated, "undersold." Where TV seeks everywhere to render its action either dramatic or melodramatic, to move the viewer by displaying constant movement, the Minimalist describes an event as one would an object, a geometric form in stasis; and he always does so from an emotional remove of light-years. Where television does and must aim always to *please,* the Catatonic writer hefts something of a finger at subject and reader alike: one has only to read a Bret Ellis sex scene (pick a page, any page) to realize that here pleasure is neither a subject nor an aim. My own aversion to Ultraminimalism, I think, stems from its naive pretension. The Catatonic Bunch seem to feel that simply by inverting the values imposed on us by television, commercial film, advertising, etc., they can automatically achieve the aesthetic depth popular entertainment so conspicuously lacks. Really, of course, the Ultraminimalists are no less infected by popular culture than other C.Y. writers: they merely choose to define their art by opposition to their own atmosphere. The attitude betrayed is similar to that of lightweight neo-classicals who felt that to be non-vulgar was not just a requirement but an assurance of value, or of insecure scholars who confuse obscurity with profundity. And it's just about as annoying.

Not that the Catatonic's discomfort with a culture of and by popularity isn't understandable. We're all at least a little uncomfortable with it—no?—probably because, as technicians like Mayer foresaw thirty years ago, escape from it has gone from impossible to inconceivable. That is, since today's popular TV culture is by its nature *mass, pan-*, it's of course going to have an impact on the styles and choices and dreams not just of a few fingerling artists and their small readerships, but of the very human collectivities about which we try to write. And this impact has been overwhelming; the new Always has changed everything. I'm going to argue that it's done so in ways that are bad and have costs. "Bad" means inimical to many of the values our communities have evolved and held and cherished and taught. "Costs" means painful changes and losses for persons. Because, see, a mysterious beast like television begins, the more sophisticated it gets, to produce and live by an antinomy, a phenomenon whose strength lies in its contradiction: though television is aimed ever and always at groups, masses, markets, collectivities, it's nevertheless true that the most powerful and lasting changes are wrought by TV on *individual persons,* each one of whom is forced every day to understand himself in relation to the Groups by virtue of which he seems to exist at all.

Think, for instance, about the way prolonged exposure to broadcast drama makes each one of us at once more self-conscious and less reflective. A culture more and more about *seeing* eventually perverts the relation of seer and seen. We watch various actors who play various characters involved in various relations and events. Seldom do we think about the fact that the single deep feature the characters share, with each other and with the actors who portray them, is that they are *watched.* The behavior of the actors, and—in a complicated way, through the drama they're inside—even the characters, is directed always at an audience for whom they behave... indeed, in virtue of whom they exist as actor or character in the first place, behind the screen's glass. We, the audience, receive unconscious reinforcement of the thesis that the most significant feature of persons is *watchableness,* and that contemporary human worth is not just isomorphic with but rooted in the phenomenon of watching. Precious distinctions between truly being and merely appearing get obfuscated. Imagine a Berkeleyan *esse-est-percipi* universe in which God is named Nielsen.

Then consider that well-known, large, "ignorant" segment of the population that believes on a day-to-day level that what happens on televised dramas is "real." This, the enormous volume of mail addressed each day to characters and not the persons who portray them, is the iceberg's extreme tip. The berg itself is a generation (New) for whom the distinction between (real) actor artificially portraying and (pretend) character genuinely behaving gets ever more tangled. The danger of the berg is badness and cost—a shift from an understanding of self as a character in a great drama whose end is meaning to an understanding of self as an actor at a great audition whose end is *seeming*, i.e., being seen.

Actually there are uncountable ways in which efficiently conceived and disseminated popular entertainment affects the existential predicaments of both persons and groups. And if "existential" seems too weighty a term to attach to anything pop, then I think you're misunderstanding what's at stake. You're invited to consider commercial dramas that deal with violence and danger and the possibility of death. There are lots, today. Each drama has a hero. He's purposely designed so that we by our nature "identify" with him. At present this is still not hard to get us to do, for we still tend to think of our own lives this way: we're each the hero of our own drama, others around us remanded to supporting roles or (increasingly) audience status.

But now try to recall the last time you saw the "hero" die within his drama's narrative frame. It's very rarely done anymore. Entertainment professionals have apparently done research: audiences find the deaths of those with whom they identify a downer, and are less apt to watch dramas in which danger is creatively connected to the death that makes danger dangerous. The natural consequence is that today's dramatic heroes tend to be "immortal" within the frame that makes them heroes and objects of identification (for the audience, VCR- and related technology give this illusion a magnetic reality). I claim that the fact that we are strongly encouraged to identify with characters for whom death is not a significant creative possibility has real costs. We the audience, and individual you over there and me right here, lose any sense of eschatology, thus of teleology, and live in a moment that is, paradoxically, both emptied of intrinsic meaning or end and quite literally *eternal.* If we're the only animals who know in advance we're going to die, we're also probably the only animals who would submit so cheerfully to the sustained denial of this undeniable and very important truth. The danger is that, as entertainment's denials of the truth get even more effective and pervasive and seductive, we will eventually forget what they're denials *of.* This is scary. Because it seems transparent to me that, if we forget how to die, we're going to forget how to live.

And if you think that contemporary literary artists, of whatever stature, are above blinking at a reality we all find unpleasant, consider the number of serious American fictional enterprises in the last decade that have dealt with what's acknowledged to be the single greatest organized threat to our persons and society. Try to name, say, two.

Maybe the real question is—how serious can people who have a *right* to be entertained permit "serious" fiction to be anymore? Because if I claimed above that the C.Y. writers' intellectual fathers held dear a contradictory blend of cutting-edge politics and old-guard aesthetics, I'm sure most of us would gladly trade it for the contradictions that are its replacement. Today's journeyman fiction writer finds himself both a lover of serious narrative and an ineluctably conditioned part of a pop-dominated culture in which the social stock of his own enterprise is falling. What we are inside of—what *comprises* us—is killing what we love.

Hyperbole? It's important to remember that most television is not just entertainment: it's also narrative. And it's so true it's trite that human beings are narrative animals: every culture countenances itself as culture via a story, whether mythopoeic or politico-economic; every whole person understands his lifetime as an organized, recountable series of events and changes with at least a beginning and middle. We need narrative like we need space-time; it's a built-in thing. In the C.Y. writers today, the narrative patterns to which literate Americans are most regularly exposed are televised. And, even on a charitable account, television is a pretty low type of narrative art. It's a narrative art that strives not to change or enlighten or broaden or reorient—not necessarily even to "entertain"—but merely and always to *engage,* to *appeal to.* Its one end—openly acknowledged—is to *ensure continued watching.* And (I claim) the metastatic efficiency with which it's done so has, as cost, inevitable and dire consequences for the level of people's tastes in narrative art. For the very *expectations* of readers in virtue of which narrative art is art.

Television's greatest appeal is that it is engaging without being at all demanding. One can rest while undergoing stimulation. Receive without giving. It's the same in all low art that has as goal continued attention and patronage: it's appealing precisely because it's at once fun and easy. And the entrenchment of a culture built on Appeal helps explain a dark and curious thing: at a time when there are more decent and good and very good serious fiction writers at work in America than ever before, an American public enjoying unprecedented literacy and disposable income spends the vast bulk of its reading time and book dollar on fiction that is, by any fair standard, trash. Trash fiction is, by design and appeal, most like televised narrative: engaging without being demanding. But trash, in terms of both quality and popularity, is a much more sinister phenomenon. For while television has from its beginnings been openly motivated by—has been *about*—considerations of mass appeal and L.C.D. and profit, our own history is chock-full of evidence that readers and societies may properly expect important, lasting contributions from a narrative art that understands itself as being about considerations more important than popularity and balance sheets. Entertainers can divert and engage and maybe even console; only artists can transfigure. Today's trash writers are entertainers working artists' turf. This in itself is nothing new. But television aesthetics, and television-like economics, have clearly made their unprecedented popularity and reward possible. And there seems to me to be a real danger that not only the forms but the *norms* of televised art will begin to supplant the standards of all narrative art. This would be a disaster.

I'm worried lest I sound too much like B. Tuchman here, because my complaints about trash are different from hers, and less sophisticated. My complaint against trash fiction is not that it's plebeian, and as for its rise I don't care at all whether postindustrial liberalism squats in history as the culprit that made it inevitable. My complaint against trash isn't that it's vulgar art, or irritatingly dumb art, but that, given what makes fiction art at all, trash is simply *unreal, empty*—and that (aided by mores of and by TV) it seduces the market writers need and the culture that needs writers away from what *is* real, full, meaningful.

Even the snottiest young *artiste,* of course, probably isn't going to bear personal ill will toward writers of trash; just as, while everybody agrees that prostitution is a bad thing for everyone involved, few are apt to blame prostitutes themselves, or wish them harm. If this seems like a non sequitur, I'm going to claim the analogy is all too apt. A prostitute is someone who, in exchange for money, affords someone else the form and sensation of sexual intimacy without any of the complex emotions or responsibilities that make intimacy between two people a valuable or meaningful human enterprise. The prostitute "gives," but—demanding nothing of comparable value in return—perverts the giving, helps render what is supposed to be a revelation a transaction. The writer of trash fiction, often with admirable craft, affords his customer a narrative structure and movement, and content that *engages* the reader—titillates, repulses, excites, transports him—without demanding of him any of the intellectual or spiritual or *artistic* responses that render verbal intercourse between writer and reader an important or even *real* activity. So when our elders tell our graduate fiction class (as they liked to do a lot) that a war for fictional art's soul is being waged in the 1980s between poetry on one side and trash on the other—to this admonishment we listen, at this we take pause. Especially when television and advertising have conditioned us to equate net worth with human worth. Sidney Sheldon, a gifted trash-master, owns jets; more people in this country write poetry than read it; the annual literary budget of the National Endowment for the Arts is less than a third of the U.S.'s yearly expenditures on military bands, less than a *tenth* of the three big networks' yearly spending on Creative Development.

Sidney Sheldon, by the way, was the Creative, Developing force behind both *I Dream of Jeannie* and *Hart to Hart.* Oprah Winfrey asks him in admiration for the secret behind his success in "two such totally different media." I say to myself, "Ha," watching.

It's in terms of economics that academic Creative Writing Programs[2] offer their least ambiguous advantages. Published writers (assuming they themselves have a graduate writing degree) can earn enough by workshop teaching to support themselves and their own fiction without having to resort to more numbing or time-consuming employment. On the student side, fellowships—some absurdly generous—and paid assistantships in teaching are usually available to almost all students. Programs tend to be a sweet deal.

And there are more such programs in this country now than anywhere anytime before. The once-lone brow of the Iowa Workshop has birthed first-rate creative departments at places like Stanford, Houston, Columbia, Johns Hopkins, Virginia, Michigan, Arizona, etc. The majority of accredited American I.H.E.s now have at least some sort of formal academic provision for students who want vocational training in fiction writing. This has all happened within the last fifteen

[2] These words are capitalized because they *understand* themselves as capitalized. Trust me on this.

years. It's unprecedented, and so are the effects of the trend on young U.S. fiction. Of the C.Y. writers I've mentioned above, I know of none who've not had some training in either a graduate or undergraduate writing department. Most of them hold M.F.A.s. Some are, even as we speak, working toward a degree called a "Creative Ph.D." Never has a "literary generation" been so thoroughly and formally trained, nor has such a large percentage of aspiring fiction writers eschewed extramural apprenticeship for ivy and grades.

And the contributions of the academy's rise in American fiction go beyond the fiscal. The workshop phenomenon has been justly credited with a recent "renaissance of the American short story," a renaissance heralded in the late seventies with the emergence of writers like the late Raymond Carver (taught at Syracuse), Jayne Anne Phillips (M.F.A. from Iowa), and the late Breece Pancake (M.F.A. from Virginia). More small magazines devoted to short literary fiction exist today than ever before, most of them either sponsored by programs or edited and staffed by recent M.F.A.s. Short story collections, even by relative unknowns, are now halfway viable economically, and publishers have moved briskly to accommodate trend.

More important for young writers themselves, programs can afford them time, academic (and parental!) legitimacy, and an environment in which to Hone Their Craft, Grow, Find Their Voice,[3] etc. For the student, a community of serious, like-

[3] On these, too: they are to Programs what *azan* are to mosques.

minded persons with whom to exchange ideas has pretty clear advantages. So, in many ways, does the fiction class itself. In a workshop, rudiments of technique and process can be taught fairly quickly to kids who might in the past have spent years in New York lofts learning basic tricks of the trade by trial and error. A classroom atmosphere of rigorous constructive criticism helps toughen young writers' hides and prepare them for the wildly disparate responses the world of real readers holds in store. Best of all, a good workshop forces students regularly to formulate consistent, reasoned criticisms of colleagues' work; and this, almost without fail, makes them far more astute about the strengths and weaknesses of their own fiction.

Still, I think it's the Program-sword's other edge that justifies the various Establishments' present disenchantment with C.Y. fiction more than anything else. The dark side of the Program trend exists, grows; and it's much more than an instantiation of the standard academic lovely-in-theory-but-mangled-in-practice conundrum. So we'll leave aside nasty little issues like departmental politics, faculty power struggles that summon images of sharks fighting for control of a bathtub, the dispiriting hiss of everybody's egos in various stages of inflation or deflation, a downright unshakable publish-or-perish mentality that equates appearance in print with talent or promise. These might be particular to one student's experience. Certain problems inherent in Programs' very structure and purpose, though, are not. For one thing, the pedagogical relation between fiction professor and fiction student has unhealthiness built right in. Writing teachers are by calling writers, not teachers. The fact that most of them are teaching not for its own sake but to support a separate and obsessive calling has got to be accepted, as does its consequence: every minute spent on class and department business is, for Program staff, a minute not spent working on their own art, and must to a degree be resented. The best teachers seem to acknowledge the conflict between their vocations, reach some kind of internal compromise, and go on. The rest, according to their capacities, either suppress the resentment or make sure they do the barely acceptable minimum their primary source of income requires. Almost all, though, take the resentment out in large part on the psyches of their pupils—for pupils represent artistic time wasted, an expenditure of a teacher's fiction-energy without fiction-production. It's all perfectly understandable. Clearly, though, feeling like a burden, an impediment to *real* art-production, is not going to be conducive to a student's development, to say nothing of his enthusiasm. Not to mention his basic willingness to engage his instructor in the kind of dynamic back-and-forth any real creative education requires, since it's usually the very-low-profile, docile, *undemanding* student who is favored, recruited, supported, and advanced by a faculty for whom demand equals distraction.

In other words, the fact that creative writing teachers must wear two hats has unhappy implications for the quality of both M.F.A. candidates and the education they receive in Programs. And it's very unclear who if anyone's to blame. Teaching fiction writing is darn hard to do well. The conscientious teacher must not only be both highly critical and emotionally sensitive, acute in his reading and articulate about his acuity: he must be all these things with regard to precisely those issues that can be communicated to and discussed in a workshop *group*. And that inevitably yields a distorted emphasis on the sorts of simple, surface concerns that a dozen or so people can talk about coherently: straightforward mechanics of traditional fiction production like fidelity to point-of-view, consistency of tense and tone, development of character, verisimilitude of setting, etc. Faults or virtues that cannot quickly be identified or discussed between bells—little things like interestingness, depth of vision, originality, political assumptions and agendas, the question whether deviation from norm is in some cases OK—must, for sound Program-pedagogical reasons, be ignored or discouraged. Too, in order to remain both helpful and sane, the professional writer/teacher has got to develop, consciously or not, an aesthetic doctrine, a static set of principles about how a "good" story works. Otherwise he'd have to start from intuitive scratch with each student piece he reads, and that way the liquor cabinet lies. But consider what this means: the Program staffer must teach the practice of art, which by its nature always exists in at least some state of tension with the rules of its practice, as essentially an applied system of rules. Surely this kind of *enforced* closure to further fictional possibilities isn't good for most teachers' own literary development. Nor is it at all good for their students, most of whom have been in school for at least sixteen years and know that the way the school game is played is: (1) Determine what the instructor wants; and (2) Supply it forthwith. Most Programs, then, produce two kinds of students. There are those few who, whether particularly gifted or not, have enough interest and faith in their fiction instincts to elect sometimes to deviate from professors' prescriptions. Many of these students are shown the door, or drop out, or gut out a couple years during which the door is always being pointed to, throats cleared, Fin. Aid unavailable. These turn out to be the lucky ones. The other kind are those who, the minute fanny touches chair, make the instructors' dicta their own—whether from insecurity, educational programming, or genuine agreement (rare)—who row instead of rock, play the game quietly and solidly, and begin producing solid, quiet work, most of which lands neatly in Dreary Camp #3, nice, cautious, boring Workshop Stories, stories as tough to find technical fault with as they are to remember after putting them down. *Here* are the rouged corpses for Dr. Gass's graveyard. Workshops *like* corpses. They *have* to. Because any class, even one in "creativity," is going to place supreme value on *not making mistakes.* And corpses, whatever their other faults, never ever screw up.[4]

I doubt whether any of this is revelatory, but I hope it's properly scary. Because Creative Writing Programs, while claiming in all good faith to train professional writers, in reality train *more teachers of Creative Writing.* The only thing a Master of Fine Arts degree actually qualifies one to do is teach...Fine

[4] Only considerations of space and legal liability restrain me from sharing with you in detail the persistent legend, at one nameless institution, of the embalmed cadaver cadged from the medical school by two deeply troubled young M.F.A. candidates, enrolled in a workshop as their proxy, smuggled pre-bell into the seminar room each week, and propped in its assigned seat, there to clutch a pencil in its white fist and stare straight ahead with an expression of somewhat rigid good cheer. The name of the legend is "The Cadaver That Got a B."

Arts. Almost all present fiction professors hold something like an M.F.A. So do most editors of literary magazines. Most M.F.A. candidates who stay in the Business will go on to teach and edit. Small wonder, then, that older critics feel in so much current C.Y. fiction the tweed breeze that could signal a veritable storm of boredom: envision if you dare a *careful, accomplished* national literature, mistake-free, seamless as fine linoleum; fiction preoccupied with norm as value instead of value's servant; fiction by academics who were taught by academics and teach aspiring academics; novel after critique-resistant novel about tenure-angst, coed-lust, cafeteria-*schmerz.*

Railing against occluded subject matter and tradition-tested style is one thing. A larger issue is whether Writing Programs and their grinding, story-every-three-weeks workshop assembly lines could, eventually, lower all standards, precipitate a broad-level literary mediocrity, fictional equivalents of what Donald Hall calls "The McPoem." I think, if they get much more popular, and do not drop the pose of "education" in favor of a humbler and more honest self-appraisal—a form of literary patronage and an occasion for literary community—we might well end up with a McStory chain that would put Ray Kroc to shame. Because it's not just the unhealthy structure of the Program, the weird creative constraints it has to impose on instructors and students alike—it's the type of student who is attracted by such an arrangement. A sheepheaded willingness to toe any line just because it's the most comfortable way to survive is contemptible in any student. But students are just symptoms. Here's the disease: in terms of rigor, demand, intellectual and emotional requirement, a lot of Creative Writing

Programs are an unfunny joke. Few require of applicants any significant preparation in history, literature, criticism, composition, foreign languages, art, or philosophy; fewer still make attempts to provide it in curricula or require it as a criterion for graduation.

Part of this problem is political. Academic departments of Creative Writing and "Straight Literature" tend to hold each other in mutual contempt, a state of affairs that student, Program, and serious-fiction audience are all going to regret a lot if it continues to obtain. Way too many students are being "certified" to go out there and try to do meaningful work on the cutting edge of an artistic discipline of whose underpinnings, history, and greatest achievements they are largely ignorant. The obligatory survey of "Writers Who Are Important to *You*" at the start of each term seems to suggest that Homer and Milton, Cervantes and Shakespeare, Maupassant and Gogol—to say nothing of the Testaments—have receded into the mists of Straight Lit; that, for far too much of this generation, Salinger invented the wheel, Updike internal combustion, and Carver, Beattie, and Phillips drive what's worth chasing. Forget Allan Bloom gnashing his teeth at high school students who pretend to no aspirations past an affordable mortgage—we're supposed to want to be *writers,* here. We as a generation are in danger of justifying Eliot at his zaniest if via a blend of academic stasis and intellectual disinterest we show to the dissatisfaction of all that culture is either cumulative or it is dead, empty on either side of a social Now that admits neither passion about the future nor curiosity about the past.

The fact that we Aspiring Voices as a generation show so little intellectual curiosity is the least defensible thing of all. But it could well be that the very thing that makes our anti-intellectualism so obscene renders it also extremely temporary. Thing in question: our generation is lucky enough to have been born into an artistic climate as stormy and exciting as anything since Pound and Co. turned the world-before-last on its head. The last few generations of American writers have breathed the relatively stable air of New Criticism and an Anglo-American aesthetics untainted by Continental winds. The climate for the "next" generation of American writers—should we decide to inhale rather than die—is aswirl with what seems like long-overdue appreciation for the weird achievements of such aliens as Husserl, Heidegger, Bakhtin, Lacan, Barthes, Poulet, Gadamer, de Man. The demise of Structuralism has changed a world's outlook on language, art, and literary discourse; and the contemporary artist can simply no longer afford to regard the work of critics or theorists or philosophers—no matter how stratospheric—as divorced from his own concerns.

Crudely put, the idea that literary language is any kind of neutral medium for the transfer of ________[5] from artist to audience, or that it's any kind of inert tool lying there passively

[5] Take your pick of Tolstoy, Schopenhauer, or Richards and insert "feeling," "freedom from phenomena," or "relevant mental condition," respectively, in the space provided.

to be well- or ill-used by a communicator of meaning, has been cast into rich and serious question. With it, too, the stubborn Romanticist view of fiction as essentially a mirror, distinguished from the real world it reflects only by its portability and mercilessly "objective" clarity, has finally taken it on the chin. Form-content distinctions are now flat planets. Language's promotion from mirror to eye, from *organikos* to organic, is yesterday's news (except in those two lonely outposts, TV and the Creative classroom) as the tide of Post-Structuralism, Marxism, Feminism, Freudianism, Deconstruction, Semiotics, Hermeneutics, and attendant -isms and -ics moves through the ("Straight") U.S. academy and into the consciousness of the conscious American adult.

The crux being that, if mimesis isn't dead, then it's on life-support courtesy of those who soon enough will be.

And what a row C.Y. writers can see among its heirs! Only about eighty years after visual-arts movements like Dada and Cubism supplanted "referential" art (no camera inventions to threaten the sovereignty of literary mimesis, see), the literature of the referent, of "psychological glow," of illusion has finally come under constructive attack from angles as disparate as they are dazzling. The refracted world of Proust and Musil, Schulz and Stein, Borges and Faulkner has, post-War, exploded into diffraction, a weird, protracted Manhattan Project staffed by Robbe-Grillet, Grass, Nabokov, Sorrentino, Bohl, Barth, McCarthy, García Márquez, Puig, Kundera, Gass, Fuentes, Elkin, Donoso, Handke, Burroughs, Duras, Coover, Gombrowicz, Le Guin, Lessing, Acker, Gaddis, Coetzee, Ozick. To name just a few. We, the would-be heirs to a gorgeous chaos, stand witness to the rise and fall of the *nouveau roman,* Postmodernism, Metafiction, the New Lyricism, the New Realism, Minimalism, Ultraminimalism, Performance-Theory. It's a freaking maelstrom, and the C.Y. writer who still likes to read a bit can't help feeling torn: if the Program is maddening in its stasis, the real world of serious fiction just *won't hold still.*

If one can stomach a good dose of simplification, though, there can be seen one deep feature shared by all the cutting-edge fiction that resonates with the post-Hiroshima revolution. That is its fall into time, a loss of innocence about the language that is its breath and bread. Its unblinking recognition of the fact that the relations between literary artist, literary language, and literary artifact are vastly more complex and powerful than has been realized hitherto. And the insight that is courage's reward—that it is *precisely* in those tangled relations that a forward-looking, fertile literary value may well reside.

This doesn't mean that Metafiction and Minimalism, the two most starkly self-conscious of the movements that exploit human beings' wary and excited new attention to language, compose or even indicate the directions in which the serious fiction of "whole new generations" will move. Both these forms strike me as simple engines of self-reference (Metafiction overtly so, Minimalism a bit sneakier); they are primitive, crude, and seem already to have reached the Clang-Bird-esque horizon of their own possibility—self-reference being just a tiny wrinkled subset of aboutness. I'm pretty convinced, though, that they're an early symptom of a dark new enlightenment, that quite soon no truly serious C.Y. writer will be able to pretend anymore that the use of literary expression for the construction of make-believe is a straightforward enterprise. We are the recipients of a knife unprecedentedly vulnerable to its own blade, and all the Writing Program prizes and *Mary Tyler Moore Show* reruns in the world can't hide what's in our hands forever.

Exciting is also confusing, and I'd be distrustful of any C.Y. snot who claimed to know where literary fiction will go during this generation's working lifetime. It's obviously true that the revolution I've just gushed about has yielded changes in outlook that are as yet primarily destructive: illusions exposed, assumptions overturned, dearly held prejudices debunked. We seem, now, to see our literary innocence taken from us without anything substantial to replace it. An age between. There's a marvelously apposite Heidegger quotation here, but I'll spare you.

The bold conclusion here, then, is that the concatenated New Generation with whom the critics are currently playing coy mistress is united by confusion, if nothing else. And this might be why so much of the worst C.Y. fiction fits so neatly into the Three Camps reviewers consign it to: Workshop Hermeticism because in confusing times caution seems prudent; Catatonia because in confusing times the bare minimal seems easy; Yuppie Nihilism because the mass culture the Yuppie inhabits and instantiates is itself at best empty and at worst evil—and in confusing times the revelation of something even this obvious is, up to a point, valuable.

Well, but it's fair to ask how valuable. Of course it's true that an unprecedented number of young Americans have big disposable incomes, fine tastes, nice things, competent accountants, access to exotic intoxicants, attractive sex partners, and are still deeply unhappy. All right. Some good fiction has held up a mercilessly powder-smeared mirror to the obvious. What troubles me about the fact that the Gold-Card-fear-and-trembling fiction just keeps coming is that, if the upheavals in popular, academic, and intellectual life have left people with any long-cherished conviction intact, it seems as if it should be an abiding faith that the conscientious, talented, and lucky artist of any age retains the power to effect change. And if Marx (sorry—last dropped name) derided the intellectuals of his day for merely interpreting the world when the real imperative was to change it, the derision seems even more apt today when we notice that many of our best-known C.Y. writers seem content merely to have reduced interpretation to whining. And what's frustrating for me about the whiners is that precisely the state of general affairs that *explains* a nihilistic artistic outlook makes it *imperative* that art *not* be nihilistic. I can think of no better argument for giving Mimesis-for-Mimesis's-Sake the chair than the fact that, for a young fiction writer, inclined by disposition and vocation to pay some extra attention to the way life gets lived around him, 1987's America is not a nice place to be. The last cohesive literary generation came to consciousness during the comparatively black-and-white era of Vietnam. We, though, are Watergate's children, television's audience, Reagan's draft-pool, and everyone's market. We've reached our majority in a truly bizarre period in which "Wrong is right," "Greed is good," and "It's better to look good than to feel good"—and when the poor old issue of trying to *be* good no longer even merits a straight face. It seems like one big echo of Mayer the fifties' ad-man: "In a world where private gratification seems the supreme value, all cats are grey."

Except art, is the thing. Serious, real, conscientious, aware, ambitious art is not a grey thing. It has never been a grey thing and it is not a grey thing now. This is why fiction in a grey time *may not be grey.* And why the titles of all but one or two of the best works of Neiman Marcus Nihilism are going to induce aphasia quite soon in literate persons who read narrative art for what makes it real.

And, besides an unfair acquaintance with many young writers who are not yet Conspicuous and so not known to you, this is why I'd be willing to bet anything at least a couple and maybe a bunch of the Whole New Generation are going to make art, maybe make great art, maybe even make great art change. One thing about the Young you can trust in 1987: if we're willing to devote our lives to something, you can rest assured we get off on it. And nothing has changed about why writers who don't do it for the money write: it's art, and art is meaning, and meaning is power: power to color cats, to order chaos, to transform void into floor and debt into treasure. The best "Voices of a Generation" surely know this already; more, they let it inform them. It's quite possible that none of the best are yet among the Conspicuous. A couple might even be... *autodidacts.* But, especially now, none of them need worry. If fashion, flux, and academy make for thin milk, at least that means the good stuff can't help but rise. I'd get ready.

—1988

bistre—yellowish-brown color (unpleasant underwear) **bittern**—wading
break of blepharitis) **blepharospasm**—spasmodic winking from eyelic
restricting Sunday activities like retail shopping, bars **bolo**—long heavy
boreal (adj.)—of or relating to the north, northern **bort**—poorly crystal
bushes, shrubs **bowline**—a knot forming a loop that does not slip **brachy**
of the length **brachydactylic**—having short fingers or toes **brachylo**
sion **bracken**—tough weedy fern that overgrows untended land
breastwork erected during siege **brickbat**—unfavorable remark, criti
available **brioche**—light-textured egg-white bread shaped into huge
of energy in an explosion **brisket**—chest of an animal / ribs and meat
cacoethes—mania or irresistible compulsion **cadelle**—small blackish
caduceus—medical emblem: snakes twined around stick **caducity**—frail
Caesar is not above grammar/grammarians" **calando**—music: gradu
caldera—large crater formed by volcanic explosion or volcanic collapse
having beautiful buttocks **calumet**—long-stemmed ceremonial pipe for
of car's wheels in chassis so they're closer at the bottom than at the top **ca**
sole—woman's sleeveless undergarment usually worn under sheer blouse
a trocar at one end that's inserted in body to remove fluid or dispense meds,
"epicanthal fold" **canticle**—religious hymn or chant w/o meter and lyrics
usually Scottish: a witch's spell or trick; a sham or fraud or deceptive move
along calves; Mary Tyler Moore's perennial pants on *Dick Van Dyke Show*
legs out **carina**—keel-shaped ridge or structure, e.g., breastbone of bird;

bird like plover **blepharitis**—inflammation of eyelids (trailer-park out-

muscle spasm **blucher**—a high shoe or half boot **blue law**—city law

Philippine machete **borborygmus**—gurgling sounds in digestive tract

lized diamond used in industry **bosky**—having an abundance of trees,

cephalic—having a short, almost round head, the width at least 80%

gy—brief, concise speech; shortened, condensed phrase and/or expres-

brail—small net for bringing fish onto boat **brattice**—partition in mine;

cism **bricolage**—something (like decor) made of whatever happens to be

bun; "woman's hair like a brioche" **brisance**—shattering effect of release

taken from chest of animal **cachou**—a pastille used to sweeten breath

beetle that destroys grain **cadent** (adj.)—having rhythm or cadence

ty of old age, senility **Caesar non supra grammaticos**—saying: "Even

al decrease in tempo and volume **calcar**—spur or spurlike projection

calenture—tropical fever once believed caused by the heat **callipygian**—

U.S. Indians **camber**—slightly arched surface, like road or snow ski; setting

melopard—giraffe; heraldic figure that's giraffe with curved horns **cami-**

cannelure—groove around the cylinder of a bullet **cannula**—a tube with

like an IV **canthus**—angle formed by upper and lower eyelids meeting; see

from Bible **cantonment**—temporary quarters for troops **cantrip** (n.)—

capri pants—tight women's slacks that go only to calves and have slit

capriole—trained horse move: jump without going forward, kicking rear

q.v. "carinated" **carnassial**—adapted for tearing flesh; "carnassial teeth"

THE EMPTY PLENUM: DAVID MARKSON'S *WITTGENSTEIN'S MISTRESS*

But what other philosopher has found the antidote to illusion in the particular and repeated humility of remembering and tracking the uses of humble words, looking philosophically as it were beneath our feet rather than over our heads?

—Stanley Cavell

There is nobody at the window in the painting of the house, by the way.

I have now concluded that what I believed to be a person is a shadow.

If it is not a shadow, it is perhaps a curtain.

As a matter of fact it could actually be nothing more than an attempt to imply depths, within the room.

Although in a manner of speaking all that is really in the window is burnt sienna pigment. And some yellow ochre.

In fact there is no window either, in that same manner of speaking, but only shape.

So that any few speculations I may have made about the person at the window would therefore now appear to be rendered meaningless, obviously.

Unless of course I subsequently become convinced that there is somebody at the window all over again.

I have put that badly.

— *Wittgenstein's Mistress,* pp. 54–55

Tell them I have had a wonderful life.

—Wittgenstein on deathbed, 1951

CERTAIN NOVELS NOT ONLY cry out for what we call "critical interpretations" but actually try to help direct them. This is probably analogous to a piece of music that both demands and defines the listener's movements, say, like a waltz. Frequently, too, the novels that direct their own critical reading concern themselves thematically with what we might consider highbrow or intellectual issues—stuff proper to art, engineering, antique lit., philosophy, etc. These novels carve out for themselves an interstice between flat-out fiction and a sort of weird cerebral *roman à clef.* When they fail they're pretty dreadful. But when they succeed, as I claim David Markson's *Wittgenstein's Mistress* does, they serve the vital and vanishing function of reminding us of fiction's limitless possibilities for reach and grasp, for making heads throb heartlike, and for sanctifying the marriages of cerebration & emotion, abstraction & lived life, transcendent truth-seeking & daily schlepping, marriages that in our happy epoch of technical occlusion and entertainment-marketing seem increasingly consummatable only in the imagination. Books I tend to associate with this INTERPRET-ME phenomenon include stuff like *Candide,* Witold Gombrowicz's *Cosmos,* Hesse's *The Glass Bead Game,* Sartre's *Nausea,* Camus's *The Stranger.* These five are works of genius of a particular kind: they shout their genius. Mr. Markson, in *Wittgenstein's Mistress,* tends rather to whisper, but his w.o.g.'s no less successful; nor—particularly given the rabid anti-intellectualism of the contemporary fiction scene—seems it any less important. It's become an important book to me, anyway. I'd never heard of this guy Markson, before, in '88. And have, still, read nothing else by him. I ordered the book mostly because of its eponymous title; I like to fancy myself a fan of the mind-bending work of its namesake. Clearly the book was/is in some way "about" Wittgenstein, given the title. This is one of the ways an INTERPRET-ME fiction clues the critical reader in about what the book's to be seen as on a tertiary level "about": the title: *Ulysses*'s title, its structure as Odyssean/Telemachean map (succeeds); Goldstein's *The Mind-Body Problem* (really terrible); Cortázar's *Hopscotch* (succeeds exactly to the extent that one ignores the invitation to hop around in it); Burroughs's *Queer* and *Junkie* (fail successfully (?)). W/r/t novels like these it's often hard to see the difference between a title and an epigraph, except for quotidian facts like the latter's longer, overter, & attributed. Another way to invite a kind of correspondence-interpretation is to drop the name of a real person like bricks throughout text, as Bruce Duffy does in his so-called "fictional" biography of Wittgenstein, the execrable 1988 *The World As I Found It,* in which, despite loud "this-is-made-up" disclaimers, Duffy brings to bear such an arsenal of historical fact and allusion that the critical reader can't but confuse the homosexuality-crazed fictional "Wittgenstein" with the real and way more complex & interesting Wittgenstein. Another way for a novel to linearize its reading is to make an intellectual shibboleth serve a repetitive narrative function: e.g., in *Candide,* Pangloss's continual "All for the best in the best of all possible worlds" is a neon sign out front of what is, except for its end, little more than a poisonously funny parody of the metaphysics of Leibniz.[1]

Kate, the monadic narrator of *Wittgenstein's Mistress,* gets a lot of her master's remarks wrong, too—the philosopher's better-known words and ideas are sprayed, skewed, all over the book, from its notebook-epigraph about sand to the *Tractatus*'s "The world is everything that is the case" to *Investigation*ary speculations on adhesive vs. magnetic "tape" that unequivocally summon the later Wittgenstein's concerns over words' "family resemblances"[2] to one another. Contra Voltaire, though, when Markson's Kate recalls lines & concepts incorrectly, her errors serve the ends not of funny propaganda but of both original

[1] ...which succumbs to the hazard of most parody and gets the point of Leibniz's best-of-all-possible-worlds stuff totally wrong.

[2] The word Wittgenstein uses as an example of family resemblance is "game": i.e., what do soccer, Monopoly, and solitaire, for all their differences, have in common by virtue of which they all correctly take the same four-letter predicate? [*Philosophical Grammar,* pp. 75, 118]

art and original interpretation. Because *Wittgenstein's Mistress,*[3] w/r/t its eponymous master, does more than just quote Wittgenstein in weird ways, or allude to his work, or attempt to be some sort of dramatization of the intellectual problems that occupied and oppressed him. Markson's book renders, imaginatively & concretely, the very bleak mathematical world Wittgenstein's *Tractatus* revolutionized philosophy by summoning via abstract argument. It is, in a weird way, the colorization of a very old film. Though Wittgenstein's philosophical stuff is far from dead or arid, *WM* nevertheless succeeds at transposing W's intellectual conundra into the piquant qualia of lived, albeit bizarrely lived, experience. The novel quickens W's early work, gives it a face, for the reader, that the philosophy does not & cannot convey...mostly because Wittgenstein's work is so hard and takes so long just to figure out on a literal level that the migrainous mental gymnastics required of his reader all but quash the dire emotional implications of W's early metaphysics. His mistress, though, asks the question her master in print does not: What if somebody really had to *live* in a *Tractatus*ized world?

I don't mean to suggest that David Markson's achievement here consists just in making abstract philosophy "accessible" to an extramural reader, or that *WM* is in itself simple. Actually, though its prose and monotone are hauntingly pedestrian, the

[3] Hereafter abbreviated *WM*

novel's diffracted system of allusions to everything from antiquity to Astroturf are a bitch to trace out, and the concentric circularity that replaces linear development as its plot's "progression" makes a digestive reading of *WM* a challenging & protracted affair. Markson's is not a pop book, and it's not decocted philosophy or a docudrama-of-the-week. Rather, for me, the novel does artistic & emotional justice to the politico-ethical implications of Ludwig Wittgenstein's abstract mathematical metaphysics, makes what is designed to be a mechanism pulse, breathe, suffer, live, etc. In so doing, it pays emotional tribute to a philosopher who by all evidence lived in personal spiritual torment over the questions too many of his academic followers have made into elaborate empty exercise. That is, Markson's *WM* succeeds in doing what few philosophers glean and what neither myriad biographical sketches nor Duffy's lurid revisionism succeeds in communicating: the consequences, for persons, of the *practice* of *theory;* the difference, say, between espousing "solipsism" as a metaphysical "position" and waking up one fine morning after a personal loss to find your grief apocalyptic, literally millennial, to being the last and only living thing on earth, with only your head, now, for not only company but environment & world, an inclined beach sliding toward a dreadful sea. Put otherwise, Markson's book transcends, for me, its review-enforced status of "intellectual tour de force" or "experimental achievement": what it limns, as an immediate study of depression & loneliness, is far too moving to be the object of either exercise or exorcism. The ways in which the book is moving, and the formal ingenuity by which it transforms metaphysics into angst and so reveals philosophy as first and last about feeling—these are enough for me, right now, to think of the novel as one of the U.S. decade's best, to deplore its relative neglect & its consignment by journals like the *NYTBR* to smarmy review by an ignorant young Carverian.[4] But add to the novel's credits a darkly pyrotechnic achievement in the animation of intellectual history—the way *WM* so completely demonstrates how one of the smartest & most important contributors to modern thought could have been such a personally miserable son of a bitch—and the book becomes, if you're the impotent unlucky sort whose beliefs inform his stomach's daily state, a special kind of great book, literally profound, and probably destined, in its & time's fullness, to be a whispering classic.

One reason *WM* whispers, as both a kind of classic and an interpretation-director, is that its charms and stratagems are very indirect. It's not only a sustained monologue by a person of gender opposite the author's, it is structured halfway between shaggy-dog joke and deadly serious allegory. A concrete example of how the prose here works appears as the second epigraph *supra*. Devices like repetition, obsessive return, free-/unfree association swirl in an uneasy suspension throughout. Yet they communicate. This studied indirection, a sustained error that practically compels misprision, is how Kate convinces us that, if she is insane, so must we be: the subtextual emotive agenda under the freewheeling disorder of isolated paragraphs, under

[4] viz. Amy Hempel, minimalist ordinaire, in the *Review*'s 22 May 1988 encyclical.

the flit of thought, under the continual struggle against the slipping sand of English & the drowning-pool of self-consciousness—a seductive order not only in but *via* chaos—compels complete & uneasy acquiescence, here. The technique rings as true as a song we can't quite place. You could call this technique "Deep Nonsense," meaning I guess a linguistic flow of strings, strands, loops, and quiffs that through the very manner of its formal construction flouts the ordinary cingula of "sense" and through its defiance of sense's limits manages somehow to "show" what cannot ordinarily be "expressed." Good comedy often functions the same way.[5] So does good advertising, today.[6] So does a surprising amount of good philosophy. So, usually on a far less explicit level than *WM*'s, can great fiction.

The start of *WM* has Kate painting messages on empty roads: "Somebody is living in the Louvre," etc. The messages are for anyone who might come along to see. "Nobody came, of course. Eventually I stopped leaving the messages." The novel's end involves the use, not the mention,[7] of such a message: "Some-

[5] Q.v. "Who's on First?"

[6] Q.v. Audi's '89 slogan for print adverts: "IT SETS THE STANDARD BY IGNORING IT."

[7] A distinction of Frege, a Wittgenstein-era titan: to mention a word or phrase is to speak about it, w/ at least implicit quotation marks: e.g., "Kate" is a four-letter name; to use a word or phrase is to mention its referent: e.g., Kate is by default the main character of *Wittgenstein's Mistress*.

body is living on this beach." Except use on what &/or whom? It's probably not right, as I think I did *supra,* to call this novel's form a "monologue."[8] Kate is typing it. It's written & not spoken. Except it's not like a diary or journal. Nor is it a "letter." Because of course a letter to whom, if there's no one else at all? Anyway, it's self-consciously written. I personally have grown weary of texts that are narrated self-consciously as written, as "texts." But *WM* is different from the Barthian/post-Derridean self-referential hosts. Here the conscious rendition of inditement not only rings true but serves essential functions. Kate is not a "writer." By vocation, apparently, a painter, Kate finds her time at the typewriter thoroughly & terribly avocational. She is shouting into her typing paper's blankness. Her missive is a function of need, not art—a kind of long message in a big bottle. I need to admit, here, that I have a weird specular stance with respect to this novel's form as *written.* I am someone who tries to write, who right now more and more seems to need to write, daily; and who hopes less that the products of that need are lucrative or even liked than simply received, read, *seen.* *WM,* in a deep-nonsensical way that's much more effective than argument or allegory'd be, speaks to why I'm starting to think most people who somehow must write must write. The need to indite, inscribe—be its fulfillment exhilarating or

[8] Unless you can empty your head of connotation and translate the word literally from the Attic Greek—then it probably has a Marksonian poignancy no other term would have...

palliative or, as is more usual, neither—springs from the doubly-bound panic felt by most persons who spend a lot of time up in their own personal heads. On one side—the side a philosopher'd call "radically skeptical" or "solipsistic"—there's the feeling that one's head *is*, in some sense, the whole world, when the imagination becomes not just a more congenial but a realer environment than the big Exterior of life on earth. Markson's book's first epigraph, from Kierkegaard's scary *Concluding Unscientific Postscript to Philosophical Fragments*, invites & imposes this first interpretation of Kate's bind and its relation to her "typing."[9] The need to get the words & voices not only *out*—outside the sixteen-inch diameter of bone that both births & imprisons them—but also *down*, trusting them neither to the insubstantial country of the mind nor to the transient venue of cords & air & ear, seems for Kate—as for anyone from a Flaubert to a diarist to a letter-fiend—a necessary affirmation of an outside, some Exterior one's written record can not only communicate with but *inhabit*. Picasso, harking to Velázquez as does Markson to Kierkegaard & Wittgenstein, did big things for the idea of visual artworks as not just representa-

[9] The ep. is "What an extraordinary change takes place... when for the first time the fact that everything depends upon how a thing is thought first enters the consciousness, when, in consequence, thought in its absoluteness replaces an apparent reality."... from "The Task of Becoming Subjective" in the *Postscript*—maybe worth noting that the form of "change" in the Danish is accusative rather than nominative & that what Markson renders as "extraordinary" appears in some other translations as "terrible" or "of thoroughgoing fear."

tions but also things, objects... but I can think of no lit.-practitioner (as opposed to New- or post-structural *theorist*) who's captured the textual urge, the emotional urgency of text as both sign and *thing*, as perfectly as has Markson here.[10] The other side of the prenominate 2-bind—the side rendered explicitly by *WM*'s opening and close—is why people who write need to do so as a mode of *communication*. It's what an abstractor like Laing calls "ontological insecurity"—why we sign our stuff, impose it on friends, mail it out in brown manila trying to get it printed. "I EXIST" is the signal that throbs under most voluntary writing—& all good writing. And "I EXIST" would have been, in my ungraceful editorial hands, the title of Markson's novel. But Markson's final choice, far better than his working *Keeper of the Ghosts*, and *far* better than his 2nd choice, *Wittgenstein's Daughter* (too clunky; deep but not nonsensical), is probably better than mine. Kate's text, one big message that someone is living on this beach, is itself obsessed & almost defined by the possibility that it does not exist, that Kate does not exist. And the novel's title, if we reflect a moment, serves ends as much thematic as allusive. Wittgenstein was gay. He never had a mistress.[11] He did, though, have a teacher and

[10] ...maybe Beckett in *Molloy*...

[11] He pretty obviously never could have had a daughter, either. But he did have intellectual "heirs," and *Wittgenstein's Daughter* would have Kate seem like one—too simple, linear, for so complex a character or her relations to masters. Plus "daughter," unlike "mistress," fails to convey the exquisite loneliness of being the linguistic

friend, one Bertrand Russell, who, with his student's encouragement, before the '20s trashed the *Cogito* tautology by which Descartes had relieved 300 years' worth of neurotic intellectuals of the worrisome doubt that they existed. Russell pointed out that the *Cogito*'s "I think and therefore am" is in fact invalid: the truth of "I think" entails only the existence of *thinking,* as the truth of "I write" yields only the existence of text. To posit an "I" that's *doing* the thinking/writing is to beg the very question Descartes had started out impaled on.... But so anyway, Kate's situation in *WM* is doubly lonely. After having spent years "looking" for people,[12] she has literally washed up on shore, now sits naked & in menses before a manual typewriter, producing words that, for her & us, render only the words themselves "ontologically secure"; the belief in either a reader for them or a (meta)physical presence producing them would require a kind of quixoticism Kate's long since lost or resigned.

What keeps the title from being cute or overheavy is that Kate really is Wittgenstein's mistress, the ghostly curator of a world of history, artifacts, & *memories*—which memories, like TV images, one can access but never really own—and of *facts,* facts about both the (former) world and her own mental habits.

beloved of a man who could not, in emotional practice, confer identity on a woman via his love.

12 ...though she never says what's true: that it was at first for a particular person, her husband, then only eventually for just anyone at all...

Hers is the affectless language of fact, and it seems less like by skill than by the inevitable miracle of something that had to be written that Markson directs our misprision in order to infuse statements that all take the form of raw data-transfer[13] with true & deep emotional import.

Kate's spare, aphoristic style, her direct & correct quotation of "The world is everything that is the case," and her obsessive need to get control of the facts that have become her interior & exterior life—all this stuff directs the reader to run not walk to Ludwig Wittgenstein's 1921 *Tractatus Logico-Philosophicus.*[14] The reason why I, who am no critic & tend to approach books I admire with all the hesitancy of the blind before walls, feel I get to assert all the flat indicatives about Kate's plight above is that so much of *WM* so clearly sends one to the *Tractatus* for critical "clarification." This isn't a weakness of the novel. Though it's kind of miraculous that it's not. And it doesn't mean that *WM* is just written "in the margins of" the *Tractatus* the way *Candide* marginalizes *The Monadology* or *Nausea* simply "dramatizes" Part Three of *L'Être et le néant.* Rather *WM,* if it is any one thing for me, is a kind of philosophical sci-fi. I.e., it's

[13] (data transferred to herself, or her self-consciousness, or to whoever may come down the pike, or to both herself and someone else, or to neither, or maybe all that's supposed to be left here is the sand of text, awaiting tides)

[14] Hereafter abbreviated *Tractatus,* and the equally famous 1953 *Philosophical Investigations* just the *Investigations,* as it's known in the industry, or *PI.*

an imaginative portrait of what it would be like actually to live in the sort of world the logic and metaphysics of Wittgenstein's *Tractatus* posit. This sort of world started out, for Wittgenstein, to be logical heaven. It ends up being (I opine) a metaphysical hell; and the way its philosophic picture rasped against the sort of life and worldview Wittgenstein the man thought worthwhile was (I claim) a big motivation for the disavowal of the *Tractatus* represented by his masterwork, 1953's *Investigations*.[15]

Basically the *Tractatus* is the first real attempt at exploring the now-trendy relation between language and the "reality" it is language's putative function to capture, map, & represent. The *Tractatus*'s project is Kantian: what must the world be like if language is even to be possible? The early Wittgenstein,[16] much under the spell of Russell and the *Principia Mathematica* that revolutionized modern logic, saw language, like math, as logic-based, and viewed the paradigmatic function of language as mirroring or "picturing" the world. From this latter belief everything in the *Tractatus* follows, just as Kate's own fetish for paintings, mirrors, & the status of mental representa-

[15] E.g., "What is the use of studying philosophy," Wittgenstein wrote to a U.S. student while working on the *Investigations* in 1946, "if all that it does for you is to enable you to talk with some plausibility about some abstruse questions of logic, etc. and if it does not improve your thinking about the important questions of everyday life?"

[16] Scholars tend to schizofy Wittgenstein, counterposing the "early" W of the *Tractatus* and the "late" W of the *Investigations, The Blue and Brown Books,* and *Philosophical Grammar.*

tions like memories & associations & perceptions forms the gessoed canvas on which her memoir *must* be sketched. The Wittgenstein of the *Tractatus* chose as the paradigm of language the truth-functional logic of Russell & Whitehead's *Principia.* His choice made practical sense, project-wise: if you're going to try to construe the world from human language, you'll be best off choosing the most perspicuous, precise type of language available—one faithful to Wittgenstein's belief that the business of language is to state facts—as well as selecting the most direct & uncontroversial relation between a language and its world of referents. The latter, I iterate & stress, is simply the relation of mirror to mirrored; and the criterion by which to judge the perspicuity of a statement is entirely & only its fidelity to that feature of the world it denotes: q.v. W's "The statement is a *picture* of the fact."[17] Now, technically, the Russellian logic that comprises language's Big Picture consists all & only of 3 things: simple logical connectives like "and," "or," & "not"; propositions or "statements"; & a view of these statements as "atomic," meaning that the truth or falsity of a complex statement like "Ludwig is affable and Bertrand is well-dressed" depends entirely on the truth value of its constituent atomic propositions—the prenominate molecular proposition is true if & only if it is true that Ludwig is friendly *and* it is true that Bertrand is dapper. The atomic propositions that are language's building blocks are, for both Russell and Wittgenstein,

[17] See the *Tractatus;* emphasis supplied.

"logically independent" of one another: they do not affect one another's truth values, only the values of those logical molecules in which they're conjoined—e.g., "L is cheerful or B is well-heeled," "It is not the case that if B is wealthy then L is cheerful," etc. Except here's the kicker: since language is & must be the world's mirror, the world is metaphysically composed only & entirely of those "facts" that statements stand for. In other words—the words of the *Tractatus*'s first & foremost line—the world is everything that is the case; the world is nothing but a huge mass of data, of logically discrete facts that have no *intrinsic* connection to one another. C.f. the *Tractatus* 1.2: "The world falls apart into facts..." 1.21: "Any one [fact] can either be the case, or not be the case, and everything else remains the same."

Mr. T. Pynchon, who has done in literature for paranoia what Sacher-Masoch did for whips, argues in his *Gravity's Rainbow* for why the paranoid delusion of complete & malevolent connection, wacko & unpleasant though it be, is preferable at least to its opposite—the conviction that *nothing* is connected to *anything* else & that *nothing* has *anything* intrinsically to do with *you*. Please see that this Pynchonian contraparanoia would be the appropriate metaphysic for any resident of the sort of world the *Tractatus* describes. And Markson's Kate lives in just such a world, while her objectless epistle "mirrors" it perfectly, manages to capture the psychic flavor both of solipsism and of Wittgenstein in the simple & affectless but surreal prose & the short aphoristic paragraphs that are also so distinctive of the *Tractatus*. Kate's textual obsession is simply to find connections between things,[18] any strands that bind the historical facts & empirical data that are all her world comprises. And always—necessarily—genuine connections elude her. All she can find is an occasional synchronicity: the fact that certain names are similar enough to be richly confusing—William Gaddis and Taddeo Gaddi, for example—or that certain lives & events happened to overlap in space & time. And even *these* fairly thin connections turn out not to be "real," features only of her imagination; and even *these* are nonetheless isolate, locked into themselves by their status as fact. When Kate recalls, for example, that Rembrandt suffered bankruptcy & Spinoza excommunication, and that, given biographical data, their paths may well have intersected at some point in the Amsterdam of the 1650s, the only encounter she can even *imagine* between them is

> "I'm sorry about your bankruptcy, Rembrandt."
> "I'm sorry about your excommunication, Spinoza."

The basic argument here is that Mr. Markson, by drawing on a definitive atomistic metaphysics and transfiguring it into art, has achieved something like the definitive anti-melodrama. He has made facts sad. For Kate's existence itself is that of an

[18] this connection-urge more fundamental and scary than the humanistic syrup of *Howard's End*'s *"Only connect"*: the latter refers to relations between persons, the former to the possibility of any extracranial universe at all...

atomic fact, her loneliness metaphysically ultimate. Her world is "empty" of all but data that are like the holes in a reticular pattern, both defined & imprisoned by the epistemic strands she knows only she can weave. And weave she does, constantly, unable to stop, self-consciously mimicking Penelope of the Attic antiquity that obsesses her. But Kate—unlike Ulysses's legit mistress—is powerless either to knit intrinsic pattern into or to dismantle what her mind has fabricated. She ends up, here, not Penelope but both Clytemnestra & Agamemnon, the Clytemnestra whom Kate describes as killing Agamemnon "after her own grief," the Agamemnon "at his bath, ensnared in that net and being stabbed through it." And since no things *present* connect either with each other or with her, Kate's memorial project in *WM* is sensible & inevitable even as it reinforces the occluded solipsism that is her plight. Via her memorial project Kate makes "external" history *her own*. I.e., rewrites it as personal. Eats it, as mad van Gogh "tried to eat his own pigments." It is not accidental that Mr. Markson's novel opens with the Genetic prepositional "In the beginning..." It is neither colorful tic nor authorial pretension that the narrator's "irreverent meditations" range from classical prosody to Dutch oils to Baroque quartets to nineteenth-century French Realism to post-Astroturf baseball. It is not an accident (though it is an allusion) that Kate has a fetish for feeding the warp & woof of tragic history into fires—she is the final historian, its tragedian and destructor, cremating each page of Herodotus (the 1st historian!) as she reads it. Nor is it cute or casual that she feels "as if I have been appointed the curator of all the world...," living in museums and placing her own paintings next to masterworks.

The curator's job—to recall, choose, arrange: to impose order & so communicate meaning—is marvelously synecdochic of the life of the solipsist, of the survival strategies apposite one's existence as monad in a world of diffracted fact.

Except a big question is: *whence facts,* if the world is "empty"?

Dalkey Archive Press's jacket copy for *WM* describes the solipsism of the Mistress as "obviously a metaphor for ultimate loneliness." And Kate is indeed awfully lonely, though her ingenuous announcements—"Generally, even then, I was lonely"—are less effective by far than the deep-nonsensical facts via which she communicates isolation's meaning—"One of those things people generally admired about Rubens, even if they were not always aware of it, was the way everybody in his paintings was always touching everybody else"; "Later today I will possibly masturbate"; "Pascal…refusing to sit on a chair without an additional chair at either side of him, so as not to fall into space." Though for me the most affecting rendition of her situation is Kate's funnysad descriptions of trying to play tennis without a partner,[19] probably the most fecund symbols of Kate's damnation to a world logically atomized in its reflective relation to language as bare data-transfer concern the narrator's obsession,

[19] plus continual reference to bunches of tennis balls bouncing all over the place made me realize tennis balls are about the best macroscopic symbol there is for the flux of atomistic fact…

marvelously American, with property & easements & houses. The following excerpt is condensed:

> I do not believe I have ever mentioned the other house.
>
> What I may have mentioned are houses in general, along the beach, but such a generalization would not have included this house, this house [unlike Kate's own] being nowhere near the water.
>
> All one can see of it from [my] upper rear window is a corner of its roof....
>
> Once I did become aware of it, I understood that there would also have to be a road leading to it from somewhere, of course.
>
> Yet for the life of me I was not able to locate the road, and for the longest time....
>
> In any case my failure to locate the road eventually began to become a wholly new sort of perplexity in my existence.[20]

It's of course tempting, given the critical imposition of Wittgenstein as referent & model & lover, to read Kate's loneliness as itself an intellectual metaphor, as just a function of the radical skepticism the *Tractatus*'s logical atomism itself imagines. Because, again, whence and wherefore the all-important "facts"

[20] pp. 88 & 89

that, for both Wittgenstein & Kate, the world "falls apart into"[21] but does *NOT* comprise? Are facts—genuine existents—intrinsic to the Exterior? admitting of countenance only via the frailties of sense-data & induction? Or, way worse, are they not perhaps perversely *de*ductive, products of the very head that countenances them as Exterior facts & as such genuinely ontic? This latter possibility—if internalized, really believed—is a track that makes stops at skepticism & then solipsism before heading straight into insanity. It's the latter possibility that informs the neurasthenia of Descartes's *Meditations* & so births modern philosophy (and with it the distinctively modern "alienation" of the individual from all wholes natural & social). Kate flirts with this Cartesian nightmare repeatedly, as in:

> What happened after I started to write about Achilles was that halfway through the sentence I began to think about a cat, instead.[22]
>
> The cat I began to think about instead was the cat outside of the broken window in the room next

[21] *Tractatus* 1.2

[22] Since I can't find any more graceful place to stick it in, let me invite you, with this line as exemplar, to see another cool formal horizon-expansion Mr. Markson effects in *WM*—the mode of presentation is less "stream of consciousness" than "stream of conscious *utterance*"; Markson's technique here shares the associative qualities of Joycean S.O.C. but differs in being *"directed"*: at what or whom it's directed becomes the novel's implicit, or anti-, plot, & accounts for a "narrative movement" that's less linear or even circular than spiral.

> to this one, at which the tape frequently scratches when there is a breeze.
>
> Which is to say that I was not actually thinking about a cat either, there being no cat except insofar as the sound of scratching reminds me of one.
>
> As there were no coins on the floor of Rembrandt's studio, except insofar as the configuration of the pigment reminded Rembrandt of them.[23]

The thing is that the painted coins that fooled Rembrandt, & Rembrandt, & Achilles, too, are all just like "the cat" here: Mr. Markson's narrator has nothing left *except* "sounds of scratching"—i.e., memory & imagination & the English language—with which to construct any sort of Exterior. Its flux is that of Kate's own head; why it resists order or population is attributable to the very desperation with which Kate tries to order & populate it: her search's fevered pathos ensures dissatisfaction. Note that by page 63, after the shine of metaphysical scrupulousness has faded, Kate goes back to talking about the unreal cat as real. The big emotional thing is that, whether her treatment of linguistic constructs as existents is out of touch with reality or simply an inevitable response to reality, the solipsistic nature of that reality, *as far as Kate's concerned,* remains unchanged. A double-bind to make Descartes, Shakespeare, & Wittgenstein all proud.

[23] p. 62

Still, as I read and appreciate *WM,* more is at stake for Kate in countenancing the possibility that her own "errors" are all that keep the world extant than questions of metaphysics or even of madness. Kate's pretty sanguine about the possibility of insanity—admits she's been mad, before, at times, "times out of mind." Actually, what are finally at stake here seem to be issues of ethics, of guilt & responsibility. One of the things that putatively so tortured Wittgenstein in the twenty years between the *Tractatus* and the *Investigations* was that a logically atomistic metaphysics admits exactly nothing of ethics or moral value or questions about what it is to be human. It's history that Wittgenstein the person cared deeply about what made things good or right or worthwhile. He did things like volunteer for the Austrian infantry in 1918, when he could & should have 4F'd out; like give his huge personal inheritance away to people, Rilke among them. A deadly serious ascetic, Wittgenstein lived his adult life in bare rooms devoid of even a lamp or coccyx-neutral chair. But it was no accident that the *Tractatus,* very much the product of the same Vienna that birthed "... two of the most powerful & symptomatic movements of modern culture: psychoanalysis and atonal music, both voices that speak of the homelessness of modern man,"[24] nevertheless itself birthed the Vienna Circle & the philosophical school of

[24] See William Barrett, "Wittgenstein the Pilgrim," in *The Illusion of Technique,* Doubleday '78.

Logical Positivism the Circle promulgated: a central tenet of Positivism being that the only utterances that made any sense at all were the well-formed data-transferring propositions of science, thus that considerations of "value" such as those of ethics or aesthetics or normative prescription were really just a confused mishmash of scientific observation and emotive utterance, such that saying "Killing is not right" really amounts just to saying "Killing: YUCK!" The fact that the metaphysics of the *Tractatus* not only couldn't take account of but pretty much denied the coherent possibility of things like ethics, values, spirituality, & responsibility had the result that "Wittgenstein, this clearheaded & intellectually honest man, was hopelessly at odds with himself."[25] For Wittgenstein was a queer sort of ascetic. He did deny his body & starve his senses—except not, as with most monkish personalities, simply to enjoy a consequent nourishment of the spirit. His big thing seems to have been denying his *self* by denying, through his essays at philosophical truth, the things most important to him. He never actually wrote anything about the exquisite tensions between atomism & attendant solipsism on the one hand & distinctively human values & qualities on the other. But, see, this is *exactly* what Mr. Markson does in *WM;* and in this way Markson's novel succeeds in speaking where Wittgenstein is mute, weaving Kate's obsession with responsibility (for the world's emptiness)

[25] Dr. James D. Wallace, unpublished response to his son's cries for help with *Wittgenstein's Mistress* and *Tractatus Logico-Philosophicus*.

gorgeously into the character's mandala of cerebral conundrum & spiritual poverty.

From this one of the specular vantages *WM* demands, Kate's central identification with the "fact" of historical personage is with Helen of Troy/Hisarlik—the Face That Launched 1,000 Ships & the body that lay behind the Trojan War's impressive casualty-count.[26] And the vehicle for this identification with Helen is a distinctively female sense of "responsibility": like *The Iliad*'s Helen, Kate is haunted by the passive sense that "everything is her fault." And Kate's repeated attempts at defending Helen against the charge of instigating exactly what emptied Ionia of men have a compulsive & shrill insistence about them that bespeak protesting too much:

> I have always harbored sincere doubts that Helen was the cause of that war, by the way.
>
> A single Spartan girl, after all.
>
> As a matter of fact the whole thing was undeniably a mercantile proposition. All ten years of it,[27]

[26] Also true that Kate identifies closely with Penelope, Clytemnestra, Eve, Agamemnon, & particularly Cassandra, the mad prophetess who warned about armed men inside empty gifts. But I'm thinking Cassandra's importance is more a function of Kate's *self-consciousness* about her own identification with Helen and feminine culpability, about which more below.

[27] (the same period of time Kate spent traversing the ancient & modern empty worlds, flopping in museums and "looking" for people)

> just to see who would pay tariff to whom, so as to be able to make use of a channel of water....
>
> Still, I find it extraordinary that young men died there in a war that long ago, and then died in the same place three thousand years after that.[28]

Issues orbiting Helen & femininity & guilt mark a sort of transition in this novel & its reading. Have I yet mentioned that a notable feature of *Wittgenstein's Mistress,* male-written, is that the novel's composed entirely of the words of a female character? And it is in terms of gender & authenticity, I think, that Mr. Markson's book becomes at once least perfect & most interesting. Most 1988ish. Most important as not just a literary transposition of a philosophic position but also a transcendence of received doctrine. Here Descartes & Kant & Wittgenstein cease being overt critical touchstones and become springboards for a flawed, moving meditation on loneliness, language, & gender.

See, Helen is "guilty" finally not because of anything she's done but because of who she is, how she appears, what she looks like; because of the effect she has, hormonally/emotionally, on men who're ready to kill & die over what they're made to feel. Kate, like Helen, is haunted by an unspoken but oppressive sense

[28] p. 59, c.f. 8–9, 22

that "...everything is her [own] fault." What everything? How close is she to the Helen she invokes?[29]

Well, first off, it's easy to see how radical skepticism—Descartes's hell & Kate's vestibule—yields at once omnipotence and moral oppression. If the World is entirely a function of Facts that not only reside in but *hail from* one's own head, one is just as Responsible for that world as is a mother for her child, or herself. This seems straightforward. But what's less clear & way richer is the peculiar slant "omniresponsibility" takes when the responsible monad in question is historically *passive,* per- & conceived as an object and not a subject—i.e., when one is a woman, one who can effect change & cataclysm not as an agent but merely as a perceived entity...perceived by historically active testosteroids whose glands positively *gush* with agency. To be an object of desire (by hirsute characters), speculation (by hirsute author), oneself the "product" of male heads & shafts is to be almost Classically feminized, less Eve than Helen, responsible without freedom to choose, act, forbear. The (my) terribly blanket assumption here is that received perceptions of women as moral agents divide into those of Hellenic and those of Evian (Eve-ish) responsibility; the claim I can support is that Markson, despite his worst intentions, manages to triumph over 400 years of post-Miltonic

[29] Evidently pretty close for readers: over half the reviews of *WM* when it came out misnamed the narrator Helen.

tradition and to present the Hellenic as the more poignant—certainly more apposite—situation of women in any system where appearance remains a "picture" or "map" of ontology. This presentation seems neither pre- nor post-feminist: it's just darned imaginative, ingenious even, and as such—despite failures of authorial vision & nerve—flies or falls on its own merits.

The degree of success with which Mr. Markson has here rendered the voice & psyche & predicament of a female, post-Positivist or otherwise, is a vexed issue. Some of the fiction I try to write is in feminine voice, and I consider myself sensitive to the technical/political problems involved in "crosswriting," and I found the female persona here compelling & real. Some female readers on whom I've foisted *WM* report finding it less so. They objected not so much to the voice & syntax (both of which are great in *WM* in a way I can't demonstrate except by quoting like twenty pages verbatim) as to some of the balder ways Mr. Markson goes about continually *reminding* the reader that Kate is a woman. The constant reference to Kate's menses, for example, was cited as clunky. Menstruation does come up a lot, & for reasons that remain narratively obscure; and if it isn't a clunky allusion to Passion or martyrdom then it's an equally clunky (because both unsubtle & otiose) reminder of gender: yes, women are persons whose vaginas sometimes bleed, but repeating & dwelling on it reminds one of bad science fiction where aliens are making continual reference to cranial antennae that—were they & the narrative voice truly alien/alien-empathetic—would be as unquestioned & quotidian a fact of life as ears or noses or hair.[30] Personally I'm neutral on the menstruation point. What I'm negative on is the particular strategy Markson sometimes employs to try to explain Kate's "female" feelings both of ultimate guilt & of ultimate loneliness. The "realistic" or character-based explanation is not, thank God, just that Kate's been left in the emotional lurch by all sorts of objectifying men, psychic abandoners who range from her husband (variously named by her Simon or Terry or sometimes Adam) to her final lover, univocally called Lucien. The proffered explanation is rather that, back in the halcyon pre-Fall days when the world was humanly populated, Kate betrayed her husband with other men, and that subsequently her little boy (variously Simon or, gulp, again Adam) died, in Mexico, possibly of TB, and that then her husband left her, about ten years ago, "time out of mind," at the same psycho-historical point at which Kate's world emptied and the diasporic quest for anyone else alive in the world at all commenced, a search that led Kate to the empty beach where she now resides and declaims to no one. Her betrayals & her son's death & husband's departure—alluded to over & over, albeit

[30] This is not my analogy, but I can't think of a better one, even though this isn't all that good; but I see the point & trust you do—it's one of those alarm-bell issues where the narrative voice is clearly communicating to a reader while pretending not to, as in like "Lord, Cragmont, the vermilion of your MOTHER tattoo is looking even more lurid against the dead-white of your prison pallor now that the circulation's returned to the legs you smashed trying to outrun a 74-car grain train in Decatur IL that balmy yet somehow also chill night in 1979"—"clunky" is the best analysis for stuff like this.

coyly—are the Evian diagnosis of her transgression & metaphysical damnation; they're presented, with an insistence impossible to ignore, as Kate's Fall[31] across gender, a Fall from the graces of a community in which she is both agent & object[32] into post-Romantic Wittgensteinian world of utter subjectivity & pathological responsibility, into the particular intellectual/emotional/moral isolation a 1988 U.S. reader associates with *men,* males alienated via agency from an Exterior we have to objectify, use up, burn the pages of in order to remain subjects, ontologi-

[31] Q.v. in this respect:

> After he knew that he had fallen, outward & down, away from the Fullness, he tried to remember what the Fullness had been....
>
> He did remember, but found he was *silent, & could not tell others.*
>
> He wanted to tell others that she leapt farthest forward & fell into a Passion *apart from his embrace.*
>
> She was in great agony, & would have been swallowed up by the sweetness, had she not reached a limit, & stopped.
>
> But the Passion *went on without her,* & *passed beyond the limit.*
>
> Sometimes he thought he was about to speak, but *the silence continued.*
>
> He wished to say: *strengthless & female fruit.*

—w/ emphasis supplied, from Valentinus's AD 199 *Pleroma,* part of the Neo-Platonic Gnosticism that functions as a metaphysical counterpoint to the anti-idealism of the *Tractatus,* & signals nicely Markson's artistic ambivalence about whether Kate's bind is ultimately Hellenic or Evian.

[32] this community being nothing other than sexual society as limned by the males who wrote scripture & epic, these males themselves interpreted & transfigured by Mr. Markson...

cally secure in shield & shaft. All this stuff I find fecund & compelling, a pregnant marriage of Attic & Christian reductions of women. But the death of her son & separation from her husband are also in *WM* presented as a very particular emotional "explanation" of Kate's psychic "condition," a peculiar reduction of Mr. Markson's own to which I kind of object. The presentation of personal history as present explanation, one that threatens to make *WM* just another madwoman monologue in the Ophelia–Rhys tradition, is oblique & ever artful, but still prominent & insistent enough to make it hard (for me) to blink its intent:

> Possibly [I was not mad] before that. [When I went south] To visit at the grave of a child I had lost... named Adam.
>
> Why have I written that his name was Adam?
>
> Simon is what my little boy was named.
>
> Time out of mind. Meaning that one can even momentarily forget the name of one's only child, who would be thirty by now?[33]
>
> As a matter of fact I believe it was when I went back to Mexico, that I [gessoed a blank canvas & then stared at it for a long time & then burned it]. In the house where I had once lived with Simon, and with Adam.

[33] p. 9

> I am basically positive that my husband [Simon/Terry] was named Adam.[34]
>
> There is no longer any problem in regard to my husband's name, by the way. Even if I never saw him again, once we separated after Simon died.[35]
>
> Although probably I did leave out this part before, about having taken lovers when I was still Adam's wife.[36]

Apparently Shiite women walk swaddled & veiled in deference to their responsibility to be invisible & so keep poor barely-keeping-it-together males from being maddened by exposure to fair sexuality. I find in *WM* the same complex & scary blend of Hellenic & Evian misogyny—Helen essentially guilty as object & Eve guilty as subject, temptress. Though I personally find the Hellenic component more interesting & a better easement into contemporary politics, I find Mr. Markson's vacillation between the two models narratively justified & psychologically neat. It is when, though, he seems to settle on the Evian as both character-archetype & narrative explanation—as the argument traced *supra* & beyond indicates—that his *Wittgenstein's Mistress* becomes most conventional as fiction. It is here, too, that for me the novel falters technically by betraying its authorial presence

[34] p. 24

[35] p. 52

[36] p. 225

as thoroughly male, *outside* Kate &/or womanhood generally. As in most cutting-edge experimental fictions, too, this *technical* flaw seriously attenuates the thematics. It seems very interesting to me that Mr. Markson has created a Kate who dwells so convincingly in a hell of utter subjectivity, yet cannot, finally, himself help but objectify her—i.e., by "explaining" her metaphysical condition as emotional/psychical, reducing her bottled missive to a mad monologue by a smart woman driven mad by the consequences of culpable sexual agency, Markson is basically subsuming Kate under one of the comparatively stock rubrics via which we guys apparently must organize & process fey mystery, feminine pathos, Strengthless & Female fruit. Kate's Fall, ostensibly one into the ghastly spiritual manifestation of a masculinely logic-bound twentieth-century metaphysic, becomes under a harsh reading little more than a(n inevitable?) stumble into alienation from the heroine's role—her self—as mother, wife, lover, *beloved.* Under this reading Kate's empty solipsism does not get to become a kind of grim independence from objectification: Kate has rather simply exchanged the role of real wife of real man for the part of nonexistent mistress of an absolute genius of objectification[37] indisposed toward heterosexual union. And I found it weird that many of the female readers who disapproved things like *WM*'s menstruation-cues as "ringing false" nevertheless approved Markson's provision of Kate's ostensible "motivation," here. Though I'm coming to accept that

[37] "The world is everything that is the case. The world falls apart into facts."

it's the petrifiedly standard critical line w/r/t fiction these U.S. days: readers want stories about very particular persons with very particular qualities in very particular circumstances whose genesis must on some level be personally-historic & psychological as well as "merely" intellectual or political or spiritual, pan-human. The successful story "transcends" its thoroughgoing individuality/idiosyncrasy via subsuming the peculiarities of character & circumstance to certain broad archetypes & mythopoeia inherited from Jung or Shakespeare or Homer or Freud or Skinner or Testament. Particularity births form; familiarity breeds content. Rarely is our uncritical inheritance of early Wittgensteinian & Logical Positivist models so obvious as in our academic & extra-mural prejudice that successful fiction encloses rather than opens up, organizes facts rather than transcends them, diagnoses rather than genuflects. Attic myths were, yes, forms of "explanation." But it's no accident that great mythos was mothered by the same culture that birthed great history—or that Kate divides her reading- & burning-time between classical histories & tragedies. To the extent that myth enriches facts & history, it serves a Positivist & factual function. But the U.S.'s own experience with myth-making & myth-worship—from Washington & cherries to Jackson & hickory to Lincoln & logs to dime novels & West as womb & soul's theater to etc., etc. to Presley & Dean & Monroe & Wayne & Reagan—an experience that informs & infects the very physics of reading, today—confirms that myth is finally compelling only in its opposition to history & data & the cingulum of Just the Facts, Ma'am. Only in that opposition can story enrich & transfigure & transcend explanation. Kate's idiosyncratic/formulaic "real" past in *WM* isn't weak as an explanation; it is for me weak & disappointing *because* it's an explanation. Just as it would have been weak & disappointing to have "explained" & particularized Kate's feelings of isolation & imprisonment, not via the idea that the typing hands she holds out in search of communion form the very barrier between Self & World they're trying to puncture, but, say, by plunking her down via shipwreck on a deserted island à la TV's Gilligan or Golding's flylord schoolboys or the Police's top-40 "Message in a Bottle."

I'm struggling to make clear, I think, that it's this masculinely prejudiced imperfection that illuminates how important & ambitious *WM* is as an experimental piece of late-'80s literature. As a would-be writer I like how the novel inverts received formulae for successful fiction by succeeding least where it conforms to them most: to the precise extent that Kate is presented here as circumstantially & historically unique, to just that extent is the novel's monstrous power attenuated. It's when Kate is *least* particular, *least* "motivated" by some artfully presented but standardly digestible Evian/Valentinian/post-Freudian trauma, that her character & plight are most e- & affecting. For (obvious tho this seems) to the extent that Kate is not motivationally unique, she can be all of us, and the empty diffraction of Kate's world can map or picture the desacralized & paradoxical solipsism of U.S. persons in a cattle-herd culture that worships only the Transparent I, of guiltily passive solipsists & skeptics trying to warm soft hands at the computer-enhanced fire of data in an Information Age where received image & enforced eros replace active countenance or sacral mystery as ends, value, meaning. Etc. The familiar bitch & moan that Markson's novel promises & comes close to transfiguring, dramatizing, *mythologizing* via bland bald fact.

I think finally the reason I object to *WM*'s attempt to give Kate's loneliness a particular "motivation" via received feminine trauma is that it's just unnecessary. For Mr. Markson has in this book succeeded already on all the really important levels of fictional conviction. He has fleshed the abstract sketches of Wittgensteinian doctrine into the concrete theater of human loneliness. In so doing he's captured far better than pseudo-biography what made Wittgenstein a tragic figure & a victim of the very diffracted modernity he helped inaugurate. Markson has written an erudite, breathtakingly cerebral novel whose prose is crystal & whose voice rivets & whose conclusion defies you not to cry. Plus he's also, in a way it'd seem for all the world he doesn't know, produced a powerfully critical meditation on loneliness's relation to language itself.

Though of course any writer's real motivations are forever occult & objects of at best lucid imagining, it's safe to point out that the post-atomist metaphysical peripety that is L. Wittgenstein's late *Philosophical Investigations* articulates philosophical concerns & assumptions so different from those of the early *Tractatus* that the *PI* amounts to less a renunciation than a kind of infanticide-by-bludgeon. For Marksonian purposes, the three important blunt instruments, near-diurnal differences between "early" & "late" Wittgenstein, concern W's enduring obsession with language-&-reality questions. One. *PI* now takes as paradigmatic of the language with which philosophers ought to be concerned not the ideal abstraction of math-logic, rather now just ordinary day-to-day language in all its general wooliness & charm.[38] Two. The *PI*'s Wittgenstein expends much energy & ink arguing against the idea of what's been called "private language." This term is the Pragmatist William James's, whom W, not an enemy to welcome, accused of looking forever "for the artichoke amongst its leaves." But *PI*'s concern to show the impossibility of private language (which it does, pretty much) is also a terrible anxiety to avoid the solipsistic consequences of mathematical logic as language-paradigm. Recall that the truth-functional schemata of math-logic & the discrete facts the schemata picture exist independent of speakers, knowers, & most of all *listeners*. *PI*'s insistence—as part of the book's movement away from what the world must be like for language to be possible & toward what language must be like given the way the world in all its babble & charm & deep nonsense actually *is*—that the existence, nay the very *idea* of language depends on some sort of communicative *community*[39]... this is about the most powerful philosophical attack on skeptic-/solipsism's basic coherence since the Descartes whose *Cogito* Wittgenstein had helped to skewer. Three. The final big difference is a new & clinical focus on the near-Nixonian trickiness of ordinary language itself. A tenet of the *PI* is that profound phil-

[38] Very cool elaborations on this sort of move are observable in J. L. Austin's *How to Do Things with Words* & Stanley Cavell's "Must We Mean What We Say?"

[39] Q.v. *PI* I, 23...

osophical stuff can be accomplished via figuring out why linguistic constructions get used as they are, & that many/most errors of "metaphysics" or "epistemology" derive from academics' & humans' susceptibility to language's *pharmakopia* of tricks & deceptions & creations. Late Wittgenstein is full of great examples of how persons are constantly succumbing to the metaphysical "bewitchment" of ordinary language. Getting lost in it. E.g., locutions like "the flow of time" create a kind of ontological UHF-ghost, seduce us into somehow seeing time itself as like a river,[40] one not just "flowing" but doing so somehow external to us, outside the things & changes of which time is really just the measure.[41] Or the ordinary predicates "game" and "rules," attached simultaneously to, e.g., jacks & gin rummy & softball & Olympiade, trick us into a specious Platonic universalism in which there is some transcendentally existent feature common to every member of the extensions of "game" or "rule" in virtue of which every member *is* a "game" or a "rule," rather than the fluid web of "family resemblances"[42] that, for Wittgenstein, perfectly justifies the

[40] Q.v. Alan Parsons Project's dirge-like "Time," late '70s.

[41] Tachyons & causality violations & the Superposition Principle all complicate W's point quite a bit, and actually there's very interesting stuff starting to appear in industrial mags about deep affinities between ordinary-language temporal locutions & cutting-edge quantum models... but anyway you get the idea.

[42] the famous & infamous *Familienahanlichkeiten* (no kidding)—c.f. *The Blue Book* 17 & 87 & 124 or *Philosophical Grammar* 75 or *PI* I, 67. For equally famous stuff on games & rules see *PI* I, 65–88.

attachment of apparently univocal predicates as nothing more or less than a type of *human behavior*—rather, that is, than any sort of transcendental reality-mapping. Wittgenstein by life's end conceived meaningful human brain-activity (i.e., philosophy) as exactly & nothing more than "...a battle against the bewitchment of our intelligence by means of language."[43] The *PI* holds that persons must or at any rate do live in a sort of linguistic dream, awash & enmeshed in ordinary language & the deceptive "metaphysics" linguistic usage & communication among persons imposes... or costs.

The above summary is pretty crude.

But actually, so, on the surface, is *Wittgenstein's Mistress*'s use & reconstitution of the *PI*'s seminal new perspective. Much of the overt master/mistress relation here again involves the resemblance-as-allusion [*sic*]. Lines in the novel like "Upstairs, one can see the ocean. Down here there are dunes, which obstruct one's view" are conscious echoes of the *PI*'s "A philosophical problem has the form: 'I don't know my way about.'"[44] Also heavily

[43] *PI* I, 109...

[44] *PI* I, 123, a profound little offering meaning roughly to point out that we are now & forever "down here" in language, inside it, on ground-level, & thus have no better a view of the Big Picture than someone earthbound in contrast to someone aloft who can look down at the earthbound guy & the terrain around him, discerning patterns against backdrops of other bigger patterns, seeing them as *patterns of something larger* instead of as the -bound man's terrain, maze, world, total...

allusive (sometimes just plain heavy) are Kate's prolonged musings on the ontological status of named things: she (as would we all) still refers to the house she burned down as a house, but she keeps wondering in what way a destroyed house is still a "house," except in virtue of language-habits from time out of mind. Or, e.g., she wonders about questions like "Where is the painting when it is in my head instead of on the wall?" & whether, were let's say no copies of *Anna Karenina* still extant (unburned) anywhere, the book would still be called *Anna Karenina.* Or marvels at facts like "One can drive through any number of towns without knowing the names of the towns."

A little of this narcissistic echo goes a long way, and Markson is sometimes unkind, allusively, on the surface. Again, though, the mistress like the master invites you/me down: what's ponderous on the first pass opens up later. It's toss-offs like the last just above that are most interesting as invitations, less allusion to a genius than gauzy prefigures of Markson's own meditations about & around some of the themes dominant in *PI.* What first strikes one as heavy or ponderous refines itself after time into a fragile note of resignation—i.e., weltschmerz as opposed to naïveté or hubris—in most of Kate's speculations on the way a name tends to "create" an object or attribute[45];

[45] note in passing that themes of nomination-as-enfranchisement, presence-as-privilege, also run through much of the feminist theory with which this novel's author reveals himself familiar...

albeit on the other hand a twinge of envy whenever she countenances the possibility of things existing without being named or subjected to predication. Why this battle occupies Kate & engages the reader has partly to do with the actual ethical pain that we may assume filled the long silence between the *Tractatus* and *PI,* but it's also attributable to an original & deeply smart exploration by Mr. Markson of something that might be called "the feminization of skepticism."

Which is probably a bad term to start throwing around in this late inning, since it requires definitions & so on; this is already pretty long.

But recall to this abstraction's ambit prenominate stuff about Helen & Eve & Cassandra & the *Tractatus,* plus the longly discussed second half of the double bind that cingulizes solipsism: radical doubt about not only the existence of objects but of *subject,* self. Kate's text, acknowledged within itself as writing, is a desperate attempt to re-create & so animate a world by *naming* it. The attempt's desperation underlies her near-anal obsession with names—of persons, personages, figures, books, symphonies, battles, towns, & roads—and it accounts for what Markson communicates so well via repetition & tone: Kate's extreme upset when she can't remember—"summon," "recall" —names well enough to make them *behave.* Her attempts at ontology-thru-nomination are a moving synecdoche of pretty much the whole history of intellectual endeavor in the whitely male West. She, no less than was Wittgenstein, or Kant, or Descartes, or Herodotus, is writing a world. The ingenious poignancy of Markson's achievement here is that Kate's modernly female vantage, in conspiracy with the very desperation that underlies her attempt at worldmaking,[46] renders her project doubly doomed. Doom 1 is what's evoked on surface: skepticism & solipsism: i.e., that there *is* no "world" to see itself mirrored in Kate's text is unhappy enough. But in *WM* Kate's memoir *itself* is "written in sand," itself subject to the "deterioration"[47] & dry rot that is such a dominant recurring image in the loops of recollection & assembly here.

I'm going to shut up right after I make this idea clear. I'm pretty sure *Wittgenstein's Mistress* is an imperfect book. Questions of voice, over-allusion, & "explanation" get to be aside, though, because of the novel's terrific emotional & political/fictional & theoretical achievement: it evokes a truth a whole lot of books & essays before it have fumbled around: (at least) for the modern female—viz. the female who understands herself as both female & modern—both sides of the solipsistic bind:

[46] i.e., she's doing it for mental survival, not for interest or acclaim or tenure...

[47] I keep waiting for feminist theorists to start talking about *deterioration* as a textual phenomenon; it would be the sort of wry joke that captures truths: "deterioration" is essentially "deconstruction" made passive, observed rather than performed, the reader the ultimate "absentee" in the post-structural totem of absence: one of the things Kate's story unpacks is the terrific power of writer-as-witness, utterly passive, unheard: it might be this more than what's argued in the main body below that's skepticism's feminist vishna.

If I exist, nothing exists outside me
But
If something exists outside me, I do not exist[48]

amount to the same thing—damnation to ghostliness among ghosts, curating a plenum of statues, mistaking echoes for voices. And, too, here both binds force on the subject just what her own dramatic predicament forces on Kate: a kind of parodic *masculinization,* one in which the Romantic Quest for the Absent Object, a desire for attainment w/r/t which *un*attainability is that desire's breath & bread, replaces an ability to be-in-the-world as neither center nor cipher, neither all-responsible nor impotent, part of one great big Family Likeness. Markson's Kate's sudden loss of interest in roads once she's found them & data once she's "mastered"[49] it is just as clunky & imperfect & human & real as say Stendhal's rush to wind up *The Charterhouse of Parma* the minute Fabrizio finally nails Clelia....And Kate's valuation, finally, only of what's unsaid, unread—burning pages once she's read them, jettisoning family once she's "responsible" for them; probably even fueling her epistle with the doomed/delicious knowledge that it's headed toward nothing—summons perfectly, again, the terrible & moving final prescription of the master's *Tractatus.*

[48] I won't waste anybody's time shouting about what a marvelous inversion of the *Cogito* & Ontological Argument this is.

[49] !!!!!

This, loosely translated, is "Anybody who understands what I'm saying eventually recognizes that it's nonsense, once he's used what I'm saying—rather like steps—to climb up past what I'm saying—he must, that is, throw away the ladder after he's used it."[50] This passage, like most of W, is only indirectly about what it's really about. It whispers & plays. It's really about the plenitude of emptiness, the importance of silence, in terms of speech, on beaches. Markson nails this idea[51]; Kate's monograph has the quality of speechlessness in a dream, the cold muteness urgency enforces, a psychic stutter. If it's true her ladder goes no place, it's also true nobody's going to throw either book away. The end. 7 January '90. Pax.

—*1990*

[50] *Tractatus* 6.54

[51] from my male p.o.v. . . .

carnelian—pale to deep red / reddish-brown **carnet**—book of postage stam
woman **Casanova de Seingalt**—full name of Casanova the lover **casuistry**
casus belli—provocation or excuse for war **catabolism**—break down
freshwater but migrating to sea to breed; could say of a guy who goes
enzyme that causes hydrogen peroxide to decompose into water and oxy
catamite—boy who has sex with a man **catamount**—mountain lion
wire hung by endpoints (phone wires) **catkin**—drooping, non-petaled
celiac (adj.)—pertaining to abdomen or abdominal cavity **cellarette**—li
dining room on second floor **cenotaph**—monument erected to dead
certes (archaic adv.)—certainly, truly **chamfer** (v.)—to bevel, cut the
etc.) **chamfron**—armor for medieval horse's head **charcuterie**—sau
charnel—repository for bodies; related to death in general: "a charnel
chemical stimulus **chenille**—fabric cords of silk or cotton, used for em
on swivels in a frame **chinch** (n.)—bedbug **chine**—backbone or spine
or harass with petty attacks **chlamydia**—also causes conjunctivitis in
an's face caused by hormonal changes, usually pregnancy **chromo**—pre
cinerarium—place for keeping ashes of a cremated body **cinnabar**—red
by a rampart **citrine**—light to moderate olive color **clabber**—curdled
w/ lovely blossoms **clathrate**—having a latticelike structure: e.g., clath
that measured time by marking the regulated flow of water through a
ply natural light to building **clerisy**—the literati; educated people as a
clinometer—device for measuring slope, angle of elevation…used

ɔs **caryatid**—architecture: a supporting column sculptured into a draped

–specious or excessively subtle reasoning intended to rationalize or mislead

ɔf complex molecules into simple ones **catadromous**—living in

o Florida or CA to have debauches as a catadromous guy **catalase**—

gen **catalpa**—type of Midwest tree w/ long pods **catamenia**—menses

:ataplasm—poultice **catenary**—inverse parabolic; imagine curve of

lowers as in willows, birches, oaks **celadon**—pale to very pale green

quor cabinet **cenacle**—a clique or circle, especially of writers; small

ɔerson whose remains are elsewhere **cerements**—burial garments

edge off; "chamfered," "chamfering" (the chamfering on wood edge,

sage, bologna: processed meat stuff, or a deli proffering such stuff

ɔdor" **chemotropism**—movement or growth of organism in response to

ɔroidery, fringing, bedspreads, rugs **cheval glass**—a long mirror mounted

ɔf animal / cut of meat including the backbone **chivvy** (v.)—to vex

:attle and sheep **chloasma**—patchy brown skin discoloration on wom-

ix meaning color: "chromoplast" **cicatrix**—area of nasty scar tissue

ɔigment gotten from mercury ore **circumvallate** (adj.)—surrounded

milk; to make (cloud) motions resembling curdling **clarkia**—show plants

ate foliage **clement**—good (w/r/t weather) **clepsydra**—ancient device

small opening **clerestory**—upper part of wall containing windows to sup-

class **clevis**—two-holed fastening device not unlike "hasp" and "staple"

in surveying **cloaca**—sewer or latrine **clochard**—tramp, vagrant

MR. COGITO

THE BEST BOOK OF 1994 is the first English translation of Zbigniew Herbert's *Mr. Cogito,* a book of poems that came out in Poland in the mid-1970s, well before Herbert's justly famous *Report from the Besieged City and Other Poems.* Mr. Cogito's a character who appears in most of Herbert's best poems—he's kind of a poetic Pnin, both intellectual and not too bright, both hopelessly confused and bravely earnest as he grapples with the Big Questions of human existence.

Zbigniew Herbert is one of the two or three best living poets in the world, and by far the best of what you'd call the "postmoderns." Since any great poem communicates an emotional urgency that postmodernism's integument of irony renders facile or banal, postmodern poets have a tough row to hoe. Herbert's Cogito-persona permits ironic absurdism and earnest emotion not only to coexist but to nourish one another. Compared to *Mr. Cogito,* the whole spectrum of American poetry—from the retrograde quaintness of the Neoformalists and *New-Yorker*-backyard-garden-meditative lyrics to the sterile abstraction of the Language Poets—looks sick. It seems significant that only writers from Eastern Europe and Latin America have succeeded in marrying the stuff of spirit and human feeling to the parodic detachment the postmodern experience seems to require. Maybe as political conditions get more oppressive here, we Americans'll get good at it, too.

—*1994*

cloche—close-fitting woman's hat, worn by e.g. flappers; a bell-shaped separated by strips of metal **cloistral/claustral**—secluded, cloistered **clo** sion and migraine **clonus**—in musculature, abnormally rapid contraction **coaming**—(nautical) raised rim or border around opening to keep water defect of eye that reduces vision **colposcope**—magnifier/camera for ex snake **commandmental**—imperative **compleat**—having a highly devel contradictory, or to prevent, forestall **coprolalia**—uncontrollable use of hill on either side **coulisse**—a grooved timber in which something slides bed as if he were having child **cradle**—like scythe, a bladed harvest tool shanghaier, somebody who tricks or coerces people into soldiering/sailor for gunnysack **crosse**—stick used in lacrosse **culex**—common mosquito **cuneal**—wedge-shaped **cupreous**—containing or resembling copper **cus** firm solid point; a cuspidate leaf (head? penis?) **cuspidor**—spittoon used to hoist cargo on and off a boat **debouche**—coming out of an enclosed paper **decollate** (v.)—to behead **décolleté**—cut low at neckline **decoup** relating to the common people **deracinate**—to pull up by the roots; to **desquamate**—to shed, peel, or come off in scales; (n.) desquamation **det** cover property wrongfully detained **dexter**—of or located on the right side as a means of obtaining compliance with a demand for justice **dhoti**—loin in monuments and tombstones (the dark shiny gray w/ luster or spa **dickey**—woman's blouse front worn under jacket, or men's detachable shir top?) **dieldrin**—poison used in insecticide **dimity**—sheer, crisp

:over for plants during frost **cloisonné**—enamelware with bands of color
niphene—drug that increases ovulation **clonidine**—drug for hyperten-
ınd relaxation **closet drama**—a play to be read rather than performed
'rom coming in **colloid**—suspension of fine particles **coloboma**—birth
ımination of vagina, used by gynecologists **colubrine**—of or resembling a
ɔped or wide-ranging skill **confute** (v.)—like refute, show to be false or
'oul language **coprolite**—petrified shit **coulee**—Midwest: a valley with a
:ouvade—culture dependent: when wife is in labor, husband takes to his
/ou swing **crazing** (n.)—a fine crack in a surface or glaze **crimp** (n.)—a
ng **crocket**—projecting ornament in architecture **croker sack**—Southern
:ulm—stem of grass or similar plant **cunctation**—procrastination, delay
ɔate—having a cusp or shaped like a cusp **cuspidate** (adj.)—tapering to
:yan—greenish blue **daltonism**—red-green colorblindness **davit**—small cranes
ırea into a wider or open one **deckle**—frame for turning wood pulp into
ıge—art of decorating a surface with paper or foil cutouts **demotic**—of or
lisplace one from his native environment **dermatoid**—resembling skin
ıue—act of unlawfully detaining personal property, or a legal action to re-
lharna—a fast conducted at the door of an offender, especially a debtor,
:loth worn by Hindu men in India **diabase**—dark gray stone mixture used
:le) **diadem**—crown worn as sign of royalty; royal power or dignity
'ront, or driver's seat in carriage, or special seats for servants in carriage (up
:otton fabric woven in stripes or checks, used for curtains and dresses

DEMOCRACY AND COMMERCE AT THE U.S. OPEN

RIGHT NOW IT'S 1530H. on 3 September, the Sunday of Labor Day Weekend, the holiday that's come to represent the American summer's right bracket. But L.D.W. always falls in the middle of the U.S. Open[1]; it's the time of the third and fourth rounds, the tournament's meat, the time of trench warfare and polysyllabic names. Right now, in the National Tennis Center's special Stadium—a towering hexagon[2] whose N, S, E, and W sides have exterior banners saying "WELCOME TO THE 1995 U.S. OPEN—*A U.S.T.A. EVENT*"—right now a whole inland sea of sunglasses and hats in the Stadium is rising to applaud as Pete Sampras and the Australian Mark Philippoussis are coming out on court, as scheduled, to

1 *"A U.S.T.A. Event."*

2 Actually, if you count the Grandstand Court's annex, the whole thing looks more like an ablated head w/ neck-stump.

labor. The two come out with their big bright athletic bags and their grim-looking Security escorts. The applause-acoustics are deafening. From down here near the court, looking up, the Stadium looks to be shaped like a huge wedding cake, and once past the gentler foothills of the box seats the aluminum stands seem to rise away on all sides almost vertically, so vertiginously steep that a misstep on any of the upper stairs looks like it would be certain and hideous death. The umpire sits in what looks like a lifeguard chair with little metal stirrups out front for his shoes,[3] wearing a headset-mike and Ray-Bans and holding what's either a clipboard or a laptop. The DecoTurf court is a rectangle of off-green marked out by the well-known configuration of very white lines inside a bigger rectangle of off-green; and as the players cross the whole thing E-W to their canvas chairs, photographers and cameramen converge and cluster on them like flies clustering on what flies like—the players ignore them in the way that only people who are very used to cameras can ignore cameras. The crowd is still up and applauding, a pastel mass of 20,000+. A woman in a floppy straw hat three seats over from me is talking on a cellular phone; the man next to her is trying to applaud while holding a box of popcorn and is losing a lot of popcorn over the box's starboard side. The scoreboards up over the Stadium's N and S rims

[3] There's always something extremely delicate and precarious and vulnerable-looking about the umpire's shoes projecting out over the court from a height in little metal stirrups—the blend of authority and precarious vulnerability is just one of the things that makes a tennis umpire such a compelling part of the whole show.

are flashing pointillist-neon ads for EVIAN. Sampras, poor-postured and chestless, smiling shyly at the ground, his powder-blue shorts swimming down around his knees, looks a little like a kid wearing his father's clothes.[4] Philippoussis, who chronologically really *is* a kid, looks hulking and steroidic walking next to Sampras. Philippoussis is 6'4" and 200+ and is crossing the court with the pigeon-toed gait of a large man who's trying not to lumber, wearing the red-and-white candy-stripe Fila shirt so many of the younger Australians favor. The PM sun is overhead to the W-SW in a sky with air so clear you can almost hear the sun combusting, and the tiny heads of the spectators way up at the top of the W bleachers are close enough to the sun's round bottom to look to be just about on fire. The players dump their long bags and begin to root through them. Their rackets are in plastic they have to unwrap. They sit in their little chairs hitting racket-faces together and cocking their heads to listen for pitch. The cameramen around them disperse at the umpire's command, some trailing snakes of cord. Ballboys take crumpled bits of racket plastic from under the players' chairs.

A lady making her way in that sideways-processional way past seats in the row right beneath me wears a shirt advising all

[4] The tentish tops and near-Bermuda-length shorts of M. Jordan and the NBA have clearly infiltrated tennis. Nearly half the men in the 128 draw are wearing clothes that seem several sizes too big, and on players as fundamentally skinny and woebegone-looking as Sampras the effect is more waifish than stylish—though I have to say that weirdly oversized clothes aren't near the visual disaster that Agassi's new clunky black sneakers (also imported from basketball fashion) are.

onlookers that they ought to Play Hard because Life Is Short. The man on her arm wears a (too-large) designer T-shirt decorated with images of U.S. currency. A firm/pleasant usher stops them halfway across the row to check their tickets. Fifteen hundred citizens of the borough of Queens are employed at the Open today. Weekend labor. The ushers are at their fat chains stretched across the Stadium tunnels, all wearing chinos and button-down shirts. The Security guys (all large and male, not a neck or a smile in sight) wear lemon-yellow knit shirts that do not flatter their guts. Chewing-gum seems to be part of Security's issued equipment. The ballboys[5] are in blue-and-white Fila, while the line judges and umpires are in (Fila) shirts of vertical red-black stripes that make them look like very hip major-sport refs. The Stadium's capacity is supposedly 20,000 and there are at least 23,000 people here, mostly to see Pete. If there were rafters people would be hanging from them, and I will be shocked if there isn't some major screaming fall-down-the-steps- or topple-backward-over-the-rim-of-the-wall-type disaster before the match is done. The crowd down here near the court is for the most part adult-looking, businessish—in the Box Seats and pricey lower stands are neckties, sockless loafers, natty slacks, sweaters w/ arms tied across chests, straw boaters, L.L. Bean fishing hats, white caps with corporate names, jeweled bandeaux, high heels, and resplendent femi-

[5] (looking more like ball-*grad-students*, here, actually—several have earrings and leg hair, and one on the south side's got a big ginger beard)

nine sunhats—with a certain very gradual casualizing as the fashion-eye travels up (and up) past the progressively cheaper seats, until the vertiginous top sections of the bleachers feature an NYC sporting event's more typical fishnet shirts and beer hats and coolers and makeshift spittoons, halter tops and fluorescent nail polish and rubber thongs, w/ attendant coarse NYC-crowd noises sometimes drifting down from way up high overhead.[6] But apparently over 50 percent of tickets for this year's Open were pre-sold to corporations, who like to use them for the cultivation of clients and the entertainment of their own executives, and there is indeed about the Stadium crowd down here something indefinable that strongly suggests Connecticut license plates and very green lawns. In sum, the socioeconomic aura here for the day's headline match is one of management rather than labor.

The players' umbrellas and chairs and big EVIAN-labeled barrels of drinks are on either side of the umpire's chair at the base of the Stadium's western cliff face, in a long thin patch of shade that ripples when the heads of the people way overhead move, and it's cool in that shade—it's cool for me, as well, in the shade of the very large man next to me, who's wearing a gorgeous

[6] The Open's crowds, I know, are legendary for being loud and vulgar and generally psycho, but I've got to say that most of the audiences for most of L.D.W.'s matches seem like people you'd be proud to take home and introduce to the folks. The odd bit of audible nastiness does sometimes issue from way up top in the Stadium's bleachers, but then usually only when there's been some missed call or flagrant injustice.

blue cord three-piecer and what seems to be a kind of huge sombrero—but the sunlight is summery, the sun (as mentioned) explosive, seeming to swell as it lowers, at 1535h. positioned about 40° above the Stadium's W battlements; and the Grandstand Court, attached to the Stadium's E flank, is knife-sliced by the well-known PM Grandstand shadow that Jim Courier is even now using to vivisect Kenneth Carlsen in full view of diners at Racquets (the impossible-to-get-into glass restaurant built into the wall that separates the Grandstand's W flank from the Stadium's E) and the 6,000+ crowd in there, a lot of whose nationalistic whistles and applause intrude into the Stadium's sonic fold and lend a kind of surreally incongruous soundtrack to Sampras and Philippoussis's exchanges as they warm up. Sampras is hitting with the casual economy that all the really top pros seem to warm up with, the serene nonchalance of a creature at the very top of the food chain. The Wimbledon champion's presence aside, this third-rounder has particular romance about it because it features two Greeks neither of whom are in fact from Greece, a kind of postmodern Peloponnesian War. Philippoussis, just eighteen, Patrick Rafter's doubles partner, ranked in the top 100 in this his first year on tour, potential superstar and actual heartthrob,[7] resem-

[7] Females in the crowds of this year's Australian Open apparently screamed and fainted and made with Beatlemania-like histrionics whenever Rafter or Philippoussis appeared, and it's true that on the court they are both extremely handsome guys; but it's also true that Mark Philippoussis, close up, looks amazingly like Gaby Sabatini—I mean *amazingly,* right down to the walk and the jaw line and the existentially affronted facial expression.

bles Sampras, somewhat—same one-handed backhand and slight loop on the forehand's backswing, same café-au-lait coloring and Groucho eyebrows and very black hair that get glossy with sweat—but the Australian is slower afoot, and in contrast to Sampras's weird boneless grace he looks almost awkward, perilously large, his shoulders square the way heavy guys with bad backs' shoulders are square. Plus he seems to have aggression-issues that need resolving: he's hitting the ball as hard as he can even in warm-up. He seems brutish, Philippoussis does, Spartan, a big slow mechanical power-baseliner[8] with chilly malice in his eyes; and against him, Sampras, who is not exactly a moonballer, seems almost frail, cerebral, a poet, both wise and sad, tired the way only democracies get tired, his expression freighted with the same odd post-Wimbledon melancholy that's dogged him all summer through Montreal, Cincinnati, etc. Thomas Enqvist's epic 2-6 6-2 4-6 6-3 7-6 (7-5) first-rounder against Marcelo Rios and Agassi's second-round squeaker against Corretja notwithstanding, it's tempting to see this upcoming match as the climax of the Open so far: two ethnically agnate and archetypally distinct foes, an opposition not just of styles of play but of fundamental orientations toward life, imagination, the uses of power... plus of course economic interests.

[8] The Open's slow DecoTurf, which various rumors allege has had some kind of extra abrasive mixed in to make it even slower for the Open, favors the power-baseline game of Agassi, Courier, et al.—even netophiles like Edberg and Krajicek have been staying back and whaling through the first two rounds.

Covering the four walls down around the Stadium Court is a kind of tarp, chlorine-blue,[9] and on it, surrounding the court, are the white proper nouns FUJIFILM, *REDBOOK* MAGAZINE, MASSMUTUAL, U.S. OPEN '95—*A U.S.T.A. EVENT,* CAFÉ de COLOMBIA (complete w/ a dotted white outline of Juan Valdez and devoted burro), INFINITI, TAMPAX, and so on.[10] Professional tennis always gets called an

[9] The Open's administration is smart about providing the right visual backdrop for world-class play. The Stadium Court at the du Maurier Ltd. in Montreal this July had yellow bleachers at the north end that, according to players, made it tough to track balls coming from that end, whereas the N.T.C.'s Stadium's got blue tarps and white chairs and gray chairs, and even the bleachers are high-contrast red—there's nothing even close to the YG part of the spectrum unless you count the pale-yellow shirts of the Security guys who stand court-side with the crossed arms and beady eyes of Secret Servicemen. (I've got to think the whole Seles thing is behind the high-profile Security here.)

[10] The tarp ads around pro tennis courts function like ads on subways, I think. Ads on subways exploit the fact that subway rides present both a lot of mental downtime and a problem with what to look at—the windows are mostly dark, and looking directly at other people on the subway is an action that the lookee can interpret in a number of ways, some of which are uncomfortable or even hazardous—and the ads up over the windows are someplace neutral and adverting to rest the eye, and so they usually get a lot of attention. And tennis is also full of downtime—periods between points, changeovers between odd games—where the eye needs diverting. Plus, during play, the tarp acts as the immediate visual background to the players, and the eyes and cameras always follow the players—including TV—so that having your company's name hovering behind Sampras as the camera tracks him is a way both to get serious visual exposure for your company and to have that name associated, even on a subliminal level, with Sampras and tennis and excellence in general, etc. It all seems tremendously sophisticated and shrewd, psychologically speaking.

international sport, but it would be more accurate to call it a *multinational* sport: fiscally speaking, it exists largely as a marketing subdivision of very large corporations, and not merely of the huge Tour-underwriting conglomerates like IBM and Virginia Slims. The hard core of most professional players' earnings comes from product endorsement. Absolutely every venue and piece of equipment associated with pro events has some kind of ad on it. Even the official names of most pro tournaments are those of companies that have bid to be a "title sponsor": the Canadian Open this year was the "du Maurier Ltd. Open" (for a Canadian cigarette company), Munich was the "BMW Open," New Haven was the "Volvo International" (next year it's to be the "Pilot Pen International"), Cincinnati the "Thriftway ATP Championship," and so on. The U.S. Open,[11] being a Slam and a national championship, doesn't have a title sponsor like Munich or Montreal; but instead of

[11] See FN#1 again—the strong sense I got was that you are never to say "The U.S. Open" in any kind of public way without also saying *"A U.S.T.A. Event."* Let's let the U.S.T.A.'s promotional appendix be implicit from now on; I don't feel like saying it over and over. The United States Tennis Association gets something like 75 percent of its yearly operating revenues from the U.S. Open, and it's probably understandable that it would want to attach its name like a remora to the tournament's flank, but the constant imposition of *"A U.S.T.A. Event"* all over the place got a little tiresome, I found, overtaxing the way relentless self-promotion is overtaxing, and I have to say I got a kind of unkind thrill out by the Main Gate's turnstiles when so many people coming in for the evening session of matches pointed up at the big sign over the Main Gate and asked each other what the hell "USTA" was, making it rhyme with a Boston pronunciation of "buster" or "Custer."

decommercializing the event, the tournament's Slam-status just makes the number of different commercial subsidizations more dizzying. The Open has an official sponsor not just for the tournament but for each of the tournament's various individual *events:* Infiniti sponsors the Men's Singles, *Redbook* the Women's Singles, MassMutual the Junior Boys, and so on.[12]

Now the umpire has ordered Play and Sampras is getting ready to serve, lifting the toe of his front foot on the toss's

[12] The names of all the various sponsors are on a big (*very* big) blue board just inside the National Tennis Center's Main Gate, with the bigger events' "presenting sponsors" on the left in huge caps, and in smaller caps on the right the names of pres. spons. of smaller events—Men's 35s Doubles, Mixed Doubles Masters—as well as other sponsors whose role is unclear beyond having paid a fee to sell concessions where appropriate and/or to have a PR booth on the grounds and a venue to call their own inside the Corporate Hospitality Areas (plus of course having their name on the v.b. blue board). Here's the whole sign's program, much reduced in scale: in the middle (natch), "1995 U.S. OPEN—*A U.S.T.A. EVENT*"; on the left: Infiniti, *Redbook,* Prudential Securities, Chase Manhattan, FujiFilm, MassMutual; on the right: American Express, AT&T, Ben Franklin Crafts, Café de Colombia, Canon, Citizen Watch Company (Citizen also has its name on all the big real-time and match-duration clocks on the Show Courts), Evian Natural Spring Water, Fila U.S.A., The Haägen-Dazs Co. Inc., Heineken, IBM, K-Swiss, *The New York Times* (which one kind of wonders, then, how objectively or aggressively the paper could report the facts if like the tournament this year were really boring or poorly managed or crooked somehow, etc.), NYNEX, Pepsi-Cola, Sony, Tampax (which, now that Virginia Slims finally got PC'd out of sponsoring the WTA, put in a bid to be the tour's new sponsor but was turned down, for reasons that haven't been made publicly explicit but are probably amusing), Tiffany and Co., Wilson Sporting Goods, good old *Tennis* magazine (which is itself owned by *The New York Times* Co., so that the *Times* sneakily gets on the Board twice), and something called the VF Corporation.

upswing in that distinctive way he has. I've never gotten to see Sampras play live before, and he's far more beautiful an athlete than he appears to be on TV. He's not particularly tall or muscley, but his serve is near-Wagnerian in its effect, and from this close up you can see that it's because Sampras has got some magic blend of flexibility and timing that lets him release his whole back and trunk into the serve—his whole *body* can snap the way normally just a wrist can snap—and that this has something to do with the hunched, coiled way he starts his service motion, lifting just the toe of his front foot and sighting over the racket like a man with a crossbow, a set of motions that looks ticcy and eccentric on TV but in person makes his whole body look like one big length of muscle, a kind of angry eel getting ready to writhe. Philippoussis, who likes between points to dance a little in place—perhaps to remind himself that he can indeed move if he needs to—awaits service without facial affect. His headband matches his candy-stripe shirt. The scoreboards' displays are now set for keeping score instead of flashing ads. Philippoussis's name eats up a large horizontal section of each board. The wall between Stadium and Grandstand (so on our E side) is topped by the press box, which runs along the wall's whole length and basically looks like the world's largest mobile home, all its windows' tinted shades now pulled against the PM sun. Three points have now yielded an ace, a service-return winner, and a long rally that ends when Philippoussis comes in on an approach that's not *quite* in the exact backhand corner and Sampras hits an incredibly top-heavy short angle past him into the ad service court. The fierceness of Sampras's backhand is something else that TV doesn't communicate well, his racket-head control more like that of one of those stocky clay-courters with forearms like joints of mutton, the topspin so heavy it distorts the ball's shape as the pass dips like a dropped thing. The malevolent but cyborgian Philippoussis hasn't betrayed anything like an actual facial expression yet. He also doesn't seem to perspire.[13] Two older guys in the row right behind me are exhorting Sampras in low tones, addressing him as "Petey," and I can't help thinking they're friends of the family or something. And propped up over the press box—so at about the height of a radio station's aerial—is the 1995 U.S. Open's own ad for itself. It's an enormous pointillist pastel print of an N.T.C. Stadium's crowd around an outsized court, the perspective weirdly foreshortened, and then with the well-known Manhattan skyline ballooning in the immediate background in a way it decidedly does not in the real Flushing,

[13] Another sort of endearing thing about Sampras is the way he always sweats through his baby-blue shorts in an embarrassing way that suggests incontinence and lets the world see just where his athletic supporter's straps are (i.e., after a while the whole upper part of the shorts is sweated through except for a drier area that's the exact shape and size of a jock). This even TV's crude pictures can capture, and I think I like it so much because it humanizes Sampras and lets me identify with him in a way that the sheer preternatural beauty of his game does not. For me, similar humanizing foibles in transcendent players included McEnroe's irrational fits of pique, Lendl's and Navratilova's habit of every once in a while getting so nervous and choking so badly on a point that they looked almost spastic and the ball would actually hit the ground *before* it reached the net, and Connors's compulsive on-court touching and adjustment of his testes within his jock, as if he needed to know just where they were at all times.

Queens; and then above and beyond the billboard is the big zucchini of the Fuji Inc. blimp floating slowly against the cerulean of far and away the best summer sky I have ever seen around New York City. Not only is the '95 Open's L.D.W. air unhumid and in the eighties, the sunshine astringent and the breeze feathery and the sky the overvivid blue of a colorized film, but the sky's air is *clean,* the air smells fine and keen and sweet the way line-dried laundry smells, the result not only of a month without rain[14] but also this weekend of a freak high-pressure front that's spiraled southwest out of Nova Scotia's upper air and is blowing the oxides and odors that are NYC's deserved own out over New Jersey. The Stadium's bowl of air gets finer and keener the higher up in the stands you go, until, standing on top of somebody's smuggled Michelob cooler in the top row of bleachers[15] and peering over the wall due east

[14] According to M. Chang's limo driver, it's been, like, the longest rainless interval of the century for NYC. I don't know whether that's true or whether New Yorkers are being enjoined from watering the mums in their window boxes or whatever, but I do know that there hasn't been one rain-delay in the whole tournament so far, and the upper-management guys from both CBS and the U.S.T.A. are going around looking pleased in a way that's just short of gloating.

[15] Ascending in the Stadium goes like this: past ten rows of dark-blue seats—actual plastic chairs, the Box Seats—then fifteen rows of light-blue seats, then eighteen rows of noticeably less comfortable gray molded-plastic seats, then (the steps by now so steep they feel the way staircases feel to a small child) uncountable rows of plain red bleachers, the land of backward Mets caps and tattoos and hightop sneakers w/ laces untied, the thick honk of Brooklyn accents, a great mass clicking of empty breeze-blown Liquor Bar cups on the cement of the bleachers' aisles...it's a climb

past the edge of the press box, looking down over the big sign that says

WELCOME TO THE 1995 U.S. OPEN
A USTA Event

you can see them, Them, coming, an enormous serpentine mass, the crowd, still at 1615h. coming, what looks from this distance like everybody in New York City who hasn't retreated to the Hamptons for the long summer weekend. The U.S. Open is a big deal for NYC. Mayor Dinkins is gone—the Dinkins who used to reroute landing patterns at LaGuardia just for the Open—but even under Rudy Giuliani, for a fortnight a city that ordinarily couldn't give two chomps of its gum for a sport as patricianly non-contact as tennis is into the game in a very big way. Thirty-year-old arbitrageurs in non-rented tuxes at the Bowery Bar dissect various men's matches and speculate on how Seles's hiatus from the game will affect her endorsement contracts now that she's back. Croatian doormen bemoan Ivanisevic's early departure. On the subway, a set of tough chicks in leather and fluorescent hair concur that even though Graf and Seles and that Spanish what's-her-face with the

during which the ears actually pop and the O_2 gets thin and the perspective on the court below becomes horrific, like a skyscraper's, the players looking insectile and the crowd moving and heaving in a nauseous way that makes the place's whole structure seem slightly to heave and sway.

hymen[16] in her name might rule, let's don't for a m.-fucking second count out the U.S.'s Zina G. 'cause this is her swan-song before the like bow-out. Or e.g. Friday, 1 September, the day after Agassi's five-set comeback against Corretja, a Lebanese driver on the Grey Line bus in from LaGuardia and a cigar-chewing old passenger he doesn't know from Adam bond over their shared assessments of Agassi's rehabilitation as a man:

"It is like he used to be brat, arrogant—you know what I am saying?"

"He grew up is what you're saying. Now he's got balls."

"Last night, this was a great game he played. This is what I am saying."

"He used to just be this hairball. Now he grew up. Now he's a *person*."[17]

But so they're coming, 40,000 yesterday and 41,000 today, ready to shell out $25–$30 for a ticket if they can even get one.[18]

[16] (*sic*—no kidding)

[17] Agassi's 1995 cybercrewcut, black sneakers, and weird new French-Resistance-fighter-style shirts have, at this year's Open, made him way more popular with male fans and only slightly less fascinatingly sexy for female fans. (Agassi's sex-symbolism's a phenomenon of deep mystery to most of the males I know, since we agree that we can all see clearly that Agassi's actually a runty, squishy-faced guy with a weird-shaped skull [which the crewcut's now made even more conspicuous] and the tiny-strided pigeon-toed walk of a schoolkid whose underwear's ridden up; and it remains completely inexplicable to us, Agassi's pull and hold on women.)

[18] The National Tennis Center Box Office opens at 1000h., and people start lining up as early as 0600 hoping to get one of the day's Grounds Passes, and the various incentives

They come by infernal and Stygian IRT subway out to the end of the #7 line, the Shea-Willets stop. They converge on NE Queens via the Van Wyck and L.I. and Whitestone Expressways, the Interborough, the Grand Central Parkway, the Cross Bay, bringing much ready cash and whatever religious medals apply to parking spaces. City dwellers navigate by limo, cab, or bus the empty canyons of L.D.W.'s Manhattan, bound for 36th St. and the Tunnel or 59th and the Queensborough Bridge, then travel forever[19] up Northern Boulevard, bringing coolers and blankets and rackets and butt-cushions with GIANTS and JETS on them and sunscreen and souvenir hats from last year's Open, up Northern Blvd. under circling air traffic until the landmarks start emerging—the squat neutron-blue ring of nearby Shea Stadium; the huge steel armillary sphere and Tinkertoy-shaped tower of the '39 World's Fairgrounds that adjoin the National Tennis Center in Flushing Meadow Corona Park[20]; or (if coming in from the S-SW) the massive exoskeleton of a whole new

and dramas in this AM line of street-savvy New Yorkers are a whole other story in themselves.

[19] (no kidding: miles and miles on Northern through the long intestine of Queens, NY, at least fifty traffic lights)

[20] This is the actual name of the park that the U.S.T.A.'s National Tennis Center is in, a name almost perfect in its unconscious capture of northeast Queens's summertime essence, connoting as it does equal parts urban sewage, suburban *pastora,* and bludgeoning sun.

N.T.C. Stadium Complex, incomplete and deeply eerie as seen from the Grand Central Pkwy., a huge exposed ribcage looming over fields of raw dirt and construction-site clutter and dumpsters from the New Style Waste Disposal Co., w/ three huge canted cranes motionlessly erect against the northern horizon. No labor is under way on the new Stadium this Labor Day Weekend except for two hard-hatted and forlornly bored Security guys patrolling inside the site's fence.

The N.T.C.'s Main Gate is on the grounds' NE side, connected to the #7 train's subway stop and parking lots by a broad blacktop promenade that leads from the commuter stations south past Park Rangers' offices and a couple of big open communitarian circles—the kind of open urban venues that look like they ought to have spurting fountains in the center, though these don't—with green benches and complex skateboarding and vigorous sinister underground commerce. At some point the promenade curves sharply west so that the Open's moving crowds pass within sight of rampant picnicking and soccer in F.M.C. Park (the "Meadow" part, apparently); then the walkway's final blacktop straightaway's enclosed by high fences topped with flags of all nations as you head for the parallel lines for actual entry at the tournament's Main Gate, the Gate's own tall fencing black iron and almost medievally secure-looking and itself topped only by good old U.S. flags, with the Open's/U.S.T.A.'s familiar greeting and self-assertion in bright brave 160-point caps on a banner hanging over the turnstiles, of which turnstiles there are six total but never more than three in actual operation. The turnstiles are only for those who already have tickets[21]—the East-Bloc-length line for AM tickets at the Box Office evaporates every day by around 1100h., when stern megaphones announce the day's sellout.

Besides the Stadium/Grandstand, there are three other N.T.C. "Show Courts," i.e., courts with serious bleachers. At 1640h., Court 16 is running men's doubles with Eltingh-Haarhuis, the world's #1 team, and its little wedge of aluminum stands isn't even full. American tennis crowds seem decisively singles-oriented. Court 17 has Korda and Kulti against the Mad Bahamian Mark Knowles[22] and his 1995 partner Daniel Nestor, the Canadian who's fun to watch because he looks so much like an

[21] Scalpers are asking and getting $125 for a Grounds Pass and (in at least one case) twice that for an eleventh-row Stadium seat for the afternoon's matches. The last straightaway of the walkway to the Gate has its healthy share of scalpers making their elliptical pitches from the grassy edge, but (weirdly) there are just as many furtive-looking parties standing at the edges asking loudly whether anyone passing by has an extra ticket for sale, or would like perhaps to sell their own, as there are scalpers. The scalpers and weird people asking to be scalped seem not even to notice one another, all of them calling softly at once, and this makes the last pre-Gate stretch of the promenade kind of surreally sad, a study in missed connection.

[22] (Knowles has the same sort of perpetually aggrieved emotional style J. P. McEnroe had, except in McEnroe the persecution complex often came off as the high-tension neurosis of a true genius, whereas with Knowles it comes off simply as whiny snarling churlish foul temper. All summer, following the Tour, the Mad Bahamian has been the only ATP player I would watch and actually hope he got beat, badly.)

anorectic Mick Jagger.[23] Court 18 has women's doubles with four players whose names I don't recognize and exactly thirty-one people in the stands. (All four of the females on 18 have bigger forearms than I do.) Natasha Zvereva, looking incomplete without Gigi, is warming up against Amy Frazier in the Grandstand. In the Stadium, Philippoussis and Sampras have split the first two sets, 6 and 5. What a big match sounds like outside the Stadium is brief strut-rattling explosions of applause and whistles and then the odd flat amplification of the umpire speaking into the abrupt silence his speaking has created. Daniel Nestor's last name, while also Hellenistic, is Homerian,[24] thus allusive to a wartime way before Athens v. Sparta. The fact that Sampras has won so many Grand Slam titles may have a lot to do with the fact that Slams' males' matches are the best of five sets. Best-of-fives require not just physical endurance but a special kind of emotional flexibility: in best-of-fives you can't play with full-bore intensity the whole time; you have to know when to kind of turn it on and when to lay back and conserve your psychic resources.[25] Philippoussis won the tie-break of a first set

[23] (Nestor seems like a pretty good egg, though.)

[24] (wise king of Pylos and all that)

[25] In 1979 I once played two best-of-five matches in one day in a weird non-U.S.T.A. junior thing in suburban Chicago, and one match went five sets and the other four, and even though I was just seventeen I walked like a very old man for days afterward. And since emotional flexibility is almost impossible for a jr., I remember noticing that all of us who'd played 3/5's left the site looking utterly wrung-out emotionally,

in which you got the impression that Sampras was sort of adjusting the idle on his game, trying to find the exact level he needed to reach to win. The suspense of the match isn't so much whether Sampras will win but how hard he'll have to play and how long it'll take him to find this out. Philippoussis hits very hard but has no imagination and even less flexibility. He's like a machine with just one gear: unless forced out of his rhythm by a wide-angle shot, he moves exclusively in forward-backward vectors. Sampras, on the other hand, seems to float like dander all over the court.[26] Philippoussis is like a great and terrible land army; Sampras is more naval, more of the drift-and-encircle school. Philippoussis is oligarchic: he has a will and seeks to impose it. Sampras is more democratic, i.e., more chaotic but also more human: his real job seems to be figuring out what his will exactly *is.* Not a lot of people remember that Athens actually lost the Peloponnesian War—it took thirty years, but Sparta finally ground them down. Nor do most people know that Athens actually *started* the whole bloody thing in the first place by picking on maritime allies of Sparta who were cutting into Athens's sea trade. Athens's clean-cut nice-guy image is a bit

hollow-eyed, with the 1,000-yard stare of pogrom-survivors. I've had a special empathic compassion for male players in Slam events ever since, when I watch.

[26] Sampras has a way of making it look like he hits a shot and dematerializes and then rematerializes someplace else in perfect position for the next shot. I have no theories about how he does this. Ken Rosewall is the only other male player in my memory who could seem to flicker in and out of existence like this. (E. Goolagong could do it, too, but not consistently.)

overdone—the whole exhausting affair was about commerce right from the beginning.

What's fun about having a U.S. Open '95 Media Pass is that you can go in and out of the Main Gate as often as you want. For paying customers there's no such luck: a sign by the turnstiles says ALL EXITS FINAL with multiple exclamation points. And the lines for entry at the three active turnstiles resemble those grim photos of trampling crowds at Third World soccer matches. Wizened little old men are paid by the tournament to stand by the turnstiles and take people's tickets—the same sort of wizened little old men you see at sporting-event turnstiles everywhere, the kind who always look like they should be wearing Shriners hats. Going through one turnstile right now at 1738h. is a very handsome bald black man in an extremely snazzy Dries Van Noten camelhair suit. Pushing hip-first through the next turnstile[27] is a woman in an electric-blue pantsuit of either silk or really good rayon. At the third active turnstile, a young foreignish-looking guy in an expensive flannel shirt w/ Ray-Bans and a cellular phone is having an argument with the turnstile's ticket-taker. The guy is claiming that he bought tickets for 3 Sept. but has mistakenly left them at home in Rye and will be *dam-ned* if he is going to be forced by a minimum-wage little wizened ticket-taker into

[27] NYC being one of the most turnstile-intensive cities in the world, New Yorkers push through turnstiles with the same sort of elegantly casual élan that really top players evince when warming up.

going all the way back to Rye to get them and then coming all the way back down here. He has his cellular phone in his hand, leaning over the ticket-taker: *surely,* he insists, there's some way to verify his ticket-holding status without his going and coming all the way back to produce the actual stupid cardboard rectangles themselves. The ticket-taker, in a blue suit that makes him look a bit like a train's conductor, is shaking his gnarled little head and has his arms raised in that simultaneously helpless but firm gesture of Can't Help You, Mac. The young man in flannel from Rye keeps flipping his cellular open and starting to dial it in a menacing way, as if threatening to get the ticket-taker in Dutch with shadowy figures from the Open's Olympian management heights the young man's got connections with; but the stolid little attendant's resolve stays firm, his face stony and his arms raised,[28] until crowd pressure from

[28] This ticket-taker, who emerged as without a doubt my favorite character at the whole '95 Open, agreed to a brief interview but wanted his name withheld—the tournament apparently really does have shadowy Olympian upper-management figures whose wrath the employees fear. This ticket-taker is sixty-one, has worked the " 'stiles" (as he calls them) at every U.S. Open since Ashe's stirring five-set defeats of both Graebner and Okker at Forest Hills in '68, thinks the Flushing Meadows N.T.C. inferior in every conceivable respect to good old Forest Hills, claims that the new half-built Stadium looming over the southern horizon is grotesque and pointless since its size will place the cheap seats at the very outer limits of human eyesight and a match seen from there will look like something seen from an incoming Boeing, plus that the new Stadium's been a boondoggle from the get-go and is lousy with corruption and malfeasance and general administrative rot—the guy is incredibly articulate and anecdotal and downright moving in his fierce attachment to a game he apparently has never once personally played, and he definitely in my opinion

customers at the flannel man's rear and flank force him to withdraw the field.

The first thing you see when you come inside the Main Gate is teams of extremely attractive young people giving away free foil packets of Colombian Coffee from really big plastic barrels with outlines of Juan Valdez & devoted burro on them. The young people, none of whom are of Colombian extraction, are cheery and outgoing but don't seem to be terribly alert, because they keep giving me new free samples every time I go out and then come in again, so that my bookbag is now stuffed with them and I'm not going to have to buy coffee for months. The next thing you see is a barker on a raised dais urging you to purchase a Daily Drawsheet for $2.00[29] and a Program+Drawsheet for a bargain $8.00. Right near the barker is a gorgeous spanking-new Infiniti automobile on a complicated stand that places the car at a kind of dramatic plunging angle. It's not clear what the relation between a fine new automobile and professional tennis is supposed to be, but the visual conjunction of car and plunging angle is extremely impressive and compelling, and there's always a dense ring of spectators around the Infiniti,

deserves a whole separate *Tennis* magazine profile next year. His stint at the Open each year is his two-week vacation from his regular job as a toll-taker at the infamous Throgs Neck Bridge between Queens and the southern Bronx, which fact may account for his flinty resolve in the face of intimidating tactics like somebody brandishing a cellular phone at him.

[29] The Daily Drawsheet has the distinction of being the single cheapest concession at the 1995 U.S. Open. A small and ice-intensive sodapop comes in second at $2.50.

looking at it but not touching it.[30] Then, over the Daily Drawsheet pitchman's right shoulder and situated suspiciously close to the Advance Ticket Window, is what has to be one of the largest free-standing autotellers in the Western world, with its own shade-awning and three separate cash stations with controls of NASA-like sophistication and complexity and enormous signs that say the autoteller's provided through the generosity of CHASE and that it is equipped to disgorge cash via the NYCE, PLUS, VISA, CIRRUS, and MASTERCARD networks of auto-withdrawal. The lines for the autoteller are so long that they braid complexly into the lines for the nearest concession stands. These concession stands seem to have undergone a kind of metastasis since last year: they now are absolutely everywhere on the N.T.C. grounds. One strongly suspects that the inside story on how a concession at the U.S. Open is acquired would turn out to involve levels of intrigue and gamesmanship that make the tournament's on-court dramas look pallid, because it's clear that the really serious separation of spectator from his cash takes place at the N.T.C.'s concession venues, all of which are doing business on the sort of scale enjoyed by coastal grocery and hardware stores during a Hurricane Warning. The free-standing little umbrella'd venues for Evian and Häagen-Dazs are small potatoes: there are entire miniature *strip-malls* of refreshment stands gauntleting almost every sidewalk and walk-

[30] Even though it's totally unguarded, people maintain the sort of respectful distance from the plunging Infiniti that one associates with museums and velvet ropes.

way and easement on the grounds—even the annular ground-level tunnel of the Stadium/Grandstand—offering sodapop for $2.50–$3.50, $3.00 water, $3.00 little paper troughs of nachos or crosshatched disk-shaped French fries whose oil immediately soaks through the trough, $3.50 beer, $2.50 popcorn,[31] etc.[32]

[31] (...this popcorn being the deep-yellow, highly salty kind that makes an accompanying beverage all but mandatory—same deal with the concessions' big hot doughy pretzels, Manhattan-street-corner-type pretzels glazed with those nuggets of salt so big that they just about have to be bitten off and chewed separately. U.S. Open pretzels are $3.00 except in the International Food Village on the Stadium's south side, a kind of compressed orgy of concession and crowded eating, where pretzel prices are slashed to $2.50 per.)

[32] Take, e.g., a skinny little Häagen-Dazs bar—really skinny, a five-biter at most—which goes for a felonious $3.00, and as with most of the food-concessions here you feel gouged and outraged about the price right up until you bite in and discover it's a seriously good Häagen-Dazs bar. The fact is that when you're hungry from the sunshine and fresh air and match-watching and gushing sympathetic saliva from watching everybody else in the crowds chow down, the Häagen-Dazs bars aren't worth $3.00 but *are* worth about $2.50. Same deal with the sodapop and popcorn; same deal with the kraut-dogs on sale from steam-billowing Coney Island Refreshment stands for what seems at first glance like a completely insane and unacceptable $4.00—but then you find out they're really long and *really* good, and that the kraut is the really smelly gloppy kind that's revolting when you're not in the mood for kraut but rapturously yummy when you are in the mood for kraut. While I grumbled both times, I bought two separate kraut-dogs, and I have to admit that they hit the old spot with a force worth at least, say, $3.25.

I should also add that Colombian Coffee was FREE at all concession stands on the N.T.C. grounds over Labor Day Weekend—part of this year's wildly aggressive Juan Valdez–marketing blitz at Flushing Meadows. This seemed like a real good deal until it turned out that 90 percent of the time the concession stands would claim to be

Now a huge roar that makes the whole Stadium's superstructure wobble signifies that the forces of democracy and human freedom have won the third set.[33] It's quite clear that

mysteriously "temporarily out" of Colombian Coffee, so that you ended up forking over $2.50 for an overiced cup of Diet Coke instead, having at this point spent way too much time in the concession line to be able to leave empty-handed. It is not inconceivable that the concession stands really were out of coffee—"FREE" representing the price at which the demand curve reaches its most extreme point, as any marketer knows—but the hardened U.S. consumer in me still strongly suspected that a coffee-related Bait and Switch was in operation at some of these stands, at which the guys behind the counter managed to give the impression that they were on some kind of Rikers Island work-release program or were moonlighting from their real occupation as late-night threatening-type lurkers at Port Authority and Penn Station.

Nevertheless, the point is that every concession stand in the N.T.C. had constant long lines in front of it and that a good 66 percent of the crowds in the Stadium and Grandstand and at the Show Courts could be seen ingesting some sort of concession-stand item at any given time.

[33] And in order to be properly impressed by the volume of concessions consumption, you need to keep in mind what a hassle it is to go get concessions when you're watching a pro match. Take the Stadium for example. You can leave your seat only during the ninety-second break between odd games, then you have to sort of slalom down crowded Stadium ramps to the nearest concession stand, hold your place in a long and Hobbesian line, hand over a gouge-scale sum, and then schlep back up the ramp, bobbing and weaving to keep people's elbows from knocking your dearly bought concessions out of your hands and adding them to the crunchy organic substratum of spilled concessions you're walking on…and of course by the time you find the ramp back to your section of seats the original ninety-second break in the action is long over—as, usually, is the next one after that, so you've now missed at least two games—and play is again under way, and the ushers at the fat chains prevent reentry, and you have to stand there in an unventilated cement corridor with a sticky and acclivated floor, mashed in with a whole lot of other people who also left to

Sampras has found his cruising altitude and that Philippoussis is going to take the first set he won and treasure it and go home to do more bench-presses in preparation for the ATP's indoor season.

I do not know who a certain Ms. or Mr. Feron is, but s/he must be a fearsomely powerful figure in the New York sports-concession industry indeed, because a good 80 percent of all concession booths at the '95 Open have signs that say FERON'S on them. This goes not only for the edible concessions—whose stands have various names but all of whose workers seem to have pale-blue FERON'S shirts on—but also for the endless rows of souvenir- and tennis-related-product booths that flank whatever of the grounds' Hellesponts aren't flanked by food booths already. The really hard-core, big-ticket souvenirs are sold on the Stadium's E side, in an area between the plunging Infiniti and the IBM Match-In-Progress Board. There's racketry and footwear and gear bags and warm-ups and T-shirts for

get concessions and are now waiting until the next break to get back to their seats, all of you huddled there with your ice melting and kraut congealing and trying to stand on tip-toe and peer ahead to the tiny chained arch of light at the end of the tunnel and maybe catch a green glimpse of ball or some surreal fragment of Philippoussis's left thigh as he thunders in toward the net or something.... New Yorkers' patience w/r/t crowds and lines and gouging and waiting is extraordinarily impressive if you're not used to it; they can all stand quiescent in airless venues for extended periods, their eyes' expressions that unique NYC combination of Zen meditation and clinical depression, clearly unhappy but never complaining.

sale at separate booths for Yonex, Fila, Nike,[34] Head, and William Serbin. There's a U.S.T.A. booth offering free U.S.T.A. T-shirts with a paid U.S.T.A. membership (which membership is essentially worthless unless you want to play in U.S.T.A.-sanctioned events, in which case you have no choice but to enlist). But any item with a "U.S. OPEN '95"–mention on it is sold exclusively out of a FERON'S booth. Of these booths there are "0/40 at FERON'S," "FERON'S U.S. Open Silks," and "FERON'S U.S. Open Specials."[35] It's not at all clear what the term "Specials" is meant to signify in terms of price: U.S. Open '95 T-shirts are $22.00 and $25.00. Tank-tops even more. Visors

[34] The single most popular souvenir at the '95 Open seems to be a plain white bandanna with that little disembodied Nike trademark wing* that goes right on your forehead if you wrap the thing just right over your head. A fashion accessory made popular by you know whom. Just about every little kid I spotted at Flushing Meadow was sporting one of these white Nike bandannas, and a fairly common sight on Sunday was a harried parent trying to tie a bandanna just right to position the Nike wing over a junior forehead while his kid stood on first one foot and then the other in impatience. (You do not want to know the retail price of these bandannas, believe me.)

* The classico-Peloponnesian implications of *Nike* and of having all these kids running around with Nike wings on their foreheads like Lenten ash seem too obvious to spend much time belaboring.

[35] There are at least four of these "U.S. Open Specials at FERON'S" booths at various high-traffic spots all over the N.T.C. grounds. The two distinctive things about the FERON'S clothing booths are (1) that they have separate registers for cash and Major Credit Card purchases, and (2) that none of the employees at any of these registers seems to be older than about eleven.

$18.00 and up. Sweatshirts are $49.00 and $54.00, depending on whether they're the dusty, acid-washed autumn colors so popular this year.

It's also clear that the sea-lanes of trade between FERON'S itself and the good old United States Tennis Association are wide open, because no official FERON'S souvenir says "U.S. Open '95" without also saying *"A U.S.T.A. Event"* right underneath.

The grounds don't exactly empty out between the end of the afternoon's slate of matches and the start of the evening's,[36] but the crowds do thin a little. Flushing Meadow gets chilly and pretty as the twilight starts. It's about 1900h., that time when the sun hasn't gone down yet but everything seems to be in something else's shadow. The ticket-takers at the Main Gate's turnstiles change shifts, and the consumers coming down the promenade are now dressed more in jeans and sweaters than shorts and thongs. Lights over all the N.T.C. courts go on together with an enormous *thunk.* The courtlight gives the underbelly of the hanging Fuji Blimp a weird ghostly glow. There's more serious, 5-Food-Group, dinnerish eating now going on at the International Food Village and in the Corporate Hospitality Areas. Sampras and Philippoussis have quit the field in the Stadium, Sampras bearing his shield and the

[36] Tickets are sold separately for the day and evening sessions, and there are very complicated mechanisms in place to keep people with day-session tickets from lurking past 2000h. and mooching free evening spectation.

Australian carried out upon his own (as it were). Arantxa Sanchez Vicario and Mary Joe Fernandez are now warming up on the Stadium Court while people in the bleachers try to stagger very carefully down the steps to get out, lugging their coolers and cushions, looking simultaneously sunburned and cold. Coming up on the Grandstand Court is a mixed-doubles match I'm looking forward to because one of the teams on the program has the marvelous name "Boogert-Oosting." Various tangential singles matches are under way on Courts 16–18, and something that's fun is to go over to these Show Courts and not to go all the way in and sit in the little sets of stands but to stand on the path outside the heavy green windscreens around the Show Courts and watch the little stripe of bare fence near the bottom for the movement of feet and to try to extrapolate from the feet's movement what's going on in each point. One unbelievably huge pair of sneakers under the screen on Court 16 turns out—sure enough—to belong to Richard Krajicek, the 6'6" Dutchman who plays like a mad crane. These shoes have to be 16EEEs at least; you wouldn't believe it. I am holding a $4.00 kraut-dog and sodapop I would very much like to find someplace isolated and quiet to consume.

It is not at all quiet outside the Main Gate as true evening falls. Not only does the combined em- and immigration of crowds for the different Sessions make the whole promenade from Gate to subway stop and parking lots resemble the fall of Saigon. It's especially unquiet out here *economically*. I don't know whether this magazine will run an aperçu of what all's going on out here as the sun falls, but I don't see why not, because it's not all that surprising. Since the 1995 U.S. Open is primarily—unabashedly—about commerce, and since commerce is by its nature *uncontainable,* it shouldn't be at all surprising that the most vigorous crepuscular commerce is taking place out here, outside the tournament's fence and Gate, in markets of all shade and hue. I have, e.g., in the last twenty minutes received three separate solicitations to buy pot (all wildly overpriced). The sweet burnt-pine smell of reefer is in the air all over out here, and one young guy in oversized fatigue pants is smoking a bone on a bench right next to a very neat and dapper old gentleman who's sitting with his hands folded primly and not giving any indication he smells anything untoward.[37] Scalpers have upped the pressure of their pitches in the lengthening shadows and are practically applying half-nelsons to anybody on the promenade who seems even possibly to be looking for something, even if that something is just a quiet isolated place to eat a kraut-dog.[38] As mentioned *supra,* I'm the proud

[37] New Yorkers also have an amazing ability to mind their own business and attend to themselves and not notice anything untoward going on, an ability that impresses me every time I come here and that always seems to lie somewhere on the continuum between Stoicism and catatonia.

[38] You'll doubtless by the way be happy to know that I did, over half an hour later, find a quiet place to hunch and gnaw supper. One of the gratuitously cool things the '95 Open does is open up a few of the minor National Tennis Center courts to regular public play once the sun's gone down. This is why some of the people in the Stadium crowd had rackets, I bet. Anyway, it seems decent of them, and you can imagine what a thrill it must be for a couple of little kids to play on a court with vestigial rubber from an afternoon of pro sneakers still on it—the civilians playing clearly feel

possessor of a U.S. Open '95 Media Pass—which consists of a necklace of nylon cord from which hangs a large plastic card w/ a direly unflattering little photo of me that hangs against my chest at about the level of a sommelier's tasting cup—and twice this evening outside the Main Gate I've been approached by somebody wanting to borrow the Media Pass and then slip it back to me through the black fence once they've strolled inside. One offer was a straight-out bribe, but the other involved a distinguished and corporate-looking gray-haired guy in green golfer's slacks who had a complex tale of woe about a tubercular niece or something who'd paid a surprise

important, and they get a lot of attention from passersby on the paths who are now conditioned to watch intently whenever they hear ball sounds, and it's interesting to watch the passersby's faces change after two or three seconds when they realize who and what they're watching. The little sets of bleachers for these minor public-play courts are, understandably, empty; and it was on one such little set of stands that I ate. A thirtyish guy and his wife were playing, the wife wearing a sun visor that looked a little gratuitous, the husband overhitting the way an afternoon of watching pros whale the hell out of the ball will make a man overhit. The only other person in the stands was one of the attractive young P.R. people who'd given me so much free coffee all day out by the M.G., sitting in her Valdez-outline T-shirt and eating something steamy out of a partitioned Styrofoam tray whose attached lid was folded back. Her professional smile and eye-twinkles were gone, so that she looked now more like the hard young New Yorker she was. As she ate she stared impassively at the husband whaling balls at his wife. She was clearly there for the same reason I was, to have some space and quiet while she ate, plus some downtime in which to rest her face from its cheery marketing expression. I felt a kind of bond between us, and from the opposite end of the bleachers where I was eating I cleared my throat and said, "Boy, it's good to find a place to be alone for a minute, isn't it?" The lady never looked around from the court as she cleared her mouth and said, "It was until a second ago."

long-distance visit to NYC and whose fondest wish was to get into the U.S. Open and that tickets were sold out, etc.[39] I observed at least one turnstile's ticket-taker (not the flinty-eyed Throgs Neck ticket-taker) receive some sort of subtle maître-d'ish payment for allowing somebody to bring in something spectators were by no stretch of the imagination allowed to bring into the N.T.C.[40] If you don't have a Stadium ticket but have the NYC savvy and financial resources, certain Stadium ushers are said (by two separate reliable sources) to be willing to place you in a vacant seat—sometimes a really up-close and desirable seat—for a sub-rosa fee, and a percentage of this fee is then apparently kicked back to a certain enterprising person or persons in the National Tennis Center who know of seats that for one reason or another aren't going to be occupied during a certain interval and relay this information to ushers (for a price). Part of the beauty of the tennis here is the way the artistry and energy are bounded by specific lines on court, but the beauty of the commerce is the way it's un- and never bounded. It's all sort of hypnotic at night. The plunging Infiniti's leather interior gets somehow mysteriously

[39] (Both these solicitations had their appeal—the straight-out-bribe one especially—and only a fear of getting caught and of having to inform *Tennis* magazine that my Media Pass had been revoked because I'd been nabbed renting it out on the black market kept me from making my own stab at '95 Open free enterprise.)

[40] You wouldn't believe me if I specified what it was, and it'd require a lot of space and context to make sense of, and this in an article that's already pretty clearly running over budget and straying from its original focused L.D.W. assignment.

illuminated when the sun goes down, so that from a distance the car seems like a beacon. Trash-can fires appear in F.M.C. Park's distance, and the #7 train's interior's also alit as it pulls into the overground Shea stop to the north. At about 2015h. there's a fracas near the I.F. Village involving some unscrupulous/enterprising employee of whatever company actually makes the " '95 Open"–emblazoned T-shirts and hats and c. for the souvenir booths, who's apparently diverted boxes and boxes of the shirts and stuff and is going around the grounds selling them on the sly at prices way below the booths' prices,[41] and N.T.C. Security's involved, as well as—incongruously—what look like two Fire Department guys in slickers and fireman hats. It's on the whole kind of a younger and rowdier and more potentially sinister crowd that's coming in for the evening session. Their faces are stonier; eye contact seems hazardous the way eye contact on subways can be hazardous. The women tend to be dressed in ways that let you know just what they'd look like without any clothes on.

Plus food: the various extracurricular food scams haven't yet been mentioned. Imagine the opportunities—not only the overpriced all-cash concession stands but the enormous tented kitchens for the Corporate Hospitality Areas and the "U.S. Open Club" for V.I.P.s and so on, the massive sizzle and clatter of high-volume prep from these kitchens off along the south parts of the Main Gate. Let's not even get into the little ease-

[41] (More power to him, on my view.)

ments behind the strips of food stands, the furtive and on the whole unauthorized-looking deliveries and removals of large boxes, the various transactions and scurryings. Forget examples of that. Here's a different incident. Let's close L.D.W. with this:

Some of the time it's hard even to know what it is you're seeing take place. In one of the big communitarian fountainless circles that the promenade opens into as it leads to the Main Gate—the circle closest to the Gate, this one is—one of the circle's green benches is controlled by gypsy-cab and -limo drivers waiting for anybody exiting who needs a gypsy-type ride back to Rye or Rockaway or wherever. Half a dozen of these guys sit on this bench in their cabbies' berets, waiting around, smoking cigars, talking shit, etc. I'm on the next bench trying to organize my notes. This is at about 2100h., late. From this circle you can see the rear flaps of some of the tented high-volume kitchens. Through one of these flaps now emerges a stocky young guy in the unmistakable tall hat and whites of a kitchen worker (though on his feet are $200 Air Jordans so new they glow in the N.T.C.'s ambient light, so he looks like he's floating). The kitchen worker's carrying a broad low cardboard box through the employee- and Media Pass-entrance in the Gate and down the promenade and across the circle, making for the bench with the cabbies. The cabbies are making gestures like: Finally, Thank God. One of the cabbies rises and moves out and meets the kitchen worker; something subtle occurs between their hands that indicates a transfer of funds; and now the cabbie bears the box back to the bench, where the rest of the drivers circle and grab and reveal that the box is full of supper—burgers, chicken legs, wieners, etc. Vague contented noises from the cabbies on the bench as they dig in.

"Goddamn rip-off," says a well-dressed Italian man next to me on my bench.

I say, "Pardon me?"

"Ripping the fucking place off," the well-dressed Italian man says, indicating with a hand gesture the kitchen worker, who's now making his way quickly back to the kitchen tent, hand in his pocket. The Italian man has a small filtered cigar in his mouth and a disgusted look and is sitting back with his legs crossed and his elbows up on the bench's back's top in that insouciant way savvy New Yorkers sit on park benches. He has heavy brows and wingtips and a Eurocut silk pinstripe suit of the type that Cagney-era gangsters wore. You half-expect him to have a white fedora and violin case. But it turns out, when he gives me his card, that he's a legit businessman, a concessioneer, here to labor instead of recreate/consume; he's scouting out possibilities for opening a couple of stands here at next year's Open, when the new Stadium's up and running and even more vigorous attendance and commerce can be foreseen. The stands he wants to open'll sell gyros, he says. He's not Italian after all.

—1996

discalced (adj.)—barefoot or wearing sandals...used to characterize ce

discarnate spirit" **disciform**—flat and rounded in shape; a disciform fungu

sloshing back and forth **dispraise** (v.)—to express displeasure, censure; (n.)

dobby (n.)—geometric figure woven into fabric; fabric with such a fig

cent—tour guide in museum or cathedral **doss**—a crude or homemade

the Alpha **dragoman**—interpreter in Middle East **drape**—clingy girlfrienc

horse through complex maneuvers w/ hands on reins and feet in stirrup

floor; decayed leaves and branches **dulcify**—to make sweet or agreeable

buk—Jewish myth: wandering soul of dead person that enters living body

with crown of thorns **eccentric**—deviating from a circular path, as in ar

the center so that it imparts reciprocal motion **eccrine**—relating to swea

molting **ecdysone**—hormone that regulates molting behavior **ecesis**—suc

covered with spines **écorché**—anatomical representation w/ skin removec

teristic species of each **ecru**—grayish yellow **effloresce**—to bloom or blo

honey to make them ingestible, tasty **ell**—wing of building at right angle

rial from another, usually with a solvent; (n.) "elution" **eluviation/eluv**

embrocate—to moisten or rub body with liniment or lotion **embrown**—tc

dive—two kinds, curly and Belgian, used in salads **enuresis**—uncontrollec

very slight differences in the intensity of stimuli, especially temperature anc

states are epiphenomena of physical neural processes ("epiphenomenal"

bodily discharge (coming?) OR a film that develops over a urine specimen

form a kind of escarpmentish angle"; a steep slope or long erosion cliff tha

tain religious orders **discarnate**—having no material body or form: "a
dished—concave; slanting toward one another at the bottom **dishing**—liquid
disapproval, censure **distemper**—a kind of paint-job using watered paint
ure **Dobro**—referring to stringed instruments like guitars and banjos **do-**
bed; dosshouse is cheap flophouse **doyen**—senior or oldest man in group;
dreidel—Jewish top w/ square body **dressage**—equestrian skill: guiding
dudeen—short-stemmed clay pipe, Scottish **duff**—organic stuff on forest
to mollify **durance**—confinement or restraint by force; imprisonment **dyb-**
and controls the living body's behavior **ecce homo**—depiction of Christ
elliptical orbit; (n.) a wheel or disc with its axis of revolution displaced from
or sweat gland **ecdysiast**—striptease artist **ecdysis**—shedding of outer skin,
cessful establishment of plant or animal species in a region **echinate**—prickly,
ecotone—transitional zone between communities containing the charac-
som **effluent**—flowing out or forth **electuary**—mix of drugs w/ sugar or
to rest; a right-angled bend in pipe or conduit **elute**—to extract one mate-
ate—sinking of dissolved material in soil when rainfall exceeds evaporation
darken **empery**—absolute dominion or sovereignty or jurisdiction **en-**
discharge of urine **epicritic** (adj.)—related to nerves w/ ability to discern
touch **epigraphy**—the study of inscriptions **epiphenomenalism**—mental
means following or consequent to something) **epistasis**—suppression of
escarpment—a steep slope in front of a fortification; "LA lawns on hillsides
yields two relatively level plains (bottom and top) of different elevations

BACK IN NEW FIRE

YOU KNOW THIS LOVE story. A gallant knight espies a fair maiden in the distant window of a forbidding-type castle. Their eyes meet—smokily—across the withered heath. Instant chemistry. And so good Sir Knight comes tear-assing toward the castle, brandishing his lance. Can he just gallop up and carry the fair maiden off? Not quite. First he's got to get past the dragon. Right? There's always a particularly nasty dragon guarding the castle, and the knight's always got to face and slay the dragon if there's to be any carrying off. But and so, like any loyal knight in the service of passion, the knight battles the dragon, all for the sake of the fair maiden. "Fair maiden" means "good-looking virgin," by the way. And so let's not be naive about what the knight's really fighting for. You can bet he's going to expect more than a breathy "My hero" from the maiden once that dragon's slain. In fact, the way the story always goes, good Sir Knight risks life and lance against the dragon not to "rescue" the good-looking virgin, but to *"win"* her. And any knight, from any era, can tell you what "win" means here.

Some of my own knightly friends see the specter of heterosexual AIDS as nothing less than a sexual Armageddon—a violent end to the casual carnalcopia of the last three decades. Some others, grim but more upbeat, regard HIV as a sort of test of our generation's sexual mettle; these guys now applaud their own casual sport-fucking as a kind of medical daredevilry that affirms the indomitability of the erotic spirit. I cite, e.g., an upbeat friend's recent letter on AIDS: "...So now nature has invented another impediment to human relations, and yet the romantic urge lives. It defies all efforts—human, moral, and viral—to extinguish it. And that's a wonderful thing. It is, in fact, possible to be encouraged by the human will to fuck, which persists despite all sorts of impediments. We shall overcome, so to speak."

Cavalier sentiments, etc. But I can't help thinking some of today's knights still underestimate both AIDS's dangers and its advantages. They fail to see that HIV could well be the salvation of sexuality in the 1990s. They don't see it, I think, because they tend to misread the eternal story of what erotic passion's all about.

The erotic will exists "*despite* impediments"? Let's go back to that knight and fair maiden exchanging lascivious looks. And here comes the knight, galloping castleward, mammoth lance at ready. Except imagine this time that there is no danger, no dragon to fear, face, fight, slay. Imagine the knight's pursuit of the maiden is wholly unimpeded—there's no dragon; the castle's unlocked; the drawbridge even lowers automatically, like a suburban garage door. And here's the fair maiden inside, wearing a Victoria's Secret teddy and crooking her finger. Does anyone else here detect a shadow of disappointment in Sir Knight's face, a slight anticlimactic droop to his lance? Does this version of the story have anything like the other's passionate, erotic edge?

"The human will to fuck"? Any animal can fuck. But only humans can experience sexual passion, something wholly different from the biological urge to mate. And sexual passion's endured for millennia as a vital psychic force in human life—not *despite* impediments but *because* of them. Plain old coitus becomes erotically charged and spiritually potent at just those points where impediments, conflicts, taboos, and consequences lend it a double-edged character—meaningful sex is both an overcoming and a succumbing, a transcendence and a transgression, triumphant and terrible and ecstatic and sad. Turtles and gnats can mate, but only the human will can defy, transgress, overcome, love: *choose.*

History-wise, both nature and culture have been ingenious at erecting impediments that give the choice of passion its price and value: religious proscriptions; penalties for adultery and divorce; chivalric chastity and courtly decorum; the stigma of illegitimate birth; chaperonage; madonna/whore complexes; syphilis; back-alley abortions; a set of "moral" codes that put sensuality on a taboo-level with defecation and apostasy...from the Victorians' dread of the body to early TV's one-foot-on-the-floor-at-all-times rule; from the automatic ruin of "fallen" women to back-seat tussles in which girlfriends struggled to deny boyfriends what they begged for in order to preserve their respect. Granted, from 1996's perspective, most of the old sexual dragons look stupid and cruel. But we need to realize that they had something big in their favor: as long as the dragons reigned, sex wasn't casual, not ever. Historically, human sexuality has been a deadly serious business—and the fiercer its dragons, the seriouser sex got; and the higher the price of choice, the higher the erotic voltage surrounding what people chose.

And then, what must have seemed suddenly, the dragons all keeled over and died. This was just around when I was born, the '60s' "Revolution" in sexuality. Sci-fi-type advances in prophylaxis and antivenereals, feminism as a political force, TV as institution, the rise of a culture of youth and its gland-intensive art and music, Civil Rights, rebellion as fashion, inhibition-killing drugs, the moral castration of churches and censors. Bikinis, miniskirts. "Free Love." The castle's doors weren't so much unlocked as blown off their hinges. Sex could finally be unconstrained, "Hang-Up"-free, just another appetite: *casual*. I was toothless and incontinent through most of the Revolution, but it must have seemed like instant paradise. For a while.

I was pre-conscious for the Revolution's big party, but I got to experience fully the hangover that followed—the erotic malaise of the '70s, as sex, divorced from most price and consequence, reached a kind of saturation-point in the culture—swinging couples and meat-market bars, hot tubs and EST, *Hustler*'s gynecological spreads, *Charlie's Angels*, herpes, kiddie-porn, mood rings, teenage pregnancy, Plato's Retreat, disco. I remember *Looking for Mr. Goodbar* all too well, its grim account of the emptiness and self-loathing that a decade of rampant casual fucking had brought on. Looking back, I realize that I came of sexual age in a culture that was starting to miss the very dragons whose deaths had supposedly freed it.

If I've got some of this right, then the casual knights of my own bland generation might well come to regard AIDS as a blessing, a gift perhaps bestowed by nature to restore some critical balance, or maybe summoned unconsciously out of the collective erotic despair of the post-'60s glut. Because the dragon is back, and clothed in a fire that can't be ignored.

I mean no offense. Nobody'd claim that a lethal epidemic is a good thing. Nothing from nature is good or bad. Natural things just *are;* the only good and bad things are people's various choices in the face of what is. But our own history shows that—for whatever reasons—an erotically charged human existence requires impediments to passion, prices for choices. That hundreds of thousands of people are dying horribly of AIDS seems like a cruel and unfair price to pay for a new erotic impediment. But it's not obviously more unfair than the millions who've died of syphilis, incompetent abortions, and "crimes of passion," nor obviously more cruel than that people used routinely to have their lives wrecked by "falling," "fornicating," "sinning," having "illegitimate" children, or getting trapped by inane religious codes in loveless and abusive marriages. At least it's not obvious to me.

There's a new dragon to face. But facing a dragon doesn't mean swaggering up to it unarmed and insulting its mom. And the erotic charge of hazard surrounding sex and HIV doesn't mean we can continue to engage in sport-fucking in the name of "courage" or romantic "will." In fact, AIDS's gift to us lies in its loud reminder that there's nothing casual about sex at all. This is a gift because human sexuality's power and meaning increase with our recognition of its seriousness. This has been what's "bad" about casual sex from the beginning: sex is never bad, but it's also never casual.

Our sexual recognition of what *is* can start with the conscientious use of protection as a gesture of love toward ourselves and our partners. But a deeper, far braver recognition of just what kind of dragon we're facing now is starting to take hold, and—far from Armageddon—is doing much to increase the erotic voltage of contemporary life. Thanks to AIDS, we're expanding our imaginations with respect to what is "sexual." Deep down, we all know that the real allure of sexuality has about as much to do with copulation as the appeal of food does with metabolic combustion. Trite though it (used to) sound, real sexuality is about our struggles to connect with one another, to erect bridges across the chasms that separate selves. Sexuality is, finally, about *imagination.* Thanks to brave people's recognition of AIDS as a fact of life, we are beginning to realize that highly charged sex can take place in all sorts of ways we'd forgotten or neglected—through non-genital touching, or over the phone, or via the mail; in a conversational nuance; in an expression; in a body's posture, a certain pressure in a held hand. Sex can be everywhere *we* are, all the time. All we need to do is really face this dragon, yielding neither to hysterical terror nor to childish denial. In return, the dragon can help us relearn what it means to be truly sexual. This is not a small thing, or optional. Fire is lethal, but we need it. The key is how we come to fire. It's not just other people you have to respect.

—*1996*

esculent—edible **espalier**—tree or shrub trained to grow in a flat plane

concrete spaces around central fountain **et ux**—Latin abbrev. for "et uxor"

development of a specific point of technique **étui**—small ornamenta

euchred us out of our life savings" **euphuism**—ornate, allusive, overpoetic

dire skin trouble **excise** (n.)—internal tax on production, manufacture

enlargement like a wart or boil **excursus**—long intellectual digression ir

some or hateful **exeleutherostomize**—to speak out freely (nonceword fron

arant sunshine"; "exhilarant coitus" **exocrine** (n.)—an externally secreting

speech in practical rhetoric **eyeteeth**—canine teeth of upper jav

fanfaronade—bragging or blustering behavior; a fanfare **fastigiate**—ha

part of fever, illness **fatuous**—unconsciously smug and foolish **felly/fe**

ment—grant of lands as a fee **fer de lance**—venomous U.S. snake (pi

mentative") **ferrule**—a ring or cap placed around a pipe to keep it fron

festoon (n.)—decoration: a string or garland, as of leaves or flowers, su

winds or waves travel **fey**—displaying an otherworldly or fairyish (coyl

territory **flake** (n.)—a frame or platform for drying produce **flambeau**—li

lar on wheel or pipe shaft, used to strengthen, hold, or attach **flitch**—lor

beam **floret**—a small or reduced-size flower, like a daisy **foliate**—of o

the posterior region of the vulva and connecting the posterior ends of the

back sections of fingers of gloves **fox** (v.)—to repair a shoe by attacl

especially political leader **fustian**—corduroyish fabric **fustic**—kind o

gabardine—sturdy, tightly woven cotton or wool fabric **galen**

against a wall; (adj.) espaliered **esplanade**—open flat place in park...like

= "and wife"; "Mr. Hoad et ux" **etude**—musical piece composed for the

case for things like needles **euchre**—card game; slang for to cheat = "he

prose style **exanthema**—skin eruption accompanying some diseases, like

sale, consumption of something **excrescence**—abnormal outgrowth or

a speech or piece of writing **execrate** (v.)—to loathe, hate, declare loath-

Greek roots) **exhilarant** (adj.)—serving to exhilarate: "warm and exhil-

gland, such as salivary or sweat gland **exordium**—introductory part of

falcate—sickle-shaped **falx**—sickle-shaped anatomical structure

ing parallel upcurving branches like lombardy poplar **fastigium**—worst

loe—the rim or section of rim of wheel that's supported by the spokes **feoff-**

viper) **fermentative**—causing fermentation ("the air in the trailer was fer-

splitting **ferule**—cane, stick, or flat board used for punishing children

pended in a curve between two points **fetch** (n.)—distance unimpeded

transcendent) look; faggy? **filibuster**—private, not military, raid of foreign

torch; a decorative candlestick **flange**—protruding rim or edge or col-

gitudinal cut in tree; a bunch of long planks bound together to make a

relating to leaves **fourchette**—small fold of mucous membrane forming

labia majora; narrow, forked strip of material connecting the front and

ng a new upper; to make beer sour by fermenting **fugleman**—leader,

yellow gotten from fustic tree (tropical U.S.) **fustigate**—criticize harshly

cal (n.)—medicine made up of 100% herbal or vegetable matter

THE (AS IT WERE) SEMINAL IMPORTANCE OF *TERMINATOR 2*

1990s MOVIEGOERS WHO HAVE sat clutching their heads in both awe and disappointment at movies like *Twister* and *Volcano* and *The Lost World* can thank James Cameron's *Terminator 2: Judgment Day* for inaugurating what's become this decade's special new genre of big-budget film: Special Effects Porn. "Porn" because, if you substitute F/X for intercourse, the parallels between the two genres become so obvious they're eerie. Just like hard-core cheapies, movies like *Terminator 2* and *Jurassic Park* aren't really "movies" in the standard sense at all. What they really are is half a dozen or so isolated, spectacular scenes—scenes comprising maybe twenty or thirty minutes of riveting, sensuous payoff—strung together via another sixty to ninety minutes of flat, dead, and often hilariously insipid narrative.

T2, one of the highest-grossing movies in history, opened six years ago. Think of the scenes we all still remember. That incredible chase scene and explosion in the L.A. sluiceway and then the liquid metal[1] T-1000 Terminator walking out of the explosion's flames and morphing seamlessly into his Martin-Milner-as-Possessed-by-Hannibal-Lecter corporeal form. The T-1000 rising hideously up out of that checkerboard floor, the T-1000 melting headfirst through the windshield of that helicopter, the T-1000 freezing in liquid nitrogen and then collapsing fractally apart. These were truly spectacular images, and they represented exponential advances in digital F/X technology. But there were at most maybe eight of these incredible sequences, and they were the movie's heart and point; the rest of *T2* is empty and derivative, pure mimetic polycelluloid.

It's not that *T2* is totally plotless or embarrassing—and it does, admittedly, stand head and shoulders above most of the F/X Porn blockbusters that have followed it. It's rather that *T2* as a dramatic narrative is slick and cliché and calculating and in sum an appalling betrayal of 1984's *The Terminator. T1,* which was James Cameron's first feature film and had a modest budget and was one of the two best U.S. action movies of the entire 1980s,[2] was a dark, breathlessly kinetic, near-brilliant piece of metaphysical Ludditism. Recall that it's A.D. 2027 and that there's been a nuclear holocaust in 1997 and that chip-driven machines now rule, and "Skynet," the archonic *diabolus ex*

[1] (actually defined in the film as "mimetic polyalloy," whatever that's supposed to mean)

[2] The '80s' other B.U.S.A.M. was Cameron's second feature, the 1986 *Aliens,* also modestly budgeted, also both hair-raising and deeply intelligent.

machina, develops a limited kind of time-travel technology and dispatches the now classically cyborgian A. Schwarzenegger back to 1984's Los Angeles to find and Terminate one Sarah Connor, the mother-to-be of the future leader of the human "Resistance," one John Connor[3]; and but that apparently the Resistance itself somehow gets one-time-only access to Skynet's time-travel technology and sends back to the same space-time coordinates a Resistance officer, the ever-sweaty but extremely tough and resourceful Kyle Reese, to try desperately to protect Ms. Sarah Connor from the Terminator's prophylactic advances,[4] and so on. It is, yes, true that Cameron's Skynet is basically Kubrick's HAL, and that most of *T1*'s time-travel paradoxes are reworkings of some fairly standard Bradbury-era science fiction themes, but *The Terminator* still has a whole lot to recommend it. There's the inspired casting of the malevolently cyborgian Schwarzenegger as the malevolently cyborgian Terminator, the role that made Ahnode a superstar and for which he was utterly and totally perfect (e.g., even his goofy 16-r.p.m. Austrian accent added a perfect little robofascist tinge to the

[3] (whose initials, for a prophesied savior of humanity, are not particularly subtle)

[4] The fact that what Skynet is attempting is in effect a retroactive abortion, together with the fact that "terminate a pregnancy" is a pretty well-known euphemism, led the female I first saw the movie with in 1984 to claim, over coffee and pie afterward, that *The Terminator* was actually one long pro-choice allegory, which I said I thought was not w/o merit but maybe a bit too simplistic to do the movie real justice, which led to kind of an unpleasant row.

Terminator's dialogue[5]). There's the first of Cameron's two great action heroines[6] in Sarah Connor, as whom the limpid-eyed and lethal-lipped Linda Hamilton also turns in the only great performance of her career. There is the dense, greasy, marvelously *machinelike* look of *The Terminator*'s mechanized F/X[7]; there are the noirish lighting and Dexedrine pace that

[5] Consider, for example, how the now-famous *"I'll be back"* line took on a level of ominous historical resonance when uttered by an unstoppable killing machine with a German accent. This was chilling and brilliant, commercial postmodernism at its best; but it is also what made *Terminator 2*'s "in-joke" of having Ahnode repeat the line in a good-guy context so disappointing.

[6] It is a complete mystery why feminist film scholars haven't paid more attention to Cameron and his early collaborator Gale Anne Hurd. *The Terminator* and *Aliens* were both violent action films with tough, competent female protagonists (incredibly rare) whose toughness and competence in no way diminished their "femininity" (even more rare, unheard of), a femininity that is rooted (along with both films' thematics) in notions of *maternity* rather than just sexuality. For example, compare Cameron's Ellen Ripley with the panty-and-tank-top Ripley of Scott's *Alien.* In fact it was flat-out criminal that Sigourney Weaver didn't win the '86 Oscar for her lead in Cameron's *Aliens.* Marlee Matlin indeed. No male lead in the history of U.S. action film even *approaches* Weaver's second Ripley for emotional depth and sheer balls—she makes Stallone, Willis, et al. look muddled and ill.

[7] (This is a ponderous, marvelously *built*-looking quality [complete with ferrous clanks and/or pneumatic hisses] that—oddly enough—at roughly the same time also distinguished the special effects in Terry Gilliam's *Brazil* and Paul Verhoeven's *RoboCop.* This was cool not only because the effects were themselves cool, but also because here were three talented young tech-minded directors who rejected the airy, hygienic look of Spielberg's and Lucas's F/X. The grimy density and preponderance of metal in Cameron's effects suggest that he's looking all the way back to Méliès and Lang for visual inspiration.)

compensate ingeniously for the low budget and manage to establish a mood that is both exhilarating and claustrophobic.[8] Plus *T1*'s story had at its center a marvelous "Appointment in Samarra"–like irony of fate: we discover in the course of the film that Kyle Reese is actually John Connor's father,[9] and thus that if Skynet hadn't built its nebulous time machine and sent back the Terminator, Reese wouldn't have been back here in '84, either, to impregnate Sarah C. This also entails that meanwhile, up in A.D. 2027, John Connor has had to send the man he knows is his father on a mission that J.C. knows will result in both that man's death and his (i.e., J.C.'s) own birth. The whole ironic mess is simultaneously Freudian and Testamental and is just *extraordinarily* cool for a low-budget action movie.

Its big-budget sequel adds only one ironic paradox to *The Terminator*'s mix: in *T2,* we learn that the "radically advanced chip"[10] on which Skynet's CPU is (will be) based actually came

[8] (Cameron would raise the use of light and pace to near-perfection in *Aliens,* where just six alien-suited stuntmen and ingenious quick-cut editing result in some of the most terrifying Teeming Rapacious Horde scenes of all time. [By the way, sorry to be going on and on about *Aliens* and *The Terminator.* It's just that they're great, great commercial cinema, and nobody talks about them enough, and they're a big reason why *T2* was such a tragic and insidious development not only for '90s film but for James Cameron, whose first two films had genius in them.])

[9] (So actually I guess it would be more like "*Luke Skywalker's* Appointment in Samarra"—nobody said this was Art-Cinema or anything.)

[10] (viz., a "neural net processor" based on an "uncooled superconductor," which I grieve to report is a conceit ripped off from Douglas Trumbull's 1983 *Brainstorm*)

(comes) from the denuded and hydraulically pressed skull of *T1*'s defunct Terminator... meaning that Skynet's attempts to alter the flow of history bring about not only John Connor's birth but Skynet's own, as well. All *T2*'s other important ironies and paradoxes, however, are unfortunately unintentional and generic and kind of sad.

Note, for example, the fact that *Terminator 2: Judgment Day,* a movie about the disastrous consequences of humans relying too heavily on computer technology, was itself unprecedentedly computer-dependent. George Lucas's Industrial Light and Magic, subcontracted by Cameron to do *T2*'s special effects, had to quadruple the size of its computer graphics department for the T-1000 sequences, sequences that also required digital-imaging specialists from around the world, thirty-six state-of-the-art Silicon Graphics computers, and terabytes of specially invented software programs for seamless morphing, realistic motion, digital "body socks," background-plate compatibility, congruences of lighting and grain, etc. And there is no question that all the lab work paid off: in 1991, *Terminator 2*'s special effects were the most spectacular and real-looking anybody had ever seen. They were also the most expensive.

T2 is thus also the first and best instance of a paradoxical law that appears to hold true for the entire F/X Porn genre. It is called the Inverse Cost and Quality Law: it states very simply that the larger a movie's budget is, the shittier that movie is going to be. The case of *T2* shows that much of the ICQL's force derives from simple financial logic. A film that would cost hundreds of millions of dollars to make is going to get financial backing if and only if its investors can be maximally—

maximally—sure that at the very least they will get their hundreds of millions of dollars back.[11] I.e., a megabudget movie *must not* fail—and "failure" here means anything less than a runaway box-office hit—and must thus adhere to certain reliable formulae that have been shown by precedent to maximally ensure a runaway hit. One of the most reliable of these formulae involves casting a superstar who is "bankable" (i.e., whose recent track record of films shows a high ROI). The studio backing for *T2*'s wildly sophisticated and expensive digital F/X therefore depends on Mr. Arnold Schwarzenegger agreeing to reprise his Terminator role. Now the ironies start to stack, though, because it turns out that Schwarzenegger—or perhaps more accurately "Schwarzenegger, Inc." or "Ahnodyne"—has decided that playing any more malevolent cyborgs would compromise the Leading Man image his elite and bankable record of ROI entails. He will do the film only if *T2*'s script is somehow engineered to make the Terminator the Good Guy. Not only is this vain and stupid and shockingly ungrateful[12]; it is also common popular knowledge, duly reported in

[11] The Industry term for getting your money back plus that little bit of extra that makes investing in a movie a decent investment is ROI, which is short for Return on Investment.

[12] Because Schwarzenegger—compared to whom Chuck Norris is an Olivier—is not an actor or even a performer. He is a body, a form—the closest thing to an actual machine in the history of the S.A.G. Ahnode's elite bankable status in 1991 was due entirely to the fact that James Cameron had had the genius to understand Schwarzenegger's essential bionism and to cast him in *T1*.

both the trades and the popular entertainment media before *T2* even goes into production. There's consequently a weird postmodern tension to the way we watch the film: we're aware of what the bankable star's demands were, and we're also aware of how much the movie cost and how important bankable stars are to a big-budget movie; and so one of the few things that keep us on the edge of our seats during the movie is our suspense about whether James Cameron can possibly weave a plausible, non-cheesy narrative that meets Schwarzenegger's career needs without betraying *T1*'s precedent.

Cameron does not succeed, at least not in avoiding heavy cheese. Recall the premise he settles on for *T2:* that Skynet once again uses its (apparently not all *that* limited) time-travel device, this time to send a far more advanced liquid metal T-1000 Terminator back to 1990s L.A., this time to kill the ten-year-old John Connor (played by the extremely annoying Edward Furlong,[13] whose voice keeps cracking pubescently and who's just clearly older than ten), and but that the intrepid human Resistance has somehow captured, subdued, and "reprogrammed" an old Schwarzenegger-model Terminator—resetting its CPU's switch from TERMINATE to PROTECT, apparently[14]—and then has somehow once *again* gotten one-

[13] It augurs ill for both Furlong and Cameron that within minutes of John Connor's introduction in the film we're rooting vigorously for him to be Terminated.

[14] A complex and interesting scene where John and Sarah actually open up the Terminator's head and remove Ahnode's CPU and do some further reprogramming—a

time access to Skynet's time-travel technology[15] and sent the Schwarzenegger Terminator back to protect young J.C. from the T-1000's infanticidal advances.[16]

Cameron's premise is financially canny and artistically

scene where we learn a lot more about neural net processors and Terminative anatomy, and where Sarah is strung out and has kind of an understandable anti-Terminator prejudice and wants to smash the CPU while she can, and where John asserts his nascent command presence and basically orders her not to—was cut from the movie's final version. Cameron's professed rationale for cutting the scene was that the middle of the movie "dragged" and that the scene was too complex: "I could account for [the Terminator's] behavior changes much more simply." I submit that the Cameron of *T1* and *Aliens* wouldn't have talked this way. But another big-budget formula for ensuring ROI is that things must be made as simple for the audience as possible; plot- and character implausibilities are to be handled through distraction rather than resolved through explanation.

[15] (around which the security must be just shockingly lax)

[16] That's the movie's main plot, but let's observe here that one of *T2*'s subplots actually echoes Cameron's Schwarzenegger dilemma and creates a kind of weird metacinematic irony. Whereas *T1* had argued for a certain kind of metaphysical passivity (i.e., fate is unavoidable, and Skynet's attempts to alter history serve only to bring it about), *Terminator 2*'s metaphysics are more active. In *T2,* the Connors take a page from Skynet's book and try to head off the foreordained nuclear holocaust, first by trying to kill Skynet's inventor and then by destroying Cyberdyne's labs and the first Terminator's CPU (though why John Connor spends half the movie carrying the deadly CPU chip around in his pocket instead of just throwing it under the first available steamroller remains unclear and irksome). The point here is that the protagonists' attempts to revise the "script" of history in *T2* parallel the director's having to muck around with *T2*'s own script in order to get Schwarzenegger to be in the movie. Multivalent ironies like this—which require that film audiences know all kinds of behind-the-scenes stuff from watching *Entertainment Tonight* and reading (umm) certain magazines—are not commercial postmodernism at its finest.

dismal: it permits *Terminator 2*'s narrative to clank along on the rails of all manner of mass-market formulae. There is, for example, no quicker or easier ingress to the audience's heart than to present an innocent child in danger, and of course protecting an innocent child from danger is Heroism at its most generic. Cameron's premise also permits the emotional center of *T2* to consist of the child and the Terminator "bonding," which in turn allows for all manner of familiar and reliable devices. Thus it is that *T2* offers us cliché explorations of stuff like the conflicts between Emotion and Logic (territory already mined to exhaustion by *Star Trek*) and between Human and Machine (turf that's been worked in everything from *Lost in Space* to *Blade Runner* to *RoboCop*), as well as exploiting the good old Alien-or-Robot-Learns-About-Human-Customs-and-Psychology-from-Sarcastic-and/or-Precocious-but-Basically-Goodhearted-Human-with-Whom-It-Bonds formula (q.q.v. here *My Favorite Martian* and *E.T.* and *Starman* and *The Brother from Another Planet* and *Harry and the Hendersons* and *ALF* and ad almost infinitum). Thus it is that the 85 percent of *T2* that is not mind-blowing digital F/X sequences subjects us to dialogue like: "Vhy do you cry?" and "Cool! My own Terminator!" and "Can you not be such a dork all the time?" and "This is intense!" and "Haven't you learned that you can't just go around killing people?" and "It's OK, Mom, he's here to help" and "I know now vhy you cry, but it's somesing I can never do"; plus to that hideous ending where Schwarzenegger gives John a cyborgian hug and then voluntarily immerses himself in molten steel to protect humanity from his neural net CPU, raising that Fonziesque thumb as he sinks below the surface,[17] and the two Connors hug and grieve, and then poor old Linda Hamilton—whose role in *T2* requires her not only to look like she's been doing nothing but Nautilus for the last several years but also to keep snarling and baring her teeth and saying stuff like "Don't fuck with me!" and "Men like you know nothing about really creating something!" and acting half-crazed with paramilitary stress, stretching Hamilton way beyond her thespian capacities and resulting in what seems more than anything like a parody of Faye Dunaway in *Mommy Dearest*—has to give us that gooey "I face the future with hope, because if a Terminator can learn the value of human life, maybe we can, too" voiceover at the very end.

The point is that head-clutchingly insipid stuff like this puts an even heavier burden of importance on *T2*'s digital effects, which now must be stunning enough to distract us from the formulaic void at the story's center, which in turn means that even more money and directorial attention must be lavished on the film's F/X. This sort of cycle is symptomatic of the insidious three-part loop that characterizes Special Effects Porn—

(1) Astounding digital dinosaur/tornado/volcano/Terminator effects that consume almost all the director's creative attention and require massive financial commitment on the part of the studio;

[17] (His hair doesn't catch on fire in the molten steel, though, which provokes intriguing speculation on what it's supposed to be made of.)

(2) A consequent need for guaranteed megabuck ROI, which entails the formulaic elements and easy sentiment that will assure mass appeal (plus will translate easily into other languages and cultures, for those important foreign sales...);

(3) A director—often one who's shown great talent in earlier, less expensive films—who is now so consumed with realizing his spectacular digital visions, and so dependent on the studio's money to bring the F/X off, that he has neither the leverage nor the energy to fight for more interesting or original plots/themes/characters.

—and thus yields the two most important corollary formulations of the Inverse Cost and Quality Law:

(ICQL(a)) The more lavish and spectacular a movie's special effects, the shittier that movie is going to be in all non-F/X respects. For obvious supporting examples of ICQL(a), see lines 1–2 of this article and/or also *Jurassic Park, Independence Day, Forrest Gump,* etc.

(ICQL(b)) There is no quicker or more efficient way to kill what is interesting and original about an interesting, original young director than to give that director a huge budget and lavish F/X resources. The number of supporting examples of ICQL(b) is sobering. Have a look, e.g., at the differences between Rodriguez's *El Mariachi* and his *From Dusk till Dawn,* between de Bont's *Speed* and *Twister,* between Gilliam's *Brazil* and *Twelve Monkeys,* between Bigelow's *Near Dark* and *Strange Days.* Or chart Cameron's industry rise and artistic decline from *T1* and *Aliens* through *T2* and *The Abyss* to—dear Lord—*True Lies.* Popular entertainment media report that Cameron's new *Titanic,* currently in post-production, is (once again) the most expensive and technically ambitious film of all time. A nation is even now pricing trenchcoats and lubricants in anticipation of its release.

—*1998*

gall—a sore or chafe caused by abrasion **gambrel**—butcher's frame fo
shoe worn by Japanese **gewgaw**—decorative trinket or bauble **gibbet**—ga
sizing or glaze made of egg whites **glissade**—gliding step in ballet **gloze**—mi
drawing that communicates nonverbally; like sign w/ pedestrian cros
Gongorism—florid, ornate literary style w/ elaborate puns and conceit
tecting the throat **Grand Guignol**—cinema that emphasizes horrifyin
bastic of speech **grapnel**—small anchor with three flukes **gravid**—pre
dill seasoning **gravure**—kind of intaglio printing **greaves**—unmel
grunion—small California fish **gueridon**—small round table **guidon**—sma
(adj.)—resembling droplets or spattered by droplets **hallux**—big to
on face **haploid**—having the same # of chromosomes as a germ = hal
ence **harridan**—querulous old woman (check?) **helotry**—condition o
mosis—flulike disease caused by inhaling spores of certain fungus, *Hi*
fireplace used for keeping food or utensils warm; a tool used for cu
having similar structure and origin though not necessarily purpose..
exhortation or urging; (n.) hortation **hoyden**—rowdy, high-spirite
ing **hyperemia**—grossly increased blood flow to a body part **hypolimn**
leaves in trees, shrubs (poplar) **hypoplasia**—incomplete development o
by the supposed treatment; "mental illness is an iatrogenic disease
illiquid—not easily converted into cash **imbricate**—having edges ove
absolute power, empire **ingress**—means or place of entering **inte**
line on a weather map connecting points of equal atmospheric pre

ıanging animals by the legs **gastine**—?? ghost?? **geta**—wooden-sole

ows **gimp**—narrow flat braid used for trimming; like fringe? **glair**—a

mize or underplay… "gloze" the embarrassing part **glyph**—crude

ng means pedestrians crossing **gomphosis**—immovable attachment

'after Luis de Góngora) **gorget**—ornamental collar; piece of armor pro-

or macabre (vs. "Gothic Horror") **grandiloquent**—pompous or bom-

ıant, especially in fish **gravlax**—appetizer w/ smoked salmon and

ed residue left after animal fat has been rendered **griot**—storyteller

lag for military unit; the soldier who carries the unit's flag **guttate**

ıanuman—monkey with eerie humanish face and Amish-looking hair

ıs many as a somatic organism **hard-bitten**—toughened by experi-

erfdom **hematite**—chief ore of iron (water w/ hematitic taste) **histoplas-**

'oplasma capsulatum **hob** (n.)—shelf or projection at back or side of

ing the teeth of machine parts, e.g., gears **homologues**—two things

e.g., flippers of seal and hands of human **hortatory**—marked by strong

girl **hustings**—places or activities associated with political campaign-

on—dense cold dead water at bottom of lake **hyponasty**—upward tilt of

organ; (adj.) hypoplastic (penis, e.g.) **iatrogenic**—caused or exacerbated

ometimes" **ilex**—holly; any trees or shrubs of the holly genus

ap like shingles or fish scales **imbrue**—to saturate or stain **imperium**—

vale—New England term for low-lying land along a river **isobar**—a

ure; two atoms having the same mass but different atomic numbers

THE NATURE OF THE FUN

The best metaphor I know of for being a fiction writer is in Don DeLillo's *Mao II,* where he describes a book-in-progress as a kind of hideously damaged infant that follows the writer around, forever crawling after the writer (i.e., dragging itself across the floor of restaurants where the writer's trying to eat, appearing at the foot of the bed first thing in the morning, etc.), hideously defective, hydrocephalic and noseless and flipper-armed and incontinent and retarded and dribbling cerebrospinal fluid out of its mouth as it mewls and blurbles and cries out to the writer, wanting love, wanting the very thing its hideousness guarantees it'll get: the writer's complete attention.

The damaged-infant trope is perfect because it captures the mix of repulsion and love the fiction writer feels for something he's working on. The fiction always comes out so horrifically defective, so hideous a betrayal of all your hopes for it—a cruel and repellent caricature of the perfection of its conception—yes, understand: grotesque because *imperfect.* And yet it's yours, the infant is, it's *you,* and you love it and dandle it and wipe the cerebrospinal fluid off its slack chin with the cuff of the only clean shirt you have left because you haven't done laundry in like three weeks because finally this one chapter or character seems like it's finally trembling on the edge of coming together and working and you're terrified to spend any time on anything other than working on it because if you look away for a second you'll lose it, dooming the whole infant to continued hideousness. And but so you love the damaged infant and pity it and care for it; but also you hate it—*hate* it—because it's deformed, repellent, because something grotesque has happened to it in the parturition from head to page; hate it because its deformity is *your* deformity (since if you were a better fiction writer your infant would of course look like one of those babies in catalogue ads for infantwear, perfect and pink and cerebrospinally continent) and its every hideous incontinent breath is a devastating indictment of *you,* on all levels... and so you want it dead, even as you dote and love and wipe it and dandle it and sometimes even apply CPR when it seems like its own grotesqueness has blocked its breath and it might die altogether.

The whole thing's all very messed up and sad, but simultaneously it's also tender and moving and noble and cool—it's a genuine *relationship,* of a sort—and even at the height of its hideousness the damaged infant somehow touches and awakens what you suspect are some of the very best parts of you: maternal parts, dark ones. You love your infant very much. And you want others to love it, too, when the time finally comes for the damaged infant to go out and face the world.

So you're in a bit of a dicey position: you love the infant and want others to love it, but that means you hope others won't see it *correctly*. You want to sort of fool people: you want them to see as perfect what you in your heart know is a betrayal of all perfection.

Or else you don't want to fool these people; what you want is you want them to see and love a lovely, miraculous, perfect, ad-ready infant and to be *right, correct,* in what they see and feel. You want to be terribly wrong: you want the damaged infant's hideousness to turn out to have been nothing but your own weird delusion or hallucination. But that'd mean you were crazy: you have seen, been stalked by, and recoiled from hideous deformities that in fact (others persuade you) aren't there at all. Meaning you're at least a couple fries short of a Happy Meal, surely. But worse: it'd also mean you see and despise hideousness in a thing *you* made (and love), in your spawn, in in certain ways *you*. And this last, best hope—this'd represent something way worse than just very bad parenting; it'd be a terrible kind of self-assault, almost self-torture. But that's still what you most want: to be completely, insanely, suicidally wrong.

But it's still all a lot of fun. Don't get me wrong. As to the nature of that fun, I keep remembering this strange little story I heard in Sunday school when I was about the size of a fire hydrant. It takes place in China or Korea or someplace like that. It seems there was this old farmer outside a village in the hill country who worked his farm with only his son and his beloved horse. One day the horse, who was not only beloved but vital to the labor-intensive work on the farm, picked the lock on his corral or whatever and ran off into the hills. All the old farmer's friends came around to exclaim what bad luck this was. The farmer only shrugged and said, "Good luck, bad luck, who knows?" A couple days later the beloved horse returned from the hills in the company of a whole priceless herd of wild horses, and the farmer's friends all come around to congratulate him on what good luck the horse's escape turned out to be. "Good luck, bad luck, who knows?" is all the farmer says in reply, shrugging. The farmer now strikes me as a bit Yiddish-sounding for an old Chinese farmer, but this is how I remember it. But so the farmer and his son set about breaking the wild horses, and one of the horses bucks the son off his back with such wild force that the son breaks his leg. And here come the friends to commiserate with the farmer and curse the bad luck that had ever brought these accursed wild horses onto his farm. The old farmer just shrugs and says, "Good luck, bad luck, who knows?" A few days later the Imperial Sino-Korean Army or something like that comes marching through the village, conscripting every able-bodied male between like ten and sixty for cannon-fodder for some hideously bloody conflict that's apparently brewing, but when they see the son's broken leg, they let him off on some sort of feudal 4-F, and instead of getting shanghaied the son stays on the farm with the old farmer. Good luck? Bad luck?

This is the sort of parabolic straw you cling to as you struggle with the issue of fun, as a writer. In the beginning, when you first start out trying to write fiction, the whole endeavor's about fun. You don't expect anybody else to read it. You're writing almost wholly to get yourself off. To enable your own fantasies and deviant logics and to escape or transform parts of yourself you don't like. And it works—and it's terrific fun. Then, if you have good luck and people seem to like what you do, and you actually get to get paid for it, and get to see your stuff professionally typeset and bound and blurbed and reviewed and even (once) being read on the AM subway by a pretty girl you don't even know, it seems to make it even *more* fun. For a while. Then things start to get complicated and confusing, not to mention scary. Now you feel like you're writing for other people, or at least you hope so. You're no longer writing just to get yourself off, which—since any kind of masturbation is lonely and hollow—is probably good. But what replaces the onanistic motive? You've found you very much enjoy having your writing liked by people, and you find you're extremely keen to have people like the new stuff you're doing. The motive of pure personal fun starts to get supplanted by the motive of being liked, of having pretty people you don't know like you and admire you and think you're a good writer. Onanism gives way to attempted seduction, as a motive. Now, attempted seduction is hard work, and its fun is offset by a terrible fear of rejection. Whatever "ego" means, your ego has now gotten into the game. Or maybe "vanity" is a better word. Because you notice that a good deal of your writing has now become basically showing off, trying to get people to think you're good. This is understandable. You have a great deal of yourself on the line, now, writing—your vanity is at stake. You discover a tricky thing about fiction writing: a certain amount of vanity is necessary to be able to do it at all, but any vanity above that certain amount is lethal. At this point 90+ percent of the stuff you're writing is motivated and informed by an overwhelming need to be liked. This results in shitty fiction. And the shitty work must get fed to the wastebasket, less because of any sort of artistic integrity than simply because shitty work will make you disliked. At this point in the evolution of writerly fun, the very thing that's always motivated you to write is now also what's motivating you to feed your writing to the wastebasket. This is a paradox and a kind of double bind, and it can keep you stuck inside yourself for months or even years, during which you wail and gnash and rue your bad luck and wonder bitterly where all the *fun* of the thing could have gone.

The smart thing to say, I think, is that the way out of this bind is to work your way somehow back to your original motivation: fun. And, if you can find your way back to the fun, you will find that the hideously unfortunate double bind of the late vain period turns out really to have been good luck for you. Because the fun you work back to has been transfigured by the unpleasantness of vanity and fear, an unpleasantness you're now so anxious to avoid that the fun you rediscover is a way fuller and more large-hearted kind of fun. It has something to do with Work as Play. Or with the discovery that disciplined fun is more fun than impulsive or hedonistic fun. Or with figuring out that not all paradoxes have to be paralyzing. Under fun's new administration, writing fiction becomes a way to go deep inside yourself and illuminate precisely the stuff you don't want to see or let anyone else see, and this stuff usually turns out (paradoxically) to be precisely the stuff all writers and readers share and respond to, feel. Fiction becomes a weird way to countenance yourself and to tell the truth instead of being a way to escape yourself or present yourself in a way you figure you will be maximally likable. This process is complicated and confusing and scary, and also hard work, but it turns out to be the best fun there is.

The fact that you can now sustain the fun of writing only by confronting the very same unfun parts of yourself you'd first used writing to avoid or disguise is another paradox, but this one isn't any kind of bind at all. What it is is a gift, a kind of miracle, and compared to it the reward of strangers' affection is as dust, lint.

—1998

isochronal—equal in duration, taking same amount of time **isomer**—two
isotropic—identical in all directions; invariant w/ respect to direction;
journal—the part of a machine shaft or axle supported by a bearing **keep**
keloid—a red raised scar from an injury **kepi**—French military cap w/ flat
or notch made by a cutting tool like an axe or saw **kidskin**—leather made
alent is "run" **laciniate**—fringed **laconic**—terse, of few words **ladder**
lamina—thin sheet, plate, or layer **laparoscopy**—using laparoscope (slen
tical, "clinker-built"(?) **last** (n.)—mold shaped like foot used by cobbler
lavabo—ritual of washing hands by priest before Eucharist **lavation**—wash
legato—music: in a smooth, even style **leptosome**—frail, skinny person
Egypt; Levantine **levator**—surgical instrument for raising depressed parts
a hare less than one year old **limbus**—a distinctive border or edge,
physiological or psychological response **limnetic**—of or occurring
stock—long forked stick for holding match…used to light cannons **linu**
lobed; a structure resembling a lobe (i.e., a rounded projection) **lob**
glasses or opera glasses with a short handle **lowboy**—towing device w/
overcast **luteous**—moderate greenish yellow **luxate**—to put out of
dark spot or discoloration in a crystal **malediction**—curse **malocclusion**—faulty
country, badlands, desert (? check before using) **Maltese cross**—four arrow
makeup **marcasite**—ornament of pyrite **marplot**—stupid meddler who
or container in which something originates **mattock**—digging tool that

molecules of same element but w/ different arrangement of atoms

isotrope, isotropy **jakes**—latrine or privy **jape**—joke, make sport of

(n.)—jail; stronghold of castle (he watched from the keep of the tree)

circular top and a visor: classic FFL hat, *Casablanca*, etc. **kerf**—a groove

from goat **kill** (n.)—Northern, Dutch term for a creek; Southern equiv-

(v.)—to run as a stocking does **lamelliform**—having the form of a thin plate

der, tubular pelvic endoscope) to treat endometriosis **lapstrake** (adj.)—nau-

lath—thin strips of wood in rows as substructure for plaster, shingles, tile

ing **lee** (n.)—place sheltered from wind; side of ship away from wind

Levant—countries bordering eastern Mediterranean from Turkey to

of a fractured skull; in anatomy, a muscle that raises a body part **leveret**—

e.g., junction of cornea and sclera of eyeball **limen**—the threshold of a

in the deeper parts of lakes or ponds **limnology**—study of lakes **lin-**

ron—herbicide to kill weeds **littoral**—of or on a shore **lobation**—being

lolly—Southern for mud hole or mire **lorgnette**—old-fashioned eye-

wheels and bed for hauling stuff behind vehicle **lowery** (adj.)—cloudy,

oint, dislocate **luxe** (n.)—condition of gross luxury, a luxury **macle**—a

contact between upper & lower teeth when jaw is closed **malpais**—bad

heads joined at point; looks like ragged tear **maquillage**—heavy theatrical

nterferes with undertaking **matrix**—womb; a surrounding environment

ooks like flat-bladed hammer **maugre**—in spite of, notwithstanding

OVERLOOKED: FIVE DIRELY UNDERAPPRECIATED U.S. NOVELS >1960

Omensetter's Luck by William H. Gass (1966)
Gass's first novel, and his least avant-gardeish, and his best. Basically a religious book. Very sad. Contains the immortal line "The body of Our Saviour shat but Our Saviour shat not." Bleak but gorgeous, like light through ice.

Steps by Jerzy Kosinski (1968)
This won some big prize or other when it first came out, but today nobody seems to remember it. *Steps* gets called a novel but it is really a collection of unbelievably creepy little allegorical tableaux done in a terse elegant voice that's like nothing else anywhere ever. Only Kafka's fragments get anywhere close to where Kosinski goes in this book, which is better than everything else he ever did combined.

Angels by Denis Johnson (1983)
This was Johnson's first fiction after the horripilative lyric poetry of *The Incognito Lounge.* Even cult fans of *Jesus' Son* often haven't heard of *Angels.* It's sort of *Jesus' Son*'s counterpoint, a novel-length odyssey of mopes and scrotes and their brutal redemptions. A totally *American* book, it's also got great prose, truly great, some of the '80s' best; e.g., lines like "All around them men drank alone, staring out of their faces."

Blood Meridian: Or the Evening Redness in the West
by Cormac McCarthy (1985)
Don't even ask.

Wittgenstein's Mistress by David Markson (1988)
W's M is a dramatic rendering of what it would be like to live in the sort of universe described by logical atomism. A monologue, formally very odd, mostly one-sentence ¶s. Tied with *Omensetter's Luck* for the all-time best U.S. book about human loneliness. These wouldn't constitute ringing endorsements if they didn't happen all to be simultaneously true—i.e., that a novel this abstract and erudite and avant-garde could also be so moving makes *Wittgenstein's Mistress* pretty much the high point of experimental fiction in this country.

—1999

maul—long-handled sledgehammer used for splitting logs, etc. **mazy**—
time of birth **medulla**—inner core of some body parts, like bone marrow is
a pipe made of this (w/ white bowl) **mensal** (adj.)—used at table, i.e., to
mere—homologous longitudinal segments that compose the body of earth
tique kitchen where biowaste is stored **milliner**—hatmaker **milt**—fish
minim—tiny or insignificant portion **moiré** (adj.)—having a wavy or rip
in which the skin absorbs all or most of the stresses to which the body is
one buyer **moratory**—authorizing delay in payment **mordacious**—given
for upholstery **Mormon cricket**—big wingless western grasshopper bad to
eggs Mornay **mudra**—series of symbolic body postures and hand move
merrymaker **muntin**—strip of wood or metal that separates & holds vari
a big rectangle, etc. (that's putting it well, Dave) **muricate**—covered with
sexual drive in elephants (Vulcans) when they're more aggressive **multi**
tes—buttocks, shanks **neap** (adj.)—from "neap tide," lowest possible tide
ing (slackers are not nidifugous) **nidify**—to build a nest **nidus**—nest for
black metallic alloy used for decorations on surfaces **numismatic**—of
nummular—shaped like a coin, circular or oval **nutation**—the act of nod
obdurate chin" **obligate** (adj.)—able to exist only in a certain kind of
orange yellow...e.g., early sunset **odonate**—dragonflyish, stiff-winged **onei**
ordurous—dungish or shitty **orgeat**—sweet flavoring, orange/almond **or**
bay window...prevalent in NE and SF houses **orotund**—full in sound, sc

labyrinthine **meconium**—dark green feces in fetus that is discharged near
medulla; (adj.) medullar **meerschaum**—dense fine white claylike substance;
dine **meridian**—noon, longitudinal circle circumscribing world **meta-**
worms, lobsters, etc. **midden**—dung hill or rubbish heap; place in an-
sperm; spermy stuff in general **minaudière**—small cosmetic case
pled surface...used of cloth **monocoque**—metal structure, like airplane,
subjected **monopsony**—a market in which there are lots of sellers for just
to biting; caustic, sarcastic **moreen**—sturdy ribbed wool or cotton used
crops **Mornay**—served w/ white sauce w/ grated cheese and seasonings:
ments in Hindu dancing & meditation **mummer**—a masked and costumed
ous panes in a window, like a window w/ four individual panes arranged in
short spines **murine**—rodentlike **must/musth**—period of heightened
voltine—producing several broods in a single season; prolific birthing **na-**
nictitate (v.)—to wink **nidifugous**—leaving the nest shortly after hatch-
eggs of insects; central point for start of infection in organism **niello**—
or relating to coins & currency **numismatist**—coin collector
ding; a wobble in a gyroscope or spinning body **obdurate**—stubborn; "an
environment **obloquy**—harsh, derisive language **ocherous**—moderate
ric—of, relating to, or suggestive of dreams **ordure**—excrement, dung
gone—theoretical life-force emanating from living things **oriel**—a small
norous; "orotund tones" **orrery**—a mechanical model of the solar system

RHETORIC AND THE MATH MELODRAMA

MATH'S CULTURAL STOCK HAS risen hard in recent years, no doubt driven by the same booming and metastatic Knowledge Economy that's turned yesterday's *non grata* nerd into today's cyber-tycoon. Call the phenomenon "Geek Chic" or "Hip(2b)^2" or whatever you will: abstract tech is now sexy, the mathematician a viable commercial hero—see for example the success of recent films like *Good Will Hunting* and *π*.

Or a better instance of math's new cachet here is Amir D. Aczel's *Fermat's Last Theorem: Unlocking the Secret of an Ancient Mathematical Problem,* which made nonfiction bestseller lists in 1996 and transformed Princeton's Andrew Wiles into a weird kind of horn-rimmed pop icon, and in the wake of which has appeared everything from Paul Hoffman's *The Man Who Loved Only Numbers* and Sylvia Nasar's *A Beautiful Mind*[1] to David

[1] These are rich and well-written biographies of the twentieth-century mathematicians Paul Erdos and John Nash, respectively.

Berlinski's *Newton's Gift* and Charles Seife's *Zero: The Biography of a Dangerous Idea.*

Though fiction, Philibert Schogt's *The Wild Numbers* and Apostolos Doxiadis's *Uncle Petros & Goldbach's Conjecture* both draw heavily on Aczel's *Fermat's Last Theorem* (as well as on G. H. Hardy's *A Mathematician's Apology*[2]). And there are other, rather striking similarities between these two novels. Both are set in the world of academic mathematics and feature characters whose specialty is number theory,[3] higher math's most purely abstract branch. Both novels revolve around their protagonists' quests to solve famous and long-standing number-theoretic problems. And both *WN* and *UPGC* have been translated by their own authors from foreign-language originals.

The facts of these two novels' close resemblance and near-simultaneous release here in the States, as well as the vigor with which their U.S. publishers are hyping them,[4] appear to

[2] This classic long essay, originally published in 1940 and re-released by Cambridge University Press in '92, is the unacknowledged father of most of the last decade's math-prose. There is very little that any of the recent books do that Hardy's terse and beautiful *Apology* did not do first, better, and with rather less fuss.

[3] (i.e., the formal study of integers/rationals, the world of Diophantine equations, of Hilbert Problems 9–12, etc.—and also the specialty of both G. H. Hardy and A. Wiles)

[4] *WN*'s cover comes with a blurb from *Fermat's Last Theorem*'s Aczel, who must have been on some kind of euphoriant medication—"I have never read a better fictional description of what it's like to work in pure math"—as well as the breathless market-

signal the inception of a whole new commercial genre—the "Math Melodrama," as it were. This is a development that should come as no surprise, given the success of some of the other titles mentioned *supra,* not to mention the commercial success in recent years of other nascent tech-intensive genres (the cyberpunk of *Neuromancer* et seq., the Clancy-style techno-thriller, the plucky-young-hackers-thwarting-evil-monolithic-institutions of *Sneakers, Hackers, The Matrix,* etc.).

As exemplified by *WN* and *UPGC* in fiction and *Fermat's Last Theorem* and *A Beautiful Mind* in non-, the Math Melodrama can be roughly characterized as combining the "Vocational Travelogue"[5] charms of genre authors like Arthur Hailey and Michael Crichton with some of the weightier allegorical functions that other genres and their heroes often serve—the

ing tag "THE LINE BETWEEN GENIUS AND MADNESS IS A THIN ONE." *UPGC*'s publisher's big tactic is to offer a $1,000,000 bounty to anyone who can prove Goldbach's Conjecture before 2002.

[5] "Vocational Travelogue" is a very shorthand way of acknowledging that for a long time one reason people used to read fiction was for a kind of imaginative tourism to places and cultures they'd never get to really see; that modernity's jetliners, TV, etc. have pretty well obsoleted this function; but that modern tech has also created such extreme vocational specialization that few people anymore are in a position to know much about any professional field but their own; and thus that a certain amount of fiction's "touristic" function now consists in giving readers dramatized access to the nuts and bolts of different professional disciplines and specialties. It is not an accident that the first important Vocational Travelogues, novels like Hailey's *Airport* and *Hotel* and Ed McBain's "police procedurals," began appearing in the late '50s and early '60s.

Western sheriff as emblem of Apollonian order, the Noir private eye as existential hero, the plucky young hacker as Odyssean trickster. The Math Melodrama's own allegorical template appears to be more classically Tragic, its hero a kind of Prometheus-Icarus figure whose high-altitude genius is also hubris and Fatal Flaw.[6] If this sounds a bit grandiose, well, it is; but it's also a fair description of the way Math Melodramas characterize the project of pure math—as nothing less than the mortal quest for Divine Truth. What's odd here is that whether a particular reader accepts this characterization or sees it as pretentious and silly will often depend less on the qualities of the Math Melodramas themselves than on certain biographical facts about the reader himself, namely how much knowledge and experience of higher math he happens to have.

This sort of oddity is, in fact, a frequent problem in reviewing or assessing "genre fiction," which is a type of narrative it's usually fair to call "the sort of thing someone who likes this sort of thing is apt to like." The evaluative criteria tend to be rather special for genre fiction. Instead of the basically *aesthetic* assay the reviewer gets to make of most literary fiction—"Is this piece of fiction *good?*"—criticism of genre fiction is ultimately more *rhetorical*—"To whom will this piece of fiction *appeal?*" In other words, as is the case with all but the broadest

[6] (Q.v. here *WN*'s marketing tag about GENIUS and MADNESS in FN4 *supra,* or *UPGC*'s flap copy's heavy description of the novel as "about the search for truth at all costs, and the heavy price of finding it" [*sic*].)

and coarsest genre fiction, the central questions about novels like *WN* and *UPGC* concern what rhetoricians call "audience": What is the intended audience for these books? And is this audience apt to find the novels satisfying on the same terms by which it finds other Math Melodramas satisfying? And if not, are there other audiences whom these books are more likely to satisfy? And so on. One reason this is a problem for reviewers is that book reviews are usually supposed to be short, clear, and relatively simple, and rhetorical criteria tend to yield very complex, sometimes even paradoxical conclusions. In the case of *The Wild Numbers* and *Uncle Petros & Goldbach's Conjecture,* the paradox is that the type of audience most likely to accept and appreciate these novels' lofty, encomiastic view of pure math is also the audience most apt to be disappointed by the variously vague, reductive, or inconsistent ways the novels handle the actual mathematics they're concerned with.

To put it in a simpler, more book review-ish way: neither of these novels is very good (one, in fact, is downright bad); but the precise *ways* in which they're not very good will vary directly with how much an individual reader already knows about the extraordinary field these two books are trying to dramatize.[7]

[7] In fairness to all concerned, this variability in readers' mathematical backgrounds is a problem for pretty much anyone trying to write general-interest prose about math, a problem that Hardy refers to as "the restrictions under which I am writing. On the one hand my examples must be very simple, and intelligible to a reader who has no specialized mathematical knowledge. . . . And on the other hand my examples should be drawn from 'pukka' mathematics, the mathematics of the working

Not just professional mathematicians, but just about anyone lucky enough ever to have studied higher math understands what a pity it is that most students never pursue the subject past its introductory levels and therefore know only the dry and brutal problem-solving of Calc I or Intro Stats (which is roughly analogous to halting one's study of poetry at the level of grammar and syntax). Modern math is like a pyramid, and the broad fundament is often not fun. It is at the higher and apical levels of geometry, topology, analysis, number theory, and mathematical logic that the fun and profundity start, when the calculators and contextless formulae fall away and all that's left are pencil & paper and what gets called "genius," viz. the particular blend of reason and ecstatic creativity that characterizes what is best about the human mind. Those who've been privileged (or forced) to study it understand that the practice of higher mathematics is, in fact, an "art"[8] and that it depends

professional mathematician." Note that this sort of thing is a problem even for rather more "special-interest" writing like this book review itself. Is it, for example, necessary to inform or remind the average *Science* reader that Fermat's Last Theorem (c. 1637) states that where n is an integer and $n > 2$, the equation $x^n + y^n = z^n$ has no nonzero integer solutions? or that Goldbach's Conjecture (or rather the "strong" G.C. as reformulated by Leonhard Euler in 1742) is that every even integer ≥ 4 can be expressed as the sum of two prime numbers, etc.? As it happens, this reviewer is not certain whether it's necessary or not, and the fact that these lines have not been deleted by *Science*'s editors (i.e., that you are reading them at all) may indicate that the editors are not totally sure either.

[8] Hardy, whose *Apology* talks about this better than anything else ever has, explains that "the mathematician's patterns, like the painter's or poet's, must be *beautiful;* the

no less than other arts on inspiration, courage, toil, etc.... but with the added stricture that the "truths" the art of math tries to express are deductive, necessary, *a priori* truths, capable of both derivation and demonstration by logical proof.[9]

It may be that mathematics is not generally recognized as one of the arts precisely because so much pyramidal training and practice is required in order to appreciate its aesthetics; math is perhaps the ultimate in acquired tastes.[10] And it's

ideas, like the colours or the words, must fit together in a harmonious way. Beauty is the first test; there is no permanent place in the world for ugly mathematics."

[9] (The assumption here will be that the typical *Science* reader already knows what *"a priori,"* "deductive truth," and "logical proof" mean and is at least roughly familiar with the relationship between pure math and formal logic... if for no other reason than that to gloss tangential stuff like this would take up enormous amounts of space and time and might well also alienate the [presumably large] percentage of *Science*'s readership who already know the stuff and are apt to find such glosses not only otiose but annoying—this reviewer can actually imagine such readers looking increasingly aggrieved and impatient and saying to themselves, *Whom does he think he's talking to?* All this is mentioned only to underscore once again the rhetorical diciness of the whole math-prose enterprise, a diciness that lies at the very center of this review's criticisms of the actual novels to be discussed, which critical discussions are upcoming very, very shortly.)

[10] It's worth noting that as so much contemporary poetry, classical music, etc. becomes ever more abstract and involute and technically complex, their own audiences get ever smaller and more specialized. With very few exceptions, the people who truly "appreciate" a piece of language-poetry or an atonal fugue are people with extensive educations in the history and theory of these arts. And this increasing exclusivity in the U.S. arts has much less to do with good old "cultural elitism" than with our era's tendency toward greater and greater specialization—it is not at all an

maybe because of math's absolute, wholly abstract Truth that so many people still view the discipline as dry or passionless and its practitioners as asocial dweebs. Some readers of *Science* will probably know all too well the frustration of trying to describe the beauty and power of Gauss's differential geometry or the Banach-Tarski Paradox to someone who remembers only the drudgery of factoring quadratic equations or the terror of a trig midterm. In fact, the weird fear and distaste that low-level math provokes in so many[11] is part of what makes the emergence of the Math Melodrama exciting: if the genre can find ways to vivify pure math and communicate the discipline's extraordinary beauty and passion to the average reader,[12] both readers and math itself stand to gain.

The ways in which Schogt's and Doxiadis's novels go about

accident that the majority of people who read contemporary poetry are themselves contemporary poets.

[11] "Math Anxiety" is now a recognized term in educational psychology, and variants of the "I'm-back-in-high-school-and-sitting-in-my-AP-Calc-final-and-I've-forgotten-to-study-or-it-turns-out-all-my-pencils-have-pimento-in-them-instead-of-graphite" nightmare are so common they're almost clichés.

[12] "Average reader" is kind of a synecdoche for "people who read mainly for diversion or entertainment." These people are American genre fiction's basic audience. It is true that Hardy's *Apology,* as well as novels from Don DeLillo's *Ratner's Star* and Thomas Pynchon's *Gravity's Rainbow* to Neal Stephenson's *Cryptonomicon* have already deployed higher math in interesting and significant ways—but books like these are belle lettres, literature, for which the audience is, again, usually small and rather specialized. Genre books are mass books and are marketed accordingly.

trying to humanize and animate math are also kind of similar. Besides both struggling to solve classic problems in number theory (the actual Goldbach Conjecture in *UPGC,* in *WN* a fictitious conundrum called "Beauregard's Wild Number Problem"[13]), the books' protagonists also both conceive of their projects almost wholly in terms of personal achievement, glory. *WN*'s Isaac Swift, a once-promising student whose pro career has stagnated, spends much time fantasizing about solving the Wild Number Problem and having "an international symposium held in my honor...and, now that I was not just a mathematician, but a famous mathematician, women would suddenly find me attractive, not just eccentric or at best amusing." And *UPGC*'s Petros Papachristos, while already a number-theorist of substantial reputation who holds an endowed chair at U. Munich, nevertheless "sought in mathematics a great, almost transcendent success, a total triumph that would bring him world fame....And to be complete, this

[13] The putative author of this problem, one "Anatole Millechamps de Beauregard" (b. 1791), is also fictitious, a kind of biographical hybrid of von Neumann and Galois, on whose florid life story—"Beauregard had a magnetic personality, and his appetite for wine, women and song was as great as for knowledge"; "One of Beauregard's closest friends caught him in bed with his wife. Blind with rage, he strangled them both"—*WN* spends most of a chapter. The specular pun of Beauregard's name, by the way, is not an accident: people in this novel are constantly saying stuff to each other like "Your findings lead directly into the high country of number theory. The view you offer is breathtaking."

triumph should be exclusively his own." Despite their different stations and attainments, the two protagonists suffer almost identically (and at great length) from the insecurity of measuring themselves against their colleagues and the fear that someone else will solve "their" problem first (Petros actually rejoices when Srinivasa Ramanujan[14] dies young of tuberculosis, simply because Ramanujan's "unique intellect was the only force he considered capable of purloining his prize"). Both protagonists' work is characterized as an anxious race against the clock and calendar; both novels make much of the fact that pure math is a "young man's game" and that the vast majority of important mathematicians do their best work before thirty-five.[15] And both heroes brood and expound at great length

[14] Like many of *UPGC*'s supporting characters, Ramanujan was a real number-theorist, an Indian savant discovered and mentored by Hardy. Robert Kanigal's *The Man Who Knew Infinity: A Life of the Genius Ramanujan* is another of the post-*Fermat* math-bios now on the market.

[15] The real source of this insight is Hardy, in his *Apology*'s famous "No mathematician should ever allow himself to forget that mathematics, more than any other art or science, is a young man's game," which *UPGC*'s narrator rips off without any attribution at all (p. 78: "Mathematics, you see, is a young man's game. It is one of the few human endeavors where youth is a necessary requirement [*sic*] for greatness"). Actually, this FN is probably the place to point out that Doxiadis's novel is filled with what appear to be little more than very slight rephrasings of stuff in Hardy's *Apology* and/or C. P. Snow's famous Foreword to it. Flipping through the two books at random, one might, e.g., compare *UPGC*'s "Anybody who claims that scientists—even the purest of the pure, the most abstract, high-flying mathematicians—are motivated exclusively by

about the particular despair of being a good but not immortally great mathematician, i.e., a mathematician brilliant enough truly to appreciate the genius of Riemann, Euler, Poincaré, et al. but not brilliant enough to be their equal. As *UPGC*'s Petros tells his nephew:

> Take Hardy and Littlewood, top-class mathematicians both of them. They possibly made the Hall

the Pursuit of Truth for the Good of Mankind, either has no idea what he's talking about or is blatantly lying" with Hardy's "So if a mathematician, or a chemist, or even a physiologist, were to tell me that the driving force in his work had been the desire to benefit humanity, then I should not believe him." Or see Hardy's "Galois died at twenty-one, Abel at twenty-seven, Ramanujan at thirty-three, Riemann at forty," and *UPGC*'s "Riemann had died at thirty-nine, Niels Henrik Abel at twenty-seven and Evariste Galois at a mere tragic twenty…"; or C. P. Snow's description of the Hardy-Littlewood team as "the most famous collaboration in the history of mathematics" vs. Doxiadis's narrator calling it "one of the most renowned partnerships in the history of mathematics." On *UPGC* pages 129–30, Doxiadis even cribs nearly word for word a deathbed exchange between Hardy and Ramanujan and tags it with the footnote "Hardy also recounts the incident in his *Mathematician's Apology* without, however, acknowledging my uncle's presence," which is not only intrusive and irritating but wrong, since it is not in the *Apology* but in Snow's Foreword to it that the scene really appears.

It's hard to know just how indictable *UPGC* is for its reliance on Hardy. It doesn't seem like outright plagiarism, because plagiarism implies sneakiness, and Doxiadis has a fully attributed Hardy-quotation right up front as the novel's epigraph. Plus it's true that much commercial genre fiction has a long history of liberating stuff from established literary works. For the record, though, it's still one of the more irksome things about *UPGC*.

> of Fame—a very *large* Hall of Fame, mind you—but even they did not get their statues erected at the grand entrance alongside Euclid, Archimedes, Newton, Euler, Gauss... *That* had been my only ambition and nothing short of the proof of Goldbach's Conjecture, which also meant cracking the deeper mystery of the primes, could possibly have lead me there. [*sic*]

while *WN*'s Isaac Swift, quite a bit lower on the academic food chain, carps to himself almost nonstop about being "well on your way to everlasting anonymity, never to be quoted and always to be seated somewhere at the back of a conference, assuming you manage to scrounge together the funds needed to attend in the first place," etc.

Interestingly, though, the most important similarity between the novels concerns the rhetorical problems of audience mentioned *supra,* while the biggest differences between *WN* and *UPGC* concern the ways the two books try to handle those problems. Oddly, the better of the two novels is also the one that seems to be the most confused and confusing about just what its audience is.

The Wild Numbers, translated from the Dutch *De wilde getallen* and its locale moved from Amsterdam to some nameless U.S. college town, is not the better novel. It's designed to be sort of a schlemiel-comedy à la Thurber's "Mitty" or Amis's *Lucky Jim. WN*'s Isaac is a mediocrity who at the start of the novel is under-published and reduced to doing scutwork calculations and "refinements" for his superstar colleague Dimitri

Arkanov[16] and at age thirty-five goes around saying stuff like "I felt old and depressed. There seemed to be no more room for dreams at my age. Everything was measured in terms of success and failure. . . . I concluded that I was a lesser human being in every respect." His prospects suddenly change when Isaac stumbles into working on "wild numbers," which are described in the translation this way:

> Beauregard had defined a number of deceptively simple operations, which, when applied to a whole number [integer?], at first resulted in fractions [rationals?]. But if the same steps were repeated often enough, the eventual outcome was once again a whole number [huh?]. Or, as Beauregard cheerfully observed: "In all numbers lurks a wild number, guaranteed to emerge when you provoke them long enough." 0 yielded the wild number 11, 1 brought forth 67, 2 itself, 3 suddenly manifested itself as 4769, 4, surprisingly, brought forth 67 again.

In an all-nighter of migrainous epiphany, Swift comes to believe he's found the long-sought answer to the Wild Number Problem, which is apparently a fictional variant of number-

[16] The work Isaac's doing for Arkanov is on "calibrator sets" and "K-reducibility," two made-up terms that figure prominently in the plot's math but are never specified or explained.

theoretic puzzles like the Twin Primes Problem[17]: "How many wild numbers are there? Are there a finite number that keep coming up, and if so, how many, or are there an infinite number?" Isaac's proof that the set of all wilds is infinite (a proof that somehow involves FN16's K-reducibility and calibrator sets as well as what are called "tame" and "pseudo-wild numbers") appears at first to be sound, and it is confirmed and lauded by Arkanov and submitted to a prestigious journal, catapulting Swift into the mathematical limelight and prompting all sorts of wacky plot-complications before it is finally discovered that the proof doesn't work after all (but by which time Isaac's found true love with a caustic divorcée who's also had horrible career reverses, so everything works out OK in the end).

The major problem with *The Wild Numbers* looks at first to be artistic but is actually rhetorical. All the book's math is, as mentioned, made up, which is not necessarily a problem—all sorts of great science fiction, from Asimov to Larry Niven, is replete with fictional math and high tech. What is a problem, though, is that the fictional math in *WN* is extremely important but also extremely vague, comprising mostly repeated and contextless verbiage—"The trick was to construct a series of infinite sets of pseudo-wild numbers such that their intersection contained wild numbers only"; "If I could only establish its K-reducibility with the aid of a suitable calibrator set!"—

[17] (Here the reviewer's assumption is that if the T.P.P. is unfamiliar or the analogy unhelpful it can just be passed over with no hard feelings on either side.)

without any definitions or even cursory fleshing-out, so that the book's math-speak ends up most resembling the absurd pseudo-jargon of bad old low-budget sci-fi movies ("Quick, Lieutenant, prepare the antigenic nanomodule for immediate stabilization flux!"). Also vague and kind of bathetic is the novel's depiction of actual mathematical work, which Isaac Swift appears to undertake only very late at night, bleary and unshaven and trembling with fatigue, "my head buzzing with complicated reasoning that led me around in circles," "fiddling around with complex equations that only a handful of people understood."[18]

Apart from its intrinsic weaknesses, the sketchy made-up math here clearly indicates that *The Wild Numbers* is meant to appeal mostly to readers with little or no high-math background, an audience that either won't know that the impressive-sounding

[18] Rather than ever being specific about what all the complicated reasoning and complex equations are, *WN* employs the metaphor of mountain-climbing to try to evoke and describe what it feels like to do higher math. Actually, "employs" is the wrong word; the book repeats, exhausts, strip-mines the metaphor, pounding it again and again—"Every step I took, no matter how small, revealed new mountain-tops and unexpected canyons in this magnificent and bizarre region of mathematics"; "Another part of me had rushed ahead: it stood on the mountain pass, catching its breath as it watched the sun rising over a land that no human eyes had ever yet beheld"—until it becomes first grating—"Having completed the climb, we threw down our heavy backpacks and wiped the sweat from our brows. We were now standing together on the mountain pass, marvelling [*sic*] at the mathematical landscape"—and finally kind of funny—"Every time, I came tumbling back into base camp, dragging an avalanche of mistaken notions down with me."

terminology is fake or won't mind that the terms never get connected to each other or anything else. This, too, is not necessarily a problem; many successful books, from Heinlein's *Stranger in a Strange Land* to Ellroy's *L.A. Confidential,* use sort of perfunctory genre-conventions as scaffolding for what are really complex and essentially human dramas (i.e., for literature). But it is true that a genre book whose particular genre-elements lack technical depth or resonance must depend, for its appeal, on other, more traditionally literary qualities like plot, character, style, etc. And this is a very real problem for *WN,* because as any kind of literary narrative it is off-the-charts bad, its characters mere 2-D types (the neurotic schlemiel, the kindly mentor, the pompous crank, the vulpine reporter, the fiancée who Doesn't Understand) and its plot howlingly implausible (e.g., for most of the book, both Isaac and Nobel-laureate Arkanov supposedly fail to spot in Isaac's proof a basic, freshman-level logical flaw, the eventual discovery of which is sort of the novel's pie-in-the-schlemiel's-face climax). Worst, or at least most distracting, is the fact that the author-translator's English seems rudimentary at best,[19] and the actual line-by-line prose of *WN* is often so stiff and clunky—"My isolated existence was making me lose all sense of measure"; "How the tiny, quivering flame of my intuition was able to withstand the numerous onslaughts of my doubts remains a mystery to me"; "She unzipped her dress, and with a few sexy

[19] (Schogt's original Dutch prose might, of course, be a thing of wonder)

wriggles, let it slide from her shoulders"—or else riddled with ESL-ish solecisms—"She pouted her lip"; "In the distance, the three white lights of the television mast flashed on and off"; "'I just don't want to stifle my thoughts to accommodate for the shortcomings of a machine'"; "I found back my love for mathematics"—or unintentionally funny—"Her tongue probing deep into my mouth left little room for mathematical reflection"—or just plain bad—"They could not help but open like flowers in the brilliant sunshine of his presence, revealing their innermost secrets to him"—as to make the reader suffer that terrible, embarrassed-for-someone-else feeling on the author's behalf.[20]

It is true that *Uncle Petros & Goldbach's Conjecture* is also self-translated[21] and its prose often awkward or stilted ("The custom of this annual meeting had been initiated by my grandfather and as a consequence had become an inviolable obligation in our tradition-ridden family"; "The next few days I

[20] *The Wild Numbers'* American publisher seems equally culpable for the prose here. If Four Walls Eight Windows, Inc. is going to let an only semi-bilingual Philibert Schogt translate his own Dutch, why didn't the FWEW editor bother to tell him that "television mast" should be "aerial" or "transmitter," that "to pout" is intransitive and "to accommodate" takes a direct object, that phrases like "Shucks" and "city slicker" and "wine, women, and song" are now not idioms but ghastly clichés, or even that—no kidding—contemporary Americans do not bow to each other in formal greeting? Where was the editor? *Was* there an editor? Who did they think was going to read this stuff?

[21] (from the original *O Theios Petros kai i Eikasia tou Golbach*)

played sick so as to be at home at the usual time of mail delivery"; "I was not made of the same mettle as he—this I realized now beyond the shadow of a doubt,"[22] etc.). But here the clunky English is mitigated somewhat by *UPGC*'s Greco-European setting and the fact that much of its action takes place before 1930. The novel's framed (or "nested") structure is itself almost Victorian: the middle-aged narrator, describing in retrospect the history of his childhood relationship with his reclusive uncle, recounts Petros's own life story in a series of flashbacks "as told to him" by the great mathematician himself. The elaborate set-up and frames notwithstanding, it is Petros Papachristos's obsessive and tormented career that drives the novel and comprises its heart.

UPGC is about as far from a schlemiel-comedy as you can get. It's more like a cross between the Myth of Icarus and Goethe's *Werther,* and it's serious as a heart attack.[23] Born in Greece around the turn of the century, Petros Papachristos is recognized as a child math prodigy and shipped across Europe to the University of Berlin, where in 1916 he receives his doctorate with a dissertation on "solving a particular variety of differential equa-

[22] And again: where was *this* book's editor?

[23] (And it's just about as subtle w/r/t its thematics, with the narrator repeatedly and *sans* irony describing his uncle as an "Ideal Romantic Hero" [caps his] and saying stuff like "Think of the biblical Tree of Knowledge or the Prometheus of mythology. People like him have surpassed the common measure; they've come to know more than is necessary to man, and for this hubris they have to pay.")

tions" that earns young Petros early acclaim because of its applications in WWI artillery targeting. It is also at U. Berlin that Petros has his first and only love affair, with his German-language tutor (a young lady by the rather unsubtle name of *Isolde*), who toys with his affections and then elopes with a Prussian officer. In not its best moment, *UPGC* tries to establish this (wince) Isolde as Petros's initial motive for tackling the Goldbach Conjecture:

> In order to win her heart back, Petros now decided, there could be no half-measures... he should have to accomplish amazing intellectual feats, nothing short of becoming a Great Mathematician. But how does one become a Great Mathematician? Simple: by solving a Great Mathematical Problem! "Which is the most difficult problem in mathematics, Professor?" he asked [his U. Berlin adviser] at their next meeting, trying to feign mere academic curiosity.

Etc., whereupon Petros devotes the remainder of his professional life to the G.C., that Everest of unsolved problems. His twenty-year labor—which ends in failure and devastation—combines periods of seclusion in Germany with extended trips to Cambridge and Vienna, in which latter there are scenes of Papachristos rubbing elbows with some of twentieth-century math's most important historical figures. The use of this *Forrest Gump*-ish device—i.e., of inserting actual famous mathematicians into the fiction's plot and dialogue—implies that *UPGC* is written for readers who are at least familiar enough with higher math to know who Hardy, Ramanujan, Gödel, and Turing are; but many of the celebrity-scenes themselves are cheesy and kind of irritating. The complex and sensitive G. H. Hardy readers know from his *Apology*, for instance, gets reduced in Doxiadis's novel to a sort of gouty old curmudgeon who spouts inanities like "Don't you forget it, Papachristos, this blasted Conjecture is *difficult!*"

Its treatment of the "real" Hardy is a good example of *UPGC*'s particular rhetorical problem: the readers who will actually know who Godfrey Harold Hardy is are *also* the readers most likely to be put off by the way the book portrays him.[24]

[24] There's a way more grievous example of this sort of thing involving Kurt Gödel and the plot's first real crisis. Alan Turing (here a wide-eyed undergrad) accidentally exposes Petros to Gödel's First Incompleteness Theorem in 1933, whereupon Petros freaks out because he fears that the Goldbach Conjecture may be one of the F.I. Theorem's "formally unprovable" propositions. This is so implausible and reductive as to be almost offensive. As *Science*'s own readership is hereby presumed (q.v. FN9) to more or less know already, Gödel's First Incompleteness Theorem is concerned with the abstract *possibility* of Completeness in axiomatic systems, and the formally unprovable propositions it succeeds in deriving are all very special self-reference-type cases—the mathematical equivalent of the "I am lying" paradox. To believe that the First Incompleteness Theorem could apply to actual number-theoretic problems like the Goldbach Conjecture is so crude and confused that there is no way that a professional mathematician of Petros's attainments could possibly entertain what the novel says is "the one and only, dizzying, terrifying question that had jumped into his mind the moment he'd heard of Gödel's result...: what if the Incompleteness Theorem also applied to *his* problem? What if Goldbach's Conjecture was unprovable?"

But then it gets even worse. Petros supposedly rushes off to Vienna and looks up Gödel—"a thin young man of average height, with small myopic eyes behind thick

And Doxiadis's novel runs into this sort of logico-rhetorical problem again and again, because its big weakness as genre fiction is its weird, ambivalent confusion about just what kind of audience it's for.

As with Schogt's *WN,* there's no better instance of this confusion than the way pure math is rendered here, although in *UPGC* the math is 100 percent real and intricately connected to the book's characters and themes. Petros's Herculean labors on his proof are recounted to the reader in the form of fireside declamations to his nephew (i.e., the narrator as a child), who's enough of a mathematical ephebe that Petros can plausibly keep stopping to deliver quick little mini-lectures on the history of number theory, from Euclid's reductio proof of the infinity of primes to the major theorems of Fermat, Euler, and Gauss on primes' distribution and succession, to the Goldbach

glasses"—and has a soap-operatic exchange that makes the reader keep wincing on behalf of everyone involved:

> "I've spent my whole life trying to prove Goldbach's Conjecture," he told him in a low, intense voice, "and now you're telling me it may be unprovable?"
>
> Gödel's pale face was now totally drained of color [*sic*].
>
> "In theory, yes—"
>
> "Damn theory, man!" Petros' shout made the heads of the Sacher café's distinguished clientèle [*sic*] turn in their direction. "I need to be *certain,* don't you understand? I have a right to know whether I'm wasting my life!" He was squeezing his arm so hard that Gödel grimaced in pain....
>
> Gödel was shaking. "I un-understand how you fe-feel, Professor," he stammered, "but I-I'm afraid that for the time being there is no way to answer yo-your question."

Conjecture and Petros's own analytic attack thereon via "the Theory of Partitions (the different ways of writing an integer as a sum)."

It gets more complicated, though, because the narrator as a grown man (i.e., the one narrating the flashbacks with Uncle P.) now has an extensive math background, and he himself laces the novel with explanatory asides on everything from Cavafy poems to the Riemann Zeta Function. The problem is that Doxiadis's decisions about what needs explicating and what doesn't are often so inconsistent as to seem bizarre, a clear sign that he's confused about audience. It's not just that there are long and irrelevant footnotes on, e.g., Gödel's method of suicide, Poincaré's theory of the unconscious, or the novel properties of the number 1,729.[25] It is that the narrator of *UPGC* will sometimes take time carefully to define very basic terms like "integers" ("the positive whole numbers 1, 2, 3, 4, 5, etc.") and "primes" ("integers that have no divisors other than 1 and themselves, like 2, 3, 5, 7, 11"), or to include patronizing asides like "It should be pointed out to the non-specialist that mathematical [text]books cannot normally be enjoyed

[25] Some of these footnotes are so weird and U.S.-reader inappropriate that it's worth giving a concrete example, such as let's say p. 41's FN to a line about the narrator enrolling in a U.S. college: "According to the American system, a student can go through the first two years of university without being obliged to declare an area of major concentration for his degree or, if he does so, is free to change his mind until the beginning of the Junior (third) year," the very meaning of which is anyone's guess.

like novels, in bed, in the bathtub, sprawled in an easy chair, or perched on the commode"—all of which clearly imply a non-math audience—while on the other hand, *UPGC* is also studded with rarefied technical phrases, such as, e.g., "*n*'s ratio to the natural logarithm," "Peano-Dedekind axiomatic system," "partial differential equation in the Clairaut form," and (no kidding) "The orders of the torsion subgroups of Ω_n and the Adams spectral sequence," that are tossed around without any kind of explanation, which (especially together with the *à clef* appearances of Gödel, Littlewood, et al.) seems to presume a highly math-literate reader.

And if all the narrator's strange elementary definitions are disregarded as mere slips or snafus, and one decides that *UPGC*'s actual intended audience is one with a solid high-math background,[26] there remains an equally strange inconsistency. This lies in the narrative's discussions of the Goldbach Conjecture itself, and of its history in the early twentieth century. For one thing, *UPGC* makes hardly mention at all of the crucial distinction between Euler's "strong Goldbach Conjecture" (see FN7 *supra*) and the Conjecture's equally famous "weak" version, which states that all odd numbers ≥ 9 are the sum of three odd primes. Nor, despite all the detailed descriptions of

[26] N.B. here that the following main-text ¶ itself is geared to a very-strong-math-background audience; nobody else is going to get the ¶'s references, and this reviewer has neither the space nor the expertise to elucidate them. So feel free to skip it if you do not fit the ¶'s demographic.

Petros's labors and all its long excursuses on pre-WWII number theory, does the novel ever once mention Euler's *phi* function (a.k.a. "totient" function) or the ingenious "sieve"-type methods that real mathematicians were using to attack the G.C. in all its forms and extensions in the 1920s and 1930s. In fact, even though *UPGC* gives us page after page on Petros's anxiety about Ramanujan's work on the G.C. (which was in reality very slight), there's no mention of any of the actual important published results of the time—e.g., Schnirelmann's 1931 proof of the upper limit of primes an even integer can be the sum of, Estermann's 1938 proof that *almost* all even numbers are the sums of two primes,[27] etc. Strangest of all: though Doxiadis's narrator spends a lot of time discussing the difference between algebraic and analytic number theory (as well as tracing out Gauss's "asymptotic" hypothesis of the Prime Number Theorem, and Hadamard and Vallée-Poussin's 1896 proof of the P.N.T. using analytic tools), there is not one reference in the book to I. M. Vinogradov, the Russian mathematician who in 1937 revolutionized analytic number theory by introducing a powerful method for getting very accurate estimates of trigonometric sums and using it to prove the weak G.C. for suffi-

[27] Interested *Science* readers can find a discussion of Schnirelmann's proof in W. Dunham's *Journey Through Genius: The Great Theorems of Mathematics* (Wiley, 1990) but will probably have to don a miner's helmet and go all the way back to *Proceedings of the London Mathematical Society Series* vol. 2 no. 44, 1938 for T. Estermann's "On Goldbach's Problem: Proof That Almost All Even Positive Integers Are Sums of Two Primes."

ciently large numbers.[28] Historically, it is Vinogradov who would have been Petros's real rival, the "unique intellect" he really feared; and it is not Gödel's but Vinogradov's Theorem that might plausibly have caused Papachristos to despair.[29]

The thing to realize here is that none of these omissions would necessarily matter had not Doxiadis chosen to make *UPGC* so dependent on actual number theory and real historical characters. As it stands, though, *UPGC* again shoots itself in the same rhetorical foot: the audience knowledgeable enough to appreciate all the "real" math and history woven into this novel is also the audience most likely to notice the strange absence in the book of so much *really* real historical work on the Conjecture. Here once again, then, is a form of the weird, contradictory-looking problem (viz., that what are necessary conditions for liking the novel are also sufficient conditions for disliking it) that pretty much destroys this book, whose author can't decide whom he's writing for.

It would be unfair to Doxiadis, though, not to acknowledge that both his novel and its flaws are far more interesting than Schogt's *WN,* and moreover that *UPGC* does include some moving and rather lovely passages—

[28] Unless you are yourself a professional mathematician, the best place to find a nonlethal discussion of this proof (which is known in number theory as "Vinogradov's Theorem"—that's how famous this guy was) is in Section C of R. K. Guy's *Unsolved Problems in Number Theory* (Springer-Verlag, 1994).

[29] N.B.: End of audience-background-and-interest-restrictive main-text ¶.

> The loneliness of the researcher doing original mathematics is unlike any other. In a very real sense of the word, he lives in a universe that is totally inaccessible, both to the greater public and to his own immediate environment. Even those closest to him cannot partake of his joys and his sorrows in any significant way, since it is all but impossible for them to understand their content.

—as well as at least one subtheme of genuine insight and originality, one that manages to go beyond anything Hardy had to say about the tragedies of math. This particular thematic line concerns Petros's ambition and his place in the mathematical community; and its allegorical touchstone appears to be not Icarus but Minos, the Cretan king who (recall) so coveted a certain great white bull, which the god Poseidon had conjured out of sea-foam to help him win the throne, that Minos broke his sworn promise to return it via religious sacrifice and instead kept the bull for himself.[30]

It is true that doing original math is "lonely." But it is also

[30] You might further recall (from, e.g., Ovid's *Metamorphoses*) that this bull ends up begetting on Minos's queen the Minotaur, a hideous teratoid monster who has to be secreted in a special labyrinth and propitiated with human flesh, and who basically symbolizes the moral rot at the heart of Minos's reign. That rot is, as Joseph Campbell describes it, a certain kind of alienated selfishness:

> The return of the bull should have symbolized Minos' selfless submission to the functions of his role. By the sacrilege of the refusal of the rite [of sacrifice], however, the individual cuts himself as a unit off from the larger

true that professional mathematicians compose a community. The reality that Petros never seems to recognize is that the "fame and immortality" he craves will depend entirely on the value of his work to other mathematicians. The role of professional community is so important in nearly all branches of scientific endeavor, in fact, that most *Science* readers can already probably affirm and appreciate what Lewis Hyde's *The Gift* tries to convey to its own more general audience:

> [T]he task of assembling a mass of disparate facts into a coherent whole clearly lies beyond the powers of a single mind or even a single generation. All such broad intellectual undertakings call for a community of scholars, one in which each individual thinker can be awash in the ideas of his comrades so that a sort of "group mind" develops, one that is capable of cognitive tasks beyond the power of any single person.

Notwithstanding all the narrator's heavy declarations that "Uncle Petros' sin was Pride" and his retreat into paralyzed seclusion "a form of burnout," "scientific battle fatigue," it emerges in *UPGC* that the real cause of Petros's tragedy is his progressive withdrawal from the professional community as his ambition to solve the Conjecture becomes a rapacity that

whole of the community.... He is the hoarder of the general benefit. He is the monster avid for the greedy rights of "my and mine."

transforms his colleagues into first rivals and then enemies. The novel's middle sections trace this progression out nicely. It starts in Cambridge, when Petros rejects an offer of professional collaboration with Hardy and Littlewood because he fears that "their problems would become his own and, what's worse, their fame would inevitably outshine his," and determines instead to work on the G.C. alone, withdrawing to Munich. There, over years of seclusion and nonstop work, privacy becomes secrecy, and Petros's fear and suspicion of other mathematicians approaches "the point of paranoia. In order to avoid his colleagues' drawing conclusions from the items he withdrew from the library, he began to . . . protect the book he really wanted by including it in a list of three or four irrelevant ones, or he would ask for an article in a scientific journal only in order to get his hands on the issue that also contained *another* article, the one he really wanted," etc. (Q.v. here also Petros's aforementioned "wild joy" at the death of Ramanujan.)

The real Minoan-type crisis, though, comes about halfway through the novel, when Petros achieves an important "intermediate result" in his progress toward the Conjecture—a "deep, pioneering theorem . . . which opened new vistas in the Theory of Numbers"—and has to decide what to do. Petros's internal debate about whether to publish the result (which is really a Hyde-vs.-Minos argument about membership in a community) is probably the novel's best moment:

> Undoubtedly, its publication would secure him recognition in the mathematical world much greater than that achieved by his method for solving differential

> equations. In fact, it would probably catapult him to the first ranks of the small but select international community of number theorists, practically on the same level as its great stars....
>
> By making his discovery public, he would also be opening the way into the [Goldbach] problem to other mathematicians who would build on it by discovering new results and expand the limits of the field in a way a lone researcher, however brilliant, could scarcely hope. The results they would achieve would, in turn, aid him in his pursuit of the proof to the Conjecture. In other words...he would be acquiring a legion of assistants in his work. Unfortunately, there was another side to this coin: one of the new unpaid (also unasked for) assistants might conceivably stumble upon a better way to apply his theorem and manage, God forbid, to prove Goldbach's Conjecture before him....
>
> He didn't have to deliberate long. The danger far outweighed the benefit. He wouldn't publish.

From here on, the die is cast. And because he is not a king, it is not his community but Petros himself who receives the inevitable punishment for this "hoarding of the general benefit."[31]

[31] Clearly, Petros's real "sin" is not "Pride" so much as plain old selfishness, Greed. It's not clear whether *UPGC*'s narrator truly fails to grasp this, or whether he is being presented as naive, or whether the whole thing's just a translation problem.

What happens is that "his" unpublished result is independently discovered by another mathematician, a development Petros finds out about only years later, from Hardy, who "expressed his amazement that Petros had not been aware of this, since its publication had caused a sensation in the circles of number theorists and brought great acclaim to its young author."[32]

As *UPGC*'s plot unfolds, this sort of Aesopian, reap-just-what-you-sow punishment gets inflicted on Petros again and again, worsening as each ego-blow increases his alienation and paranoia and sends him deeper into a kind of professional solipsism. Far more than any supposed misreading of Gödel's First Incompleteness Theorem, it is this solipsism that leads to Petros's "failure"—as both a mathematician and a person—and he ends up rather like Milton's Satan, not just alone but Alone, sustaining himself on the sort of megalomaniacal self-pity that creative people everywhere know and dread: "I, Petros Papachristos, never having published anything of value, will go down in mathematical history—or rather will *not* go down in it—as having achieved nothing. This suits me fine, you know. I have no regrets. Mediocrity would never have satisfied me. To an ersatz, footnote kind of immortality, I prefer… total obscurity!" Despite the confused and confusing math-

[32] Obvious though it is, Doxiadis appears to fear that his audience won't get the compact irony here, so he has Hardy then rather sniffily advise Petros "that it might in the future be more profitable for him to stay in closer contact with his scientific colleagues."

labyrinth it's hidden inside, the embedded story of Petros's fall is a kind of monstrous gem, one in whose facets readers of many different backgrounds and tastes might see parts of themselves reflected. Apparent implication: if math can be art, so sometimes can genre.

—2000

oscitancy—the act of yawning **osculate**—to kiss **osier**—willow trees w/

coarse cotton fabric used for grain sacks, upholstery, drapes **outland**—ou

old, primitive: paleontrope? **palliate**—lessen severity, relieve symptom

decoration in classical moldings, reliefs, vase paintings **parallax**—ap

server's position & new line of sight **paraphilia**—unhealthy sexua

pareve—kosher w/r/t diet **parfleche**—untanned animal hide soaked in

material **parget**—plaster, roughcast, used to coat walls and insides of chin

ring or halo **parol** (n.)—oral utterance; (adj.) legal by word of mouth

ders...big w/ Elizabethan women **pas de deux**—dance for two, especiall

infatuation (icky British syllabic) **pasquinade**—lampoon posted in pub

pastern—part of dog or horse's foot between hoof and fetlock **pa**

or cup or pan **patelliphobia**—fear of bowls, cups, basins, and tubs **pa**

pawky—shrewd or cunning in humorous manner (mostly British

wheel to impart forward motion or prevent backward motion **peau de**

peen (v.)—to hammer or bend w/ peen ("the windshield peened with rain"

robe or cloak w/ fur trim or all fur **pellagra**—disease from lack of n

with pellagra **pendent** (adj.)—hanging down; awaiting settlement; penc

until debt is paid **pepo**—fruit of watermelon, squash, pumpkin, w/

cover or coat with liquid, color, light **peritrichous**—having a band o

richous mustache" **perorate**—conclude speech formally; speak at grea

flowered plant **piaffer**—horse trick where horse trots in plac

rodlike twigs used in basketry; or one of these twigs **osnaburg**—heavy

lying areas of a country, the provinces **paleo**—prefix meaning ancient,

palmary (adj.)—outstanding, great **palmette**—stylized palm leaf used as

parent change in the direction of an object caused by change in the ob-

perversion **parbuckle**—sling for raising or lowering objects vertically

lye to get hair off and then dried on a stretcher; a shield made of this

neys **parhelion**—bright spot appearing on either side of sun, or luminous

not written **partlet**—collared ruffled covering for neck and shoul-

in ballet **pase**—one-handed bullfighting maneuver **pash**—a romantic

lic (used of tabloids: "story of O.J.'s trial served up in lurid pasquinade")

tille—small medicated or flavored tablet **patelliform**—shaped like a dish

tois—regional dialect **pavane**—slow, courtly dance of 1500s and 1600s

pawl—hinged or pivoted device adapted to fit into the notch of a ratchet

soie—soft silk or satin fabric with dull finish **peculate**—to embezzle

pelerine—short classy woman's cape w/ points on collar **pelisse**—long

acin: skin eruptions, stomach trouble; pellagrous; pellagrin = person

ing **peonage**—system in which debtors are bound in servitude to creditors

hard rind and flattened seeds **perciatelli**—thick spaghetti **perfuse**—to

cilia around the mouth as certain protozoans: "a woman with a perit-

grandiloquent length **pettitoes**—pig feet as food **phlox**—Midwestern

w/ legs rising very high **pima cotton**—good lightweight cotton

THE BEST OF THE PROSE POEM

- Physical dimensions of *The Best of The Prose Poem: An International Journal* anthology in cm: 15 × 22.5 × 2.
- Weight of anthology in grams: 419.
- Total # of words in anthology: 85,667.
- Total # of words devoted to actual prose poems: 69,986.
- *Rain Taxi*'s length-limit for review of *Best of The P.P.:* 1,000 words.
- Form of review: indexical/statistical/schematic.
- Official name of this new, transgeneric critical form: the Indexical Book Review.
- Tactical reason for review form: The words preceding each item's colon technically constitute neither subjective complement nor appositive nor really any recognized grammatical unit at all; hence none of these antecolonic words should count against *R.T.*'s rigid 1,000-word limit.
- Other, better-known and/or currently fashionable transgeneric literary forms: the Nonfiction Novel, the Prose Poem, the Lyric Essay, etc.

- Basic aesthetic/ideological raison d'être of the above forms: to comment on, complicate, subvert, defamiliarize, transgress against, or otherwise fuck with received ideas of genre, category, and (especially) formal conventions/constraints. (See by analogy the historical progression *rhymed accentual-syllabic verse* → *blank verse* → *vers libre,* etc.)
- Big paradox/oxymoron behind this raison and the current trendiness of transgeneric forms: In fact, these putatively "transgressive" forms depend heavily on received ideas of genre, category, and formal conventions, since without such an established context there's nothing much to transgress against. Transgeneric forms are therefore most viable—most interesting, least fatuous—during eras when literary genres themselves are relatively stable and their conventions well-established and -codified and no one seems much disposed to fuck with them. And ours is not such an era.
- From eminent prose poet Russell Edson's definition of "Prose Poem" in a famous essay on the form called "Portrait of the Writer as a Fat Man: Some Subjective Ideas or Notions on the Care and Feeding of Prose Poems": "A poetry freed from the definition of poetry, and a prose free of the necessities of fiction; a personal form disciplined not by other literature but by unhappiness; thus a way to be happy."
- From C. Hugh Holman and William Harmon's *A Handbook to Literature, Sixth Edition*'s definition of "Prose Poem": "A poem printed as prose, with both margins justified."
- Obvious but crucial distinction: between a prose poem as an individual artwork and the Prose Poem as an actual literary genre.

- Signs that some person/persons are trying to elevate a certain transgressive literary form or hybrid into an actual genre: Literary journals start having special issues devoted to the form, then whole new journals exclusively devoted to the form spring up (often with the form's name somewhere in their titles), and various "Best of" anthologies from these new journals begin hitting the market. A critical literature starts to assemble itself around the form, much of that criticism consisting in apologiae, encomiums, and (paradoxically) definitions, codifications, and lists of formal characteristics (→ conventions). Some writers start identifying themselves professionally as practitioners of the form. Finally, the form begins to get treated as a separate/special category for the purposes of book publishing, prizes and awards, academic appointments, etc.
- Within pages of *Best of The P.P.*, total number of ads for, references to, and lists of other journals/collections/articles/anthologies/presses devoted to the Prose Poem: 78.
- Bio-note on anthology's editor: "Peter Johnson is founder and editor of *The Prose Poem: An International Journal.* His latest books of prose poems are *Pretty Happy!* (White Pine Press, 1997) and *Love Poems for the Millennium* (Quale Press, 1998). He received an NEA for Creative Writing in 1999."
- From bio-notes on random *Best of The P.P.* contributors: "Ellen McGrath Smith is a Ph.D. candidate in literature at Duquesne University, where she is completing a doctoral dissertation that deals with the American prose poem"; "Mark Vinz is the author of... a book of prose poems, *Late Night Calls.* He is also co-editor of *The Party Train: A*

Collection of North American Prose Poetry, published by New Rivers Press."

- First sentence of Peter Johnson's Introduction to anthology: "In editing *The Best of The Prose Poem: An International Journal,* I feel humble and defensive at the same time."
- Total # of pages in anthology, including editor's Intro, prenominate p.p. ads and lists, and bio-notes on contributors: 288.
- Total # of pages devoted to actual prose poems: 227.
- Total # of prose poems in anthology: 204.
- Arrangement of constituent p.p.'s: alphabetical by author.
- Average number of words in a constituent p.p.: 342.3 (mean), 309 (median).
- Longest p.p. in anthology: John Yau's "The Newly Renovated Opera House on Gilligan's Island," 1,049 words.
- Shortest p.p. in anthology: G. Chambers & R. Federman's "A Little Request," 53 words.
- Constituent p.p.'s that, like "The Newly Renovated Opera House on Gilligan's Island," have titles that turn out to be way more interesting than the poems themselves: "T. S. Eliot Was a Negro," "That UFO That Picked on Us," "The Big Deep Voice of God," "The Prodigal Son Is Spotted on the Grassy Knoll," "Lullaby for the Elderly," "The Leopard's Mouth Is Dry and Cold Inside."
- Some random relevant questions: Are the pieces in, e.g., Lydia Davis's *Break It Down* or Diane Williams's *Excitability* prose poems? Is Eliot's "Hysteria" a prose poem? What about the three long prose pieces in Ashbery's *Three Poems*? Are the little italicized entr'actes in Hemingway's *In Our*

Time prose poems? Are Kawabata's "Palm-of-the-Hand Stories"? Is Kafka's "A Little Fable"? What about Cormac McCarthy's dreamy, anapestic prologue to *Suttree*? What about the innumerable ¶s in Faulkner that scan perfectly as iambic-pentameter sonnets? Why are so many tiny and self-consciously lyrical stories published these days as "short-shorts" or "flash fictions" and not as prose poems?

- Approximate % of *Best of The P.P.*'s 9-page Introduction that Peter Johnson spends talking about how fiendishly difficult he finds it to define "Prose Poem": 75+.
- Representative excerpts from this discussion: "Just as black humor straddles the fine line between comedy and tragedy, so the prose poem plants one foot in prose, the other in poetry, both heels resting precariously on banana peels"; "When I first began writing prose poems and consciously considering prose poetry as a distinct genre, I thought of the platypus, that lovable yet homely Tasmanian hybrid, but then came to see the weakness of that comparison. The platypus's genetic code is predetermined. It can't all of a sudden grow an elephant's trunk out of its backside."
- From Holman and Harmon's *Handbook to Literature*'s definition of "Prose Poem": "The point seems to be that a writing in prose, even the most prosaic,[1] is a poem if the author says so."

[1] (N.B.: from *The American Heritage Dictionary, Fourth Edition*'s definition of "prosaic": "consisting or characteristic of prose"; "lacking in imagination and spirit, dull.")

- From anthology's bio-notes on contributors: (1) "Aloysius Bertrand (1807–1841) has sometimes been called 'The Father of the Modern Prose Poem,' though he never used the term to describe his own work"; (2) "Barry Silesky is the author of *One Thing That Can Save Us,* prose poems (called short-short fiction by Coffee House Press)."
- Of the 144 contributors to *Best of The P.P.,* total # who are, like M. Aloysius Bertrand, now dead: 14.
- Total # of contributors who have also published work in literary organ called *Flash Fiction:* 6.
- Total # of contributors who do/did edit literary journals, anthologies, and/or small presses: 21.
- Titles of published books listed in bio-note for anthology contributor Nin Andrews: *The Book of Orgasms* and *Spontaneous Breasts.*
- Average # of prose poems from each *Best of The P.P.* contributor: 1.42 (mean), 1.58 (median).
- Examples of particularly well-known or eminent contributors, with # of included p.p.'s from each: Russell Edson, 7; David Ignatow, 4; Charles Simic, 4; James Tate, 4; Robert Bly, 2; Maxine Chernoff, 2; Larry Levis, 2; Henri Michaux, 2; Stuart Dybek, 1; Bill Knott, 1; Gabriela Mistral, 1; Pablo Neruda, 1.
- Total # of above p.p.'s that seem like they're anywhere even remotely close to their eminent contributors' best work: 3.
- Total # of times Peter Johnson quotes or refers to Russell Edson in his Introduction: 13.
- Another typical sentence from Peter Johnson's Intro: "To me, literary theory, like philosophy, provides few answers;

instead, and most importantly, it creates an endless internal and external dialogue which forces us to constantly reevaluate our standards."

- Highest conceivable grade that anthology's Introduction would receive in an average university Lit./Composition class: B-.
- Total # of anthology's 204 prose poems that are good/alive/powerful/interesting enough to persist in reader's mind more than 60 seconds after completion: 31.
- Of these 31, # that are so great you end up not even caring what genre they're supposed to be part of: 9.
- Of these 9, # that are by one Jon Davis, a poet whom this reviewer'd never heard of before but whose pieces in this anthology are so off-the-charts terrific that the reviewer has actually gone out and bought the one Jon Davis book mentioned in his bio-note and may very well decide to try to advertise it in this magazine, at reviewer's own expense if necessary—that's how good this guy is: 5.
- Of the remaining 4 great pieces here, # that are by the late David Ignatow and concern his impending death and are so totally beautiful and merciless that you can't forget them even if you want to: 2.
- Other contributors, previously unknown to reviewer, who have good/alive/powerful/interesting pieces in anthology: Gary Fincke ("The History of Passion Will Tumble This Week"), Jennifer L. Holley ("The Rubbing"), Jay Meek ("Leaving the Roadside Motel"), Fred Muratori ("From *Nothing in the Dark*"), J. David Stevens ("The Sign"), Helen Tzagoloff ("Mail-Order Bride").

- Some of the common features of the 31 g/a/p/i pieces in anthology: (1) Even without line breaks or standard prosodic constraints, the p.p.'s seem tightly controlled; they possess both a metrical and a narrative logic. (2) Their sentences tend to be short, almost terse. (3) Many of the p.p.'s are subtly iambic; what meter and alliteration there is is unheavy and tends to make the piece read faster rather than slower. (4a) The pieces' realistic imagery is concrete, its descriptions compact and associations tautly drawn. (4b) The pieces' surreal imagery/associations never seem gratuitously weird; i.e., they end up making psychological or emotional sense given what the p.p.'s about. (5) Any puns, entendres, metapoetic allusions, or other forms of jeu d'esprit come off as relevant/serious and never seem like their main purpose is to make the writer appear clever. (6) The pieces' tone tends to be intimate rather than formal (meaning, in other words, that the p.p.'s exploit one of the big advantages of much good prose, which is the reader's impression of a human being actually sitting right there talking to him). (7) They all have actual narratives and/or Dramatic Situations. (8) If there's an argument, the argument is tight, comprehensible, and if not persuasive then at least interesting. (9) The good 31 are all, without exception, moving.
- Examples of opening lines of constituent p.p.'s that have some or all of the above qualities: "Only a picture window stands between us and the full force of gusts that lift the branches of the red pine" (Thomas R. Smith's "Windy Day

at Kabekona"); "It's of no consequence to the grass that it withers, secure in its identity" (David Ignatow's "Proud of Myself"); "This is not an elegy because the world is full of elegies and I am tired of consoling and being consoled" (Jon Davis's "The Bait").

- Total # of anthology contributors who are employed as Poet in Residence at a children's hospital: 1.
- # who are described in bio-note as "the *enfant terrible* of Greek Surrealism": 1.
- # who have the last names Johnson or Smith: 6.
- Total % of anthology prose poems that are primarily about death/loss/life's transience: 57.1.
- % about sex: 16.6.
- % about love: 0.2.
- % about cooking: 0.2.
- Square root of book's ISBN: 43,520.065.
- Of *Best of The P.P.*'s 173 unmemorable or otherwise ungreat prose poems, total % that deploy as topoi or include as important characteristics (1) bitter or unhappy childhood memories: 21.3; (2) an object, scene, or tableau that is described, analogized, troped, associated, and ruminated over until the establishment of its status as a metaphor seems to be the p.p.'s only real aim: 50.6; (3) references to or discussions of Poetry itself: 12.1; (4) ultrararefied allusions to, e.g., Théophile Gautier, Paul Quéré, Sibelius's "Swan of Tuonela," etc.: 13.8; (5) heavy-handed use of anaphora, ploce, repetend, and/or alliteration: 20.7; (6) assorted jeux d'esprit whose main purpose seems to be

to make the poet appear clever: 15.5; (7a) surreal/fabulist conceits and descriptions whose obvious point is the psycho-affective disorder of the modern world: 21.8; (7b) surreal/fabulist conceits and descriptions whose point or even relation to anything else in the p.p. is indiscernible: 48.3; (8a) surreal or free-associative transitions between sentences or ¶s: 51.7... (8b) which transitions themselves have no discernible point or resonance and make the whole p.p. seem at once pretentious and arbitrary: 46.6; and (9) just plain bad, clunky writing, no matter what genre or era it is: 51.7.

- Examples of above feature (9) from randomly selected anthology p.p.'s: "I don't know how you feel about it, but for years and years, from the point of view of a person practicing my own, would-be benignly optimistic profession—that of a struggling manufacturer of colorful and sometimes even relatively amusing toys—I've felt that this constant placing of myself into bad moods by the conventional world, practically amounts to theft!" (Michael Benedikt's "The Toymaker Gloomy but Then Again Sometimes Happy"); "She intended to be epic with repercussions this time, so through mostly legal methods she hastened his entrapment" (Brian Swann's "The Director"); "No good, the slow resisting of rage, the kindly cupping of each hand in prayer while facing the shot-up outskirts of the town, as though to hold water out to a thirsty sniper, and see the rifle laid down, and water taken as a final covenant" (Robert Hill Long's "Small Clinic at Kilometer 7").
- Total # of zeroes in anthology's Library of Congress Control Number: 5.

- Total # of postcolonic words left before *RT*'s 1,000-word limit is exceeded: 267, minus this phrase's own 5[2] words.
- Most common problems with the substantial % of the book's prose poems that are mediocre/bad: (1) The p.p.'s argument/theme/point/project is either too obvious or too obscure; (2) The p.p. lacks formal control, logic; it comes off flabby, arbitrary, dull—see, e.g., "All over the world the shooting goes on. Then the doorbell rings and the pain is actually gone. With the notes buried in the counter's daily junk pile, you had no idea you'd even entered. Now it's another city. No paradise, but all the blood, sex, he, she, flushed away. It's not all luck" (Barry Silesky's "Saved").
- How problem (2) directly above is related to what reviewer sees as the most serious, paradoxical problem for the Prose Poem per se: Like all self-consciously transgressive poetic forms, the p.p. is, by both definition and intent, anti-formal. That is, it is distinguished as a form primarily by what it lacks, viz. stuff like line breaks, enjambment, formal rhyme- or metrical schemes, etc. At the same time, a prose poem very consciously calls itself a *poem,* which of course sends the reader a message, namely that this is a particular kind of literary art that demands a particular kind of reading—slow, careful, with extra attention paid to certain special characteristics. Not least of these special

[2] (Numerals don't count as words either, obviously.)

characteristics are the compression and multivalence of the poem's syntax and the particular rhythms and tensions of the poem's music. These are what give a poem the weird special urgency that both justifies and rewards the extra work a reader has to put into reading it. And see that it's nearly always *formal* features that create and convey this poetic urgency: e.g., the tension of the line breaks against the lines' own punctuation and meter, the use of breaks and enjambment and metrical scheme to control speed, emphasis, multivalence of expression, etc. W/r/t *Best of The P.P.,* the absence of formal controls seems like the major reason why so many of its constituent p.p.'s seem not just non-urgent but incoherent; most of them literally fall apart under the close, concentrated attention that poetry's supposed to demand.[3]

- Paradoxical consequence of above paradoxical problem for the 31 p.p.'s in the book that really are rich and alive and fine: It makes them seem even better, and not just better in comparison to the dross that surrounds them. It's more like the 173 mediocre/bad p.p.'s here help the reader appreciate the terrible, almost impossible disadvantages of the p.p.

[3] N.B. that this sort of problem is endemic to many of the trendy literary forms that identify/congratulate themselves as transgressive. And it's easy to see why. In regarding formal conventions primarily as "rules" to rebel against, the Professional Transgressor fails to see that conventions often *become* conventions precisely because of their power and utility, i.e., because of the paradoxical freedoms they permit the artist who understands how to use (not merely "obey") them.

form, which then makes the pieces from Davis, Ignatow, et al. seem less like just successes than like miracles. The experience of reading a piece like Davis's "The Frogs" or Stevens's "The Sign" or Ignatow's "My Own House," of watching the p.p. somehow achieve poetry's weird blend of logic and magic with hardly any of poetry's regular assets or tools, helps us to understand the allure of transgressive forms for writers,[4] and maybe to remember that most formal conventions themselves start out as "experiments."

- Source of metaphorical description of a prose poem as "a cast-iron aeroplane that can actually fly," which image conveys the miraculous feel of the anthology's best p.p.'s way better than the purely expository review ¶ just above does: Russell Edson, as duly quoted by Peter Johnson, whose Introduction however can't leave the perfect image alone to ramify in the reader's head but has to gloss it with "Edson's metaphor and his comment on literary definitions are attractive to poets because he champions the unconscious and the personal imagination in its attempt to escape literary and cultural contamination."
- Probability that, if this reviewer were named Peter Johnson, he would publish under either "Pete" or his first two initials: 100%.

[4] (Imagine offering a gymnast the chance to levitate and hang there unsupported, or an astronaut the prospect of a launch w/o rocket.)

- Indexical Book Review coda: Another famous R. Edson pronouncement, although this time one that P. Johnson, Ed.—for rather obvious professional reasons[5]—does not quote in his Introduction: "What makes us so fond of [the p.p.] is its clumsiness, its lack of expectation or ambition. Any way of writing that isolates its writer from worldly acceptance offers the greatest creative efficiency. Isolation from other writers, and isolation from easy publishing."

—2001

[5] Just in case these reasons [as well as the anthology's real intended audience] are not yet obvious, q.v. the following announcement, variations of which appear in regular font on *Best of The P.P.*'s editorial page, in bold at the end of Johnson's Intro, *again* in bold in an ad for *The P.P.* after the contributors' bio-notes, and yet *again,* in a bold font so big it takes up the whole page, at the very end of the anthology:

> ***The Prose Poem: An International Journal*** **will be reading for Volume 10 between December 1, 2001 and March 1, 2002. Unsolicited work submitted before this date will be returned unread. Please include an SASE and a two-sentence biographical note. Please send no more than 3 to 5 poems.**

pinchbeck—any cheap imitation; zinc and copper alloy used as fake gold

apes **pityriases**—skin disease w/ flaking of oily scales **pizzle**—penis **plas**

ing **plication**—act or process of folding; condition of being folded **plim**

plus fours—loose knickers bagging below the knees; worn by old-time

cold-blooded, as in fish or reptile **pongid**—ape family that includes go

especially one who, holding many offices, fulfills none of them **poppet**

motion **porringer**—shallow cup or bowl with a handle **porte-cochère**—en

over a driveway at the entrance of a building to provide shelter **porti**

application of learning **prevenient**—coming before, preceding **primipa**

ing firstborn or eldest child **prion**—microscopic protein particle similar to

scrapie, and mad cow disease, spongiform brain diseases **privity**—se

prolapse—to fall or slip out of place **ptosis**—abnormal lowering or droop

area **purlieus**—outskirts, environs **putrescine**—foul-smelling ptomaine

from ankle to knee…a gaiter **pyknic**—having a short, stocky phy

rachis—main axis or shaft, as in spinal column or trunk of tree or main

radiolarian—type of marine protozoan **ramify** (v.)—to have complicating

own" **ratables**—income from property taxes **ratoon**—a shoot sprouting

or confused **recrudesce**—to break out anew after period of quiescence **rec**

retroussé—turned up at the end, used to describe noses **revetment**—a

related to Rhine or area around it **riata**—a lariat, a lasso **rigorism**—harsh

rimple—a fold or wrinkle **rinderpest**—horrible disease of cattle

pinguid—fat, oily; used of liquid or food **pithecoid**—of or resembling

tron—the front of a man's dress shirt; quilted protective chest pad in fenc-

soll—primitive sneaker; rubber-soled boating shoe **plover**—wading bird

golfers **pococurante** (adj.)—careless, indifferent, easy **poikilothermic**—

rilla, chimpanzee, orangutan **Poobah**—pompous, ostentatious official,

valve—intake or exhaust valve that plugs and unplugs its opening w/ axial

trance leading thru building into enclosed courtyard; an enclosure

co—long porch, w/ columns, often leading to front door **praxis**—custom,

ra—woman who's pregnant for the first time **primogeniture**—state of be-

virus but lacking nucleic acid: causes terrible crystalline changes in brain,

cret, special knowledge between two or more people; (adj.) privitive

ing of upper eyelid; (adj.) ptotic **purlieu**—an outlying or neighboring

produced in decaying animal tissue **puttee**—strip of cloth wound spirally

sique **quadrate**—square or rectangular...four sides & four angles

stem of flower **raclette**—cheese melted onto bread or potatoes: Swiss dish

consequences, "a universe of sexual experience as richly ramified as our

from a plant base, as in banana, sugarcane **ravel** (v.)—to become tangled

to—right-hand page of book **retroflex**—bent, curved, or bent backward

facing, as of masonry, used to support an embankment **Rhenish**—

ness or strictness **rime**—thin coating of ice or mud; rimey, rimed

ringent—having gaping liplike parts like the shells of certain bivalves

TWENTY-FOUR WORD NOTES

Utilize A noxious puff-word. Since it does nothing that good old *use* doesn't do, its extra letters and syllables don't make a writer seem smarter; rather, using *utilize* makes you seem either like a pompous twit or like someone so insecure that she'll use pointlessly big words in an attempt to look sophisticated. The same is true for the noun *utilization,* for *vehicle* as used for *car,* for *residence* as used for *house,* for *presently, at present, at this time,* and *at the present time* as used for *now,* and so on. What's worth remembering about puff-words is something that good writing teachers spend a lot of time drumming into undergrads: "formal writing" does not mean gratuitously fancy writing; it means clean, clear, maximally considerate writing.

If Most dictionaries' usage notes for *if* are long and involved; it might be English's hardest conjunction. From experience born of personal humiliation, I inform you that there are two main ways to mess up with *if* and make your writing look weak. The first is to use *if* for *whether.* They are not synonyms—*if* is used to express a conditional, *whether* to introduce alternative possibilities. True, abstract grammatical distinctions are hard to keep straight in the heat of composition, but in this case there's a wonderfully simple test you can use: If you can coherently insert an "[or not]" after either the conjunction or the clause it introduces, you need *whether.* Examples: "He didn't know whether [or not] it would rain"; "She asked me straight out whether I was a fetishist [or not]"; "We told him to call if [or not? no] he needed a ride [or not? no]." The second kind of snafu involves a basic rule for using commas with subordinating conjunctions (which are what *if* is one of). A subordinating conjunction signals the reader that the clause it's part of is dependent—common sub. conjunctions include *before, after, while, unless, if, as,* and *because.* The relevant rule is easy and well worth remembering: Use a comma after the subordinating conjunction's clause only if that clause comes before the independent clause that completes the thought; if the sub. conj.'s clause comes after the independent clause, there's no comma. Example: "If I were you, I'd put down that hatchet" vs. "I'd put down that hatchet if I were you."

Pulchritude A paradoxical noun because it refers to a kind of beauty but is itself one of the ugliest words in the language. Same goes for the adj. form *pulchritudinous.* They're part of a tiny elite cadre of words that possess the opposite of the qualities they denote. *Diminutive, big, foreign, fancy* (adj.), *classy, colloquialism,* and *monosyllabic* are some others; there are at least a dozen more. Inviting your school-age kids to list as many paradoxical words as they can is a neat way to deepen their relationship to English and help them see that words are both symbols for real things and real things themselves.

Mucous An adjective, not synonymous with the noun *mucus.* It's worth noting this not only because the two words are fun but because so many people don't know the difference. *Mucus* means the unmentionable stuff itself. *Mucous* refers to (1) something that makes or secretes mucus, as in "The next morning, his mucous membranes were in rocky shape indeed," or (2) something that consists of or resembles mucus, as in "The mucous consistency of its eggs kept the diner's breakfast trade minimal."

Toward It might seem pedantic to point out that *toward* is the correct U.S. spelling and *towards* is British. On the other hand, so many writers at all levels seem ignorant of the difference that using *toward* becomes a costless, unpretentious way to signal your fluency in American English. It's the same with *gray* (U.S.) and *grey* (Brit.), though so many Americans have been using them interchangeably for so long that some U.S. dictionaries now list *grey* as a passable variant. This is not likely to happen with *toward/towards,* though—at least not in our lifetimes. Nor will it happen with using *as* to mean *since* or *because,* which a lot of U.S. students like to do because they think it makes their prose look classier ("As Dostoevsky is so firmly opposed to nihilism, it should come as no surprise that he so often presents his novels' protagonists with moral dilemmas"). As of 2003, the causal *as* is acceptable only in British English, and even there it's OK only if the dependent *as*-clause comes at the start of the sentence, since if it comes in the middle the *as* can look temporal and cause confusion ("I declined her offer as I was on my way to the bank already").

That There is widespread ignorance about how to use *that* as a relative pronoun, and two common *that*-errors are so severe that teachers, editors, and other high-end readers will make unkind judgments about you if you commit them. The first is to use *which* when you need *that.* Writers who do this usually think the two relative pronouns are interchangeable but that *which* makes you look smarter. They aren't, and it doesn't. For writers, the abstract rule that *that* introduces restrictive elements and *which* introduces nonrestrictive elements is probably less helpful than the following simple test: If there needs to be a comma before the rel. pron., you need *which;* otherwise, you need *that.*[1] Examples: "We have a massive SUV that we

[1] **Bonus Factoid and Suggestion:** It so happens that you can occupy a bright child for most of a very quiet morning by challenging her to use *that* five times in a row in a

purchased on credit last month"; "The massive SUV, which we purchased on credit last month, seats us ten feet above any other driver on the road." The second error, even more common, is way worse. It's using *that* when you need *who* or *whom.* (Examples: "She is the girl that he's always dreamed of"; "Daddy promised the air rifle to the first one of us that cleaned out the hog pen.") There's a very basic rule: *Who* and *whom* are the relative pronouns for people; *that* and *which* are the rel. pronouns for everything else. It's true that there's a progressive-type linguistic argument to be made for the thesis that the "error" of using *that* with people is in fact the first phase of our language evolving past the *who/that* distinction, that a universal *that* is simpler and will allow English to dispense with the archaic incommodious subject-*who*-vs.-object-*whom* thing. This sort of argument is interesting in theory; ignore it in practice. As of 2003, misusing *that* for *who* or *whom,* whether in writing or speech, functions as a kind of class-marker—it's the grammatical equivalent of wearing NASCAR paraphernalia or liking pro wrestling. If you think that last assertion is snooty or extreme, please keep

single coherent sentence, to which stumper the solution is all about the present distinction: "He said that that *that* that that writer used should really have been a *which.*" (You can up the challenge to six in a row if the kid is old enough to know about the medial-question-mark-in-sentence trick: "He said that? that that *that* that that writer used should have been a *which?*")

in mind that the hideous *PTL Club*'s initials actually stood for "People That Love."

Effete Here's a word on which some dictionaries and usage authorities haven't quite caught up with the realities of literate usage. Yes, the traditional meaning of *effete* is "depleted of vitality, washed out, exhausted"—and in a college paper for an older prof. you'd probably want to use it in only that way. But a great many educated people accept *effete* now also as a pejorative synonym for *elite* or *elitist,* one with an added suggestion of effeminacy, over-refinement, pretension, and/or decadence; and in this writer's opinion it is not a boner to use *effete* this way, since no other word has quite its connotative flavor. Traditionalists who see the extended definition as an error often blame Spiro Agnew's characterization of some liberal group or other as an "effete corps of impudent snobs," but there are deeper reasons for the extension, such as that *effete* derives from the Latin *effētus,* which meant "worn out from bearing children" and thus had an obvious feminine connotation. Or that historically *effete* was often used to describe artistic movements that had exhausted their vitality, and one of the main characteristics of a kind of art's exhaustion was its descent into excessive refinement or foppery or decadence.

Dialogue Noun-wise, the interesting thing about *dialogue* is that it means "a conversation or exchange between two or more people," so it's not wrong to say something like "The council engaged in a long dialogue about the proposal."

Avoid modifying it with certain adjectives, though—*constructive dialogue* and *meaningful dialogue* have, thanks mainly to political cant, become clichés that will make readers' eyes glaze over. Please also avoid using *dialogue* as a verb—ever. This is despite the facts that (1) Shakespeare used it as a verb, and (2) There are all sorts of other accepted verbalizations of nouns in English that work the same way; e.g., *to diet* is reduced from "to go on a diet," *to trap* from "to catch in a trap," and so on. Maybe in thirty years, *to dialogue* will be just as standard, but as of now it strikes most literate readers as affected and jargonish. Same with *to transition;* same with *to parent.*

Privilege Even though some dictionaries OK it, *to privilege* is currently used only in a particular English subdialect that might be called academese. Example: "The patriarchal Western canon privileges univocal discourse situated within established contexts over the polyphonic free play of decentered utterance." The contemporary form of this subdialect originated in literary and social theory but has now metastasized throughout much of the humanities. There is exactly one situation in which you'd want to use *to privilege, to situate, to interrogate* + some abstract noun phrase, or pretty much any construction that's three times longer than it needs to be—this is in a university course taught by a prof. so thoroughly cloistered, insecure, or stupid as to believe that academese is good intelligent writing. A required course, one that you can't switch out of. In any other situation, run very fast the other way.

Myriad As an adj., *myriad* means (1) an indefinitely large number of something ("The Local Group comprises myriad galaxies") or (2) made up of a great many diverse elements ("the myriad plant life of Amazonia"). As a noun, it's used with an article and *of* to mean a large number ("The new CFO faced a myriad of cash-flow problems.") What's odd is that some authorities consider only the adjective usage correct—there's about a 50-50 chance that a given copyeditor will query *a myriad of*—even though the noun usage has a much longer history. It was only in nineteenth-century poetry that *myriad* started being used as an adj. So it's a bit of a stumper. It's tempting to recommend avoiding the noun usage so that no readers will be bugged, but at the same time it's true that any reader who's bugged by *a myriad of* is both persnickety and wrong—and you can usually rebut snooty teachers, copyeditors, et al. by directing them to Coleridge's "Myriad myriads of lives teemed forth."

Dysphesia This is a medical noun with timely non-medical applications. We often use *aphasia* to refer to a brain-centered inability to use language, which is close but not identical to the medical meaning. *Dysphesia* can be similarly extended from its technical definition to mean really severe difficulties in forming coherent sentences. As anyone who's listened to our current president knows, there are speakers whose lack of facility goes way beyond the range of *clumsy* or *inarticulate.* What G. W. Bush's public English really is is *dysphesiac.*

Unique This is one of a class of adjectives, sometimes called "uncomparables," that can be a little tricky. Among other uncomparables are *precise, exact, correct, entire, accurate, preferable, inevitable, possible, false;* there are probably two dozen in all. These adjectives all describe absolute, non-negotiable states: something is either false or it's not; something is either inevitable or it's not. Many writers get careless and try to modify uncomparables with comparatives like *more* and *less* or intensives like *very*. But if you really think about them, the core assertions in sentences like "War is becoming increasingly inevitable as Middle East tensions rise," "Their cost estimate was more accurate than the other firms'," and "As a mortician, he has a very unique attitude" are nonsense. If something is inevitable, it is bound to happen; it cannot be bound to happen and then somehow even more bound to happen. *Unique* already means one-of-a-kind, so the adj. phrase *very unique* is at best redundant and at worst stupid, like "audible to the ear" or "rectangular in shape." Uncomparable-type boners can be easily fixed—"War is looking increasingly inevitable"; "Their cost estimate was more nearly accurate"; "he has a unique attitude"—but for writers the hard part is noticing such errors in the first place. You can blame the culture of marketing for some of this difficulty. As the number and rhetorical volume of U.S. ads increase, we become inured to hyperbolic language, which then forces marketers to load superlatives and uncomparables with high-octane modifiers (*special* → *very special* → *Super-special!* → ***Mega-Special!!***), and so on.

A deeper issue implicit in the problem of uncomparables is the dissimilarities between Standard Written English and the language of advertising. Advertising English, which probably deserves to be studied as its own dialect, operates under different syntactic rules than SWE, mainly because AE's goals and assumptions are different. Sentences like "We offer a totally unique dining experience," "Come on down and receive your free gift," and "Save up to 50 percent...and more!" are perfectly OK in Advertising English—but this is because Advertising English is aimed at people who are not paying close attention. If your audience is by definition involuntary, distracted, and numbed, then *free gift* and *totally unique* stand a better chance of penetrating—and simple penetration is what AE is all about. The goals and assumptions of Standard Written English are obviously way more complex, but one SWE axiom is that your reader is paying close attention and expects you to have done the same.

Beg In its main function, *to beg* serves as an improved modern synonym for the old *crave,* which now sounds very affected. Both verbs mean to request earnestly and from a kind of subordinate position—one begs a favor but demands a right. *Beseech* and *implore* are close to *beg,* but both imply a little extra anxiety and/or urgency. The only really egregious way you can screw up with this word is to misuse the phrase *beg the question.* This phrase does not—repeat, not—mean "invite the following obvious question," and sentences like "This begs the question, why are our elected leaders silent on this issue?" are both increasingly common and deeply wrong. The idiom *beg the question* is the compressed Anglicization of the Latin *petitio principii,* which is the name of a particular kind of logical fallacy in which one bases a conclusion on a premise that turns out to be just as debatable as the conclusion. Genuine examples of begging the question are "The death penalty is the proper punishment for murder because those who kill forfeit their own right to life" and "True wisdom is speaking and acting judiciously." Because of its extremely specific origin and meaning, *beg the question* will never mean "invite the question" no matter how widespread the usage becomes. Nor, strictly speaking, will it mean "avoid or ignore the real issue," even though a subsidiary def. of *beg* is "to dodge or evade." If you want to accuse someone of missing the point, you can say "You're begging the real issue" or something, but it's not right to use even this sense of *beg* with *question* unless you are sure that you're talking about a case of *petitio principii.*

Critique I went to college in the mid-1980s, and there I was taught that there's no such verb as *to critique.* The profs. who hammered this into me (both over fifty) explained that *to criticize* meant "to judge the merits and defects of, to analyze, to evaluate" and that *critique* (n.) was the noun for "a specific critical commentary or review." Now, though, the dictionary's primary def. of *to criticize* is usually "to find fault with"; i.e., the verb has taken on increasingly negative connotations. Thus some usage authorities now consider *to critique* to be OK; they argue that it can minimize confusion by denoting the neutral, scholarly-type assessment that used to be what *criticize* meant. Here's the thing, though: it's still only some usage experts who accept *to critique.* Dictionaries' usage panels are usually now split about 50-50 on sentences like "After a run-through, the playwright and director both critiqued the actor's delivery." And it's not just authorities. A fair percentage of educated people still find *to critique* either wrong or irksome. Why alienate smart readers unnecessarily? If you're worried that *criticize* will seem deprecatory, you can say *evaluate, explicate, analyze, judge*... or you can always use the old bury-the-main-verb trick and do *offer a critique of, submit a critique of,* etc.

Focus *Focus* is now the noun of choice for expressing what people used to mean by *concentration* ("Sampras's on-court focus was phenomenal") and *priority* ("Our focus is on serving the needs of our customers"). As an adj., it seems often to serve as an approving synonym for *driven* or *monomaniacal:* "He's the most focused warehouse manager we've ever had." As a verb, it seems isomorphic with the older *to concentrate:* "Focus, people!"; "The Democrats hope that the campaign will focus on the economy"; "We need to focus on finding solutions instead of blaming each other," etc. W/r/t those last two sample sentences, notice how the verb phrase *to focus on* can take as its object either a thing-noun ("economy") or a gerund ("finding"), and how its meaning and grammatical structure are slightly different in the two cases. With a noun, *to focus on* means "to concentrate attention or effort on," i.e., the direct object is built right into the verb phrase; but with a gerund it means "to direct toward a particular goal"—there's always a direct object like "attention/efforts/energies" that's suppressed but understood, and the gerund actually functions as an indirect object. Given the speed with which *to focus* has supplanted *to concentrate,* it's a little surprising that nobody objects to its somewhat jargony New Age feel—but nobody seems to. Maybe it's because the word is only one of many film and drama terms that have entered mainstream usage in the last decade, e.g., *to foreground* (= to feature, to give top priority to); *to background* (= to downplay, to relegate to the back burner); *scenario* (= an outline of some hypothetical sequence of events), and so on.

Impossibly This is one of those adverbs that's formed from an adjective and can modify only adjectives, never verbs. Modifying adjectives with these sorts of adverbs—*impossibly fast, extraordinarily yummy, irreducibly complex, unbelievably obnoxious*—is a hypereducated speech tic that translates well to writing. Not only can the adverbs be as colorful/funny/snarky as you like, but the device is a quick way to up the formality of your prose without sacrificing personality—it makes whoever's narrating sound like an actual person, albeit a classy one. The big caveat is that you can't use these special-adv.-with-adj. constructions more than once every few sentences or your prose starts to look like it's trying too hard.

Individual As a noun, this word has one legitimate use, which is to distinguish a single person from some larger group: "One of the enduring oppositions of British literature is that between the individual and society"; "She's a real individual." It is not a synonym for *person* despite the fact that much legal, bureaucratic, and public-statement prose uses it that way—which is to say that it looms large in turgid crap like "Law-enforcement personnel apprehended the individual as he was attempting to exit the premises." *Individual* for *person* and *an individual* for *someone* are pretentious, deadening puff-words. (For more on puff-words, please see the note at *utilize.*)

Fervent A beautiful and expressive word that combines the phonological charms of *verve* and *fever.* Lots of writers, though, think *fervent* is synonymous with *fervid,* and most dictionary defs. don't do much to disabuse them. The truth is that there's a hierarchical trio of zeal-type adjectives, all with roots in the Latin verb *fervēre* (= to boil). Even though *fervent* can also mean extremely hot, glowing (as in "Fingering his ascot, Aubrey gazed abstractedly at the brazier's fervent coals"), it's actually just the baseline term; *fervent* is basically synonymous with *ardent. Fervid* is the next level up; it connotes even more passion/devotion/eagerness than *fervent.* At the top is *perfervid,* which means extravagantly, rabidly, uncontrollably zealous or impassioned. *Perfervid* deserves to be used more, not only for its internal alliteration and metrical pizzazz but because its deployment usually shows that the writer knows the differences between the three *fervēre*-words.

Loan If you use *loan* as a verb in anything other than ultra-informal speech, you're marking yourself as ignorant or careless. As of 2004, the verb *to lend* never comes off as fussy or pretentious, merely as correct.

Feckless A totally great adjective. One reason that slippage in the meaning of *effete* is OK is that we can use *feckless* to express what *effete* used to mean. *Feckless* primarily means deficient in efficacy, i.e., lacking vigor or determination, feeble; but it can also mean careless, profligate, irresponsible. It appears most often now in connection with wastoid youths, bloated bureaucracies—anyone who's culpable for his own haplessness. The great thing about using *feckless* is that it lets you be extremely dismissive and mean without sounding mean; you just sound witty and classy. The word's also fun to read because of the soft-*e* assonance and the *k* sound—the triply assonant noun form is even more fun.

All of Other than as an ironic idiom for "no more than" (e.g., "Sex with Edgar lasted all of a minute"), does *all of* have any legit uses? The answer is both complicated and personally humbling. An irksome habit of many student writers is automatically to stick an *of* between the adjective *all* and any noun that follows—"All of the firemen slid down the pole," "She sent cards to all of her friends"—and I have spent a decade telling undergrads to abjure this habit, for two reasons. The first is that an excess of *of*'s is one of the surest signs of flabby or maladroit writing, and the second is that the usage is often wrong. I have promulgated the following rule: Except for the ironic-idiom case, the only time it's correct to use *all of* is when the adj. phrase is followed by a pronoun—"All of them got cards"; "I wanted Edgar to have all of me"—unless, however, the relevant pronoun is possessive, in which case you must again omit the *of,* as in "All my friends despise Edgar." Only a few weeks ago did I learn (from a bright student who got annoyed enough at my hectoring to start poring over usage guides in the hopes of finding something I'd been wrong about that she could raise her hand at just the right moment in class and embarrass me with [which she did, and I was, and deserved it—there's nothing more ridiculous than a pedant who's wrong]), however, that there's actually one more complication to the first part of the rule. With *all* plus a noun, it turns out that the medial *of* is required if that noun is possessive, as in "All of Edgar's problems stem from his childhood," "All of Dave's bombast came back to haunt him that day." I doubt I will ever forget this.

Bland Here's an adj. that the dictionaries are behind on. *Bland* was originally used of people to mean "suave, smooth, unperturbed, soothingly pleasing" (cf. *blandish, blandishment*), and of things to mean "soft, mild, pleasantly soothing, etc." Only incidentally did it mean "dull, insipid, flavorless." As of 2004, though, *bland* nearly always has a pejorative tinge. Outside of one special semi-medical idiom ("The ulcerous CEO was placed on a bland diet"), *bland* now tends to imply that whatever's described was trying to be more interesting, piquant, stirring, forceful, magnetic, or engaging than it actually ended up being.

Noma This medical noun signifies an especially icky ulcerous infection of the mouth or genitals. Because the condition most commonly strikes children living in abject poverty/squalor, it's a bit like scrofula. And just as the adj. *scrofulous* has gradually extended its sense to mean "corrupt, degenerate, gnarly," so *nomal* seems ripe for similar extension; it could serve as a slightly obscure or erudite synonym for "scrofulous, repulsive, pathetically gross, grossly pathetic"...you get the idea.

Hairy There are maybe more descriptors for various kinds of hair and hairiness than any other word-set in English, and some of them are extremely strange and fun. The more pedestrian terms like *shaggy, unshorn, bushy, coiffed,* and so on we'll figure you already know. The adj. *barbigerous* is an extremely uptown synonym for *bearded. Cirrose* and *cirrous,* from the Latin *cirrus* meaning "curl" or "fringe" (as in *cirrus clouds*), can both be used to refer to somebody's curly or tufty or wispy/feathery hair—Nicolas

Cage's hair in *Adaptation* is cirrose. *Crinite* means "hairy or possessed of a hair-like appendage," though it's mainly a botanical term and would be a bit eccentric applied to a person. *Crinose,* though, is a people-adj. that means "having a lot of hair," especially in the sense of one's hair being really long. The related noun *crinosity* is antiquated but not obsolete and can be used to refer to somebody's hair in an amusingly donnish way, as in *Madonna's normally platinum crinosity is now a maternal brown. Glabrous,* which is the loveliest of all hair-related adjectives, means having no hair (on a given part) at all. Please note that *glabrous* means more baby's-bottom-hairless than bald or shaved, though if you wanted to describe a bald person in an ironically fancy way you could talk about his *glabrous dome* or something. *Hirsute* is probably the most familiar upmarket synonym for *hairy,* totally at home in any kind of formal writing. Like that of many hair-related adjectives, *hirsute*'s original use was in botany (where it means "covered with coarse or bristly hairs"), but in regular usage its definition is much more general. Not so with the noun *hirsutism,* though, which is still semi-medical and means having a truly pathological amount of hair and/or hair that's unusually or unevenly distributed—the point is that the noun's not really a synonym for *hairiness. Hispid* means "covered with stiff or rough little hairs" and could apply to a military pate or unshaved jaw. *Hispidulous* is mainly just a puffed-up form of *hispid* and should be avoided. *Lanate* and *lanated* mean "having or being composed of woolly hairs." A prettier and slightly more familiar way to describe woolly hair is with the adjective *flocculent.* (There's also *floccose,* but this is used mainly of odd little hairy fruits like kiwi and quince.) Then there are the *pil*-based words, all derived from the Latin *pilus* (=hair). *Pilose,* another fairly common adj., means "covered with fine soft hair." Deceptively similar-looking is *pilous,* which is a more hardcore-science adj. that the *Oxford English Dictionary* defines as "characterized by or abounding in hair, hairy," citing as an example the following (unexplained, thus kind of troubling) sentence: *It is covered with a rough pilous epidermis. Pilous*'s own similarity to *pileous* is not deceptive, since the latter, a medical adjective, means "consisting of or pertaining to hair"; e.g., certain hair-intensive cancerous growths are classified as *pileous tumors.* On the other hand, pileous tumors are sometimes also called *piliferous tumors,* wherein the latter adj. means "having or producing hair" (in botany, *piliferous* means "tipped with a hair," as in certain weird leaves). There's also *piligerous,* which means "covered or clothed in hair" and is used primarily of animals, and *piliated,* which comes from the plural of *pilus* and is used to describe certain kinds of hairy or fringe-intensive bacteria. Last but not least is the noun *pilimiction,* which names a hopefully very rare medical disorder "in which piliform or hair-like bodies are passed in the urine." Outside of maybe describing some kind of terribly excruciated facial expression as *pilimictive,* however, it's hard to imagine a mainstream use for *pilimiction.* (One *pil*-word N.B.: It so happens that the adjective *pubescent* literally means "covered with soft downy hairs," so technically it qualifies as a synonym for *pilose;* but as of 2004 almost no reader will take *pubescent* this way, so I'd stick with *pilose.*) *Tomentose* means "covered with dense little matted hairs"—baby chimps, hobbits' feet, and Robin Williams are all tomentose. *Ulotrichous,* which is properly classed with *lannate* and *flocculent,* is an old and extremely fancy term for "crisply woolly hair." Be advised that it is also, if not exactly a racist adj., certainly a racial one—A. C. Haddon's *Races of Man,* from the early 1900s, famously classified races according to three basic hair types: *leiotrichous* (straight), *cymotrichous* (wavy), and *ulotrichous.*

Now go do the right thing.

N.B. If you're thinking of using any of the more esoteric adjectives here, you'd be well advised to keep an *OED* close at hand. This is not simply a gratuitous plug of another Oxford U. Press product. The fact is that some of these hair-related terms aren't in other dictionaries; plus, the terms are often specialized enough that you're going to want not just an abstract definition but a couple sample sentences so that you can see how the words are actually used. Only the *OED* has both defs. and in-context samples for just about every significant word in the language. Actually, why not screw appearances and just state the obvious: No really serious writer should be without an *OED,* whether it's bought or stolen or hacked into the online version of or whatever you need to do. Nothing else comes close.

—*2004*

riparian—having to do with rivers **rostrate** (adj.)—having a beaklike people mixed together; (v.) to crease or fold **ruddled** (adj.)—red-shot, waste, icky ground, especially w/r/t plants **rue**—fragrant weeds **ru** wrinkle, or crease, as in lining of stomach; (adj.) rugate **runnel**—a creek about one's own misdeeds **sacerdotal**—of or relating to priests **satyroma** to say," "namely" (like "viz."?); abbreviations are sc., scil., ss. **sciolism**—pre or split easily; "a scissile mineral," "a scissile peptide bond" **scored**—scarred **per**—opening for draining off water **septage**—waste found in septic tank dry **seriate**—arranged or occurring in a series or in rows **seria** covered with soft silky hairs **serrate**—having or forming a row of sharp rows...used with troops **sessile**—in botany, leaf that's stalkless and attached a barnacle **seta**—a stiff hair or bristle; (pl.) setae **settle** (n.)—wood **Shavian**—characteristic of George Bernard Shaw **Sheraton**—1800s **shirr** (v.)—to gather cloth into decorative rows by parallel stitching **shiva** *a Wonderful Life*) **shrive**—to obtain absolution **shriven**—absolved **sic pas** **silent butler**—box w/ handle and hinged cover for collecting ashes and pocket material) **silex**—silica or finely ground tripoli used as an inert emoluments **sinistrorse**—growing upward in a spiral that turns from right of straw **skive** (v.)—to cut thin layers off **sloe-eyed**—having slanted dark staircase **soigné** (adj.)—sophisticated, elegant, fashionable: "a soigné little **somniferous**—sleep-inducing **son et lumière**—theater show at night in

part **rowen**—a second crop, as of hay, in a season **ruck**—a multitude of bloody (ruddle is ferrous red dye) **ruderal** (adj.)—growing in garbage, **fous**—color: reddish, from pinkish to orangeish **ruga**—bio term for fold, or narrow channel for water **ruth**—compassion or pity for another; sorrow **niac**—male version of nymphomaniac **scilicet**—adverb, Latin for "that is tentious air of scholarship; superficial knowledgeability **scissile** (adj.)—cut or marked in parallel lines **scotopia**—ability to see in dark **scup-** **septectomy**—removal of all or part of septum **sere** (adj.)—withered, **tim**—Latin adverb: one after another, in a series **sericeous**— little teethy things **serried**—pressed or crowded together, especially in directly at base; in zoology, permanently attached, not free-moving, like en bench with high back and storage space under the seat type of furniture, simple, straight lines, long legs; tall, narrow desks, etc. **ree**—Midwestern: noisy mock serenade for newlyweds (cops in rain in *It's* **sim**—"thus everywhere"; used to show something recurs throughout text crumbs **silesia**—sturdy twill used for linings and pockets (white greebly paint filler **simony**—buying or selling ecclesiastical pardons, offices, or to left: "a sinistrorse vine" **skell**—homeless derelict **skep**—beehive made eyes **soffit**—underside of a structural component like a beam, arch, or restaurant" **soilure** (adj.)—dirty, soiled **somnifacient**—sleep-inducing outdoor setting, usually a historical setting, and related to history of a place

BORGES ON THE COUCH

THERE'S AN UNHAPPY PARADOX about literary biographies. The majority of readers who will be interested in a writer's bio, especially one as long and exhaustive as Edwin Williamson's *Borges: A Life,* will be admirers of the writer's work. They will therefore usually be idealizers of that writer and perpetrators (consciously or not) of the intentional fallacy. Part of the appeal of the writer's work for these fans will be the distinctive stamp of that writer's personality, predilections, style, particular tics and obsessions—the sense that *these* stories were written by *this* author and could have been done by no other.[1] And

[1] Of course, Borges's famous "Pierre Menard, Author of the *Quixote*" makes sport of this very conviction, just as his later "Borges and I" anticipates and refutes the whole idea of a literary biography. The fact that his fiction is always several steps ahead of its interpreters is one of the things that make Borges so great, and so modern.

yet it often seems that the person we encounter in the literary biography could not possibly have written the works we admire. And the more intimate and thorough the bio, the stronger this feeling usually is. In the present case, the Jorge Luis Borges who emerges in Williamson's book—a vain, timid, pompous mama's boy, given for much of his life to dithery romantic obsessions—is about as different as one can get from the limpid, witty, pansophical, profoundly adult writer we know from his stories. Rightly or no, anyone who reveres Borges as one of the best and most important fiction writers of the last century will resist this dissonance, and will look, as a way to explain and mitigate it, for obvious defects in Williamson's life study. The book won't disappoint them.

Edwin Williamson is an Oxford don and esteemed Hispanist whose *Penguin History of Latin America* is a small masterpiece of lucidity and triage. It is therefore unsurprising that his *Borges* starts strong, with a fascinating sketch of Argentine history and the Borges family's place within it. For Williamson, the great conflict in the Argentine national character is that between the "sword" of civilizing European liberalism and the "dagger" of romantic gaucho individualism, and he argues that Borges's life and work can be properly understood only in reference to this conflict, particularly as it plays out in his childhood. In the nineteenth century, grandfathers on both sides of his family had distinguished themselves in important battles for South American independence from Spain and the establishment of a centralized Argentine government, and Borges's mother was obsessed with the family's historical glory. Borges's father, a man stunted by the heroic paternal shadow in which he lived, evidently did things like give his son an actual dagger to use on bullies at school and send him to a brothel for devirgination. The young Borges failed both these "tests," the scars of which marked him forever and show up all over the place in his fiction, Williamson thinks.

It is in these claims about personal stuff encoded in the writer's art that the book's real defect lies. In fairness, it's just a pronounced case of a syndrome that seems common to literary biographies, so common that it might point to a design flaw in the whole enterprise. *Borges: A Life*'s big problem is that Williamson is an atrocious reader of Borges's work; his interpretations amount to a simplistic, dishonest kind of psychological criticism. You can see why this problem might be intrinsic to the genre. A biographer wants his story to be not only interesting but literarily valuable.[2] In order to ensure this, the bio has to make the writer's personal life and psychic travails seem vital to his work. The idea is that we can't correctly interpret a piece of verbal art unless we know the personal and/or psychological circumstances surrounding its creation. That this is simply assumed as an axiom by many biographers is one problem; another is that the approach works a lot better on some writers than on others. It works well on Kafka—Borges's only modern

[2] Actually, these two agendas dovetail, since the only reason anybody's interested in a writer's life is because of his literary importance. (Think about it—the personal lives of most people who spend fourteen hours a day sitting there alone, reading and writing, are not going to be thrill-rides to hear about.)

equal as an allegorist, with whom he's often compared—because Kafka's fictions are expressionist, projective, and personal; they make artistic sense only as manifestations of Kafka's psyche. But Borges's stories are very different. They are designed primarily as metaphysical arguments[3]; they are dense, self-enclosed, with their own deviant logics. Above all, they are meant to be impersonal, to transcend individual consciousness—"to be incorporated," as Borges puts it, "like the fables of Theseus or Ahasuerus, into the general memory of the species and even transcend the fame of their creator or the extinction of the language in which they were written." One reason for this is that Borges is a mystic, or at least a sort of radical Neo-Platonist—human thought, behavior, and history are all the product of one big Mind, or are elements of an immense kabbalistic Book that includes its own decoding. Biography-wise, then, we have a strange situation in which Borges's individual personality and circumstances matter only insofar as they lead him to create artworks in which such personal facts are held to be unreal.

Borges: A Life, which is strongest in its treatments of Argentine history and politics,[4] is at its very worst when Williamson is

[3] This is part of what gives Borges's stories their mythic, precognitive quality (all cultures' earliest, most vital metaphysics is mythopoeic), which quality in turn helps explain how the stories can be at once so abstract and so moving.

[4] The biography is probably most valuable in its account of Borges's political evolution. A common bit of literary gossip about Borges is that the reason he wasn't awarded a

discussing specific pieces in light of Borges's personal life. Unfortunately, he discusses just about everything Borges ever wrote. Williamson's critical thesis is clear: "Bereft of a key to their autobiographical context, no one could have grasped the vivid significance these pieces actually had for their author." And in case after case, the resultant readings are shallow, forced, and distorted—as indeed they must be if the biographer's project is to be justified. Random example: "The Wait," a marvelous short-short that appears in 1949's *The Aleph,*

Nobel Prize was his supposed support for Argentina's ghastly authoritarian juntas of the 1960s and '70s. From Williamson, though, we learn that Borges's politics were actually far more complex and tragic. The child of an old liberal family, and an unabashed leftist in his youth, Borges was one of the first and bravest public opponents of European fascism and the rightist nationalism it spawned in Argentina. What changed him was Perón, whose creepy right-wing populist dictatorship aroused such loathing in Borges that he allied himself with the repressively anti-Perón *Revolución Libertadora.* Borges's situation following Perón's first ouster in 1955 is full of unsettling parallels for American readers. Because Peronism still had great popularity with Argentina's working poor, the exiled dictator retained enormous political power, and would have won any democratic national election held in the 1950s. This placed believers in liberal democracy (such as J. L. Borges) in the same sort of bind that the United States faced in South Vietnam a few years later—how do you promote democracy when you know that a majority of people will, if given the chance, vote for an end to democratic voting? In essence, Borges decided that the Argentine masses had been so hoodwinked by Perón and his wife that a return to democracy was possible only after the nation had been cleansed of Peronism. Williamson's analysis of the slippery slope this decision put Borges on, and his account of the hatchet job that Argentina's leftists did on Borges's political reputation in retaliation for his defection (such that by 1967, when the writer came to Harvard to lecture, the students practically expected him to have epaulettes and a riding crop), make for his book's best chapters.

takes the form of a layered homage to Hemingway, gangster movies, and the Buenos Aires underworld. An Argentine mobster, in hiding from another mobster and living under the pursuer's name, dreams so often of his killers' appearance in his bedroom that, when the assassins finally come for him, he

> gestured at them to wait, and he turned over and faced the wall, as though going back to sleep. Did he do that to awaken the pity of the men that killed him, or because it's easier to endure a terrifying event than to imagine it, wait for it endlessly—or (and this is perhaps the most likely possibility) so that his murderers would become a dream, as they had already been so many times, in that same place, at that same hour?

The distant interrogative ending—a Borges trademark—becomes an inquisition into dreams, reality, guilt, augury, and mortal terror. For Williamson, though, the real key to the story's significance appears to be that "Borges had failed to win the love of Estela Canto.... With Estela gone, there seemed nothing to live for," and he represents the story's ending all and only as a depressed whimper: "When his killers finally track him down, he just rolls over meekly to face the wall and resigns himself to the inevitable."

It is not merely that Williamson reads every last thing in Borges's oeuvre as a correlative of the author's emotional state. It is that he tends to reduce all of Borges's psychic conflicts and personal problems to the pursuit of women. Williamson's theory here involves two big elements: Borges's inability to stand up to his domineering mother,[5] and his belief, codified in a starry-eyed reading of Dante, that "it was the love of a woman that alone could deliver him from the hellish unreality he shared with his father and inspire him to write a masterpiece that would justify his life." Story after story is thus interpreted by Williamson as a coded dispatch on Borges's amorous career, which career turns out to be sad, timorous, puerile, moony, and (like most people's) extremely boring. The formula is applied equally to famous pieces, such as "'The Aleph' (1945), whose autobiographical subtext alludes to his thwarted love for Norah Lange," and to lesser-known stories like "The Zahir":

> The torments described by Borges in this story... are, of course, displaced confessions of the extremity of his plight. Estela [Canto, who'd just broken up with him] was to have been the "new Beatrice," inspiring him to create a work that would be "the Rose without purpose, the Platonic, intemporal Rose," but here he was again, sunk in the unreality of the labyrinthine self, with no prospect now of contemplating the mystic Rose of love.

[5] Be warned that much of the mom-based psychologizing seems right out of *Oprah,* e.g., "However, by urging her son to realize the ambitions she had defined for herself, she unwittingly induced a sense of unworthiness in him that became the chief obstacle to his self-assertion."

Thin though this kind of explication is, it's preferable to the reverse process by which Williamson sometimes presents Borges's stories and poems as "evidence" that he was in emotional extremities. Williamson's claim, for instance, that in 1934, "after his definitive rejection by Norah Lange, Borges... came to the brink of killing himself" is based entirely on two tiny pieces of contemporaneous fiction in which the protagonists struggle with suicide. Not only is this a bizarre way to read and reason—was the Flaubert who wrote *Madame Bovary* eo ipso suicidal?—but Williamson seems to believe that it licenses him to make all sorts of dubious, humiliating claims about Borges's interior life: "'The Cyclical Night,' which he published in *La Nación* on October 6, reveals him to be in the throes of an acute personal crisis"; "In the extracts from this unfinished poem...we can see that the reason for wishing to commit suicide was literary failure, stemming ultimately from sexual self-doubt." Bluck.

Again, it is primarily because of Borges's short stories that anyone will care enough to read about his life. And while Edwin Williamson spends a lot of time detailing the explosive success that Borges enjoyed in middle age, after the 1961 International Publishers' Prize, shared with Samuel Beckett, introduced his work to the United States and Europe,[6] there is little

[6] Williamson's chapters on Borges's sudden world fame will be of special interest to those American readers who weren't yet alive or reading in the mid-1960s. I was lucky enough to discover Borges as a kid, but only because I happened to find *Labyrinths,*

in his book about just why Jorge Luis Borges is an important enough fiction writer to deserve such a microscopic bio. The truth, briefly stated, is that Borges is arguably the great bridge between modernism and postmodernism in world literature. He is modernist in that his fiction shows a first-rate human mind stripped of all foundations in religious or ideological certainty—a mind turned thus wholly in on itself.[7] His stories are inbent and hermetic, with the oblique terror of a game whose rules are unknown and its stakes everything.

And the mind of those stories is nearly always a mind that lives in and through books. This is because Borges the writer is, fundamentally, a reader. The dense, obscure allusiveness of his fiction is not a tic, or even really a style; and it is no accident that his best stories are often fake essays, or reviews of fictitious books, or have texts at their plots' centers, or have as protagonists Homer or Dante or Averroës. Whether for seminal artistic reasons or neurotic personal ones or both, Borges collapses reader and writer into a new kind of aesthetic agent, one who makes stories out of stories, one for whom reading is

an early English-language collection of his most famous stories, on my father's bookshelves in 1974. I believed that the book was there only because of my parents' unusually fine literary taste and discernment—which verily they do possess—but what I didn't know was that by 1974 *Labyrinths* was also on tens of thousands of other U.S. homes' shelves, that Borges had actually been a sensation on the order of Tolkien and Gibran among hip readers of the previous decade.

[7] Labyrinths, mirrors, dreams, doubles—so many of the elements that appear over and over in Borges's fiction are symbols of the psyche turned inward.

essentially—consciously—a creative act. This is not, however, because Borges is a metafictionist or cleverly disguised critic. It is because he knows that there's finally no difference—that murderer and victim, detective and fugitive, performer and audience are the same. Obviously, this has postmodern implications (hence the pontine claim above), but Borges's is really a mystical insight, and a profound one. It's also frightening, since the line between monism and solipsism is thin and porous, more to do with spirit than with mind per se. And, as an artistic program, this kind of collapse/transcendence of individual identity is also paradoxical, requiring a grotesque self-obsession combined with an almost total effacement of self and personality. Tics and obsessions aside, what makes a Borges story Borgesian is the odd, ineluctable sense you get that no one and everyone did it. This is why, for instance, it is so irksome to see Williamson describe Borges's "The Immortal" and "The Writing of the God"—two of the greatest, most scalp-crinkling mystical stories ever, next to which the epiphanies of Joyce or redemptions of O'Connor seem pallid and crude—as respective products of Borges's "many-layered distress" and "indifference to his fate" after various idealized girlfriends dump him. Stuff like this misses the whole point. Even if Williamson's claims are true, the stories so completely transcend their motive cause that the biographical facts become, in the deepest and most literal way, irrelevant.

—2004

sopor—abnormally deep, lethargic sleep **sordino**—a mute for an in salad **sortilege**—sorcery, witchcraft, divination **sough** (n.)—a soft leaves **souk**—open-air Arab market **spagyric**—relating to or rese Greek spinach pie **spandrel**—triangular space between arch's exte good cleavage (used of minerals) **spavined** (adj.)—marked by de caves ("speleothems") **spirituel**—having a refined mind or wit **spolia** **sprat**—small edible fish **stanchion**—upright pole, post, or support **stertor**—a heavy snoring sound in respiration **stob**—short piece of parts, like crickets and locusts **succor**—assistance in time of distress **su** sarcastic adverb **sural**—of or relating to calf of leg **surbase**—baseboard camp follower who sold provisions to soldiers **swage**—tool used in bend fabrics with a soft nap **tailing**—refuse after ore has been processed **ta** **gram**—intricate Chinese puzzle w/ squares and diagonals **taran** (adj.)—having symptoms that develop slowly or appear long after incep **demalion**—a ragamuffin, person wearing ragged clothing **taxon**—a tax how the movement of earth on its axis and around sun causes night urgent but ineffectual attempt to pee or shit **thallophyte**—algaeish su **bus**—clot in blood vessel or heart **toby**—a drinking mug in the shape of or cotton **trecento**—the 14th century, esp. w/r/t Italian art and lit **treil** produced by rapid repetition of a single tone **trencherman**—gour mining **tribade** (n.)—lesbian **tribology**—study of friction, lubrication,

strument **soricine**—looking like a shrew **sorrel**—fancy greens for murmuring or rustling sound; (v.) to make such a sound...wind, surf, mbling alchemy **spall**—chip or flake of rock or ore **spanakopita**—rior curves and the rectangular framework around it **spathic**—having struction, ruin; junkyard full of spavined cars **speleology**—study of tion—plundering or despoiling **Sprachgefü hl**—"feeling for language" **sternutation**—sneezing, a sneeze **sternutatory**—causing sneezing wood-like stake; Southern **stridulation**—noise produced by moving body **pernal**—coming from or related to heavens, celestial; q.v. "supernally" as **suspire** (v.)—to sigh **susurration**—soft whispering sound **sutler**—army ing or shaping cold metal **swanskin**—any of several flannel or cotton **lus**—sloping pile of loose stone at base of cliff; also "anklebone" **tan-tism**—disorder where you have uncontrollable need to dance **tardive** tion; used of disease **tarn**—small mountain lake formed by glacier **tatter-**onomic group like phylum, class, species **tellurion**—a device that shows & day & seasons **tenebrosity**—gloominess, darkness **tenesmus**—per-simple plants w/ no differentiation between root, stem, leaf **throm-**a stout man wearing a three-cornered hat **toile**—sheer fabric like linen **lage**—decorative trellis for vines **tremolo**—like vibrato, a tremulous event mand, hearty eater **trepan**—rock-boring tool used for sinking shafts in and wear of surfaces in relative motion **trichoid**—resembling hair

DECIDERIZATION 2007— A SPECIAL REPORT

I THINK IT'S UNLIKELY that anyone is reading this as an introduction. Most of the people I know treat Best American anthologies like Whitman's Samplers. They skip around, pick and choose. There isn't the same kind of linear commitment as in a regular book. Which means that the reader has more freedom of choice, which of course is part of what America's all about. If you're like most of us, you'll first check the table of contents for names of writers you like, and their pieces are what you'll read first. Then you'll go by title, or apparent subject, or sometimes even first line. There's a kind of triage. The guest editor's intro is last, if at all.

This sense of being last or least likely confers its own freedoms. I feel free to state an emergent truth that I maybe wouldn't if I thought that the book's sales could really be hurt or its essays' audience scared away. This truth is that just about every important word on *The Best American Essays 2007*'s front cover turns out to be vague, debatable, slippery, disingenuous, or else "true" only in certain contexts that are themselves slippery and hard to sort out or make sense of—and that in general the whole project of an anthology like this requires a degree of credulity and submission on the part of the reader that might appear, at first, to be almost un-American.

...Whereupon, after that graceless burst of bad news, I'm betting that most of whichever readers thought that maybe this year they'd try starting out linearly with the editor's intro have now decided to stop or flip ahead to Jo Ann Beard's "Werner," the collection's first essay. This is actually fine for them to do, because Beard's is an unambiguously great piece—exquisitely written and suffused with a sort of merciless compassion. It's a narrative essay, I think the subgenre's called, although the truth is that I don't believe I would have loved the piece any less or differently if it had been classed as a short story, which is to say not an essay at all but fiction.

Thus one constituent of the truth about the cover is that your guest editor isn't sure what an essay even is. Not that this is unusual. Most literary readers take a position on the meaning of "essay" rather like the famous one that U.S.S.C. Justice Potter Stewart took on "obscene": we feel that we pretty much know an essay when we see one, and that that's enough, regardless of all the noodling and complication involved in actually trying to define the term "essay." I don't know whether gut certainty is really enough here or not, though. I think I personally prefer the term "literary nonfiction." Pieces like "Werner" and Daniel Orozco's "Shakers" seem so remote from the sort of thing that Montaigne and Chesterton were doing when the essay was being codified that to call these pieces essays seems to make the term too broad to really signify. And yet Beard's and Orozco's pieces are so arresting and alive and good that they end up being salient even if one is working as a guest essay editor and sitting there reading a dozen Xeroxed pieces in a row before them and then another dozen in a row after them—essays on everything from memory and surfing and Esperanto to childhood and mortality and Wikipedia, on depression and translation and emptiness and James Brown, Mozart, prison, poker, trees, anorgasmia, color, homelessness, stalking, fellatio, ferns, fathers, grandmothers, falconry, grief, film comedy—a rate of consumption that tends to level everything out into an undifferentiated mass of high-quality description and trenchant reflection that becomes both numbing and euphoric, a kind of Total Noise that's also the sound of our U.S. culture right now, a culture and volume of info and spin and rhetoric and context that I know I'm not alone in finding too much to even absorb, much less to try to make sense of or organize into any kind of triage of saliency or value. Such basic absorption, organization, and triage used to be what was required of an educated adult, a.k.a. an informed citizen—at least that's what I got taught. Suffice it here to say that the requirements now seem different.

A corollary to the above bad news is that I'm not really even all that confident or concerned about the differences between nonfiction and fiction, with "differences" here meaning formal or definitive, and "I" referring to me as a reader.[1] There are, as it happens, intergenre differences that I know and care about as a writer, though these differences are hard to talk about in a way that people who don't try to write both fiction and nonfiction will understand. I'm worried that they'll sound cheesy and melodramatic. Although maybe they won't. Maybe, given the ambient volume of your own life's noise, the main difference will make sense to you. Writing-wise, fiction is scarier, but nonfiction is harder—because nonfiction's based in reality, and today's felt reality is overwhelmingly, circuit-blowingly huge and complex. Whereas fiction comes out of nothing. Actually, so wait: the truth is that both genres are scary; both feel like they're executed on tightropes, over abysses—it's the abysses that are different. Fiction's abyss is silence, *nada.* Whereas nonfiction's abyss is Total Noise, the seething static of every particular thing and experience, and one's total freedom of infinite

[1] A subcorollary here is that it's a bit odd that Houghton Mifflin and the Best American series tend to pick professional writers to be their guest editors. There are, after all, highly expert professional readers among the industry's editors, critics, scholars, etc., and the guest editor's job here is really 95 percent readerly. Underlying the series' preference for writers appears to be one or both of the following: (a) the belief that someone's being a good writer makes her *eo ipso* a good reader—which is the same reasoning that undergirds most blurbs and MFA programs, and is both logically invalid and empirically false (trust me); or (b) the fact that the writers the series pick tend to have comparatively high name recognition, which the publishers figure will translate into wider attention and better sales. Premise (b) involves marketing and revenue and is thus probably backed up by hard data and thought in a way that (a) isn't.

choice about what to choose to attend to and represent and connect, and how, and why, & c.

There's a rather more concrete problem with the cover's word "editor," and it may be the real reason why these editorial introductions are the least appealing candy in the box. *The Best American Essays 2007*'s pieces are arranged alphabetically, by author, and they're essentially reprints from magazines and journals; whatever (light) copyediting they receive is done in-house by Houghton Mifflin. So what the cover calls your editor isn't really doing any editing. My real function is best described by an epithet that may, in future years, sum up 2006 with the same grim efficiency that terms like "Peace with Honor," "Iran-Contra," "Florida Recount," and "Shock and Awe" now comprise and evoke other years. What your editor really is here is: the Decider.

Being the Decider for a Best American anthology is part honor and part service, with "service" here not as in "public service" but rather as in "service industry." That is, in return for some pay and intangible assets, I am acting as an evaluative filter, winnowing a very large field of possibilities down to a manageable, absorbable Best for your delectation. Thinking about this kind of Decidering[2] is interesting in all kinds of different ways[3]; but the general point is that professional

[2] (usage *sic,* in honor of the term's source)

[3] For example, from the perspective of Information Theory, the bulk of the Decider's labor actually consists of *excluding* nominees from the final prize collection, which

filtering/winnowing is a type of service that we citizens and consumers now depend on more and more, and in ever-increasing ways, as the quantity of available information and products and art and opinion and choices and all the complications and ramifications thereof expands at roughly the rate of Moore's Law.

The immediate point, on the other hand, is obvious. Unless you are both a shut-in and independently wealthy, there is no way you can sit there and read all the contents of all the 2006 issues of all the hundreds of U.S. periodicals that publish literary nonfiction. So you subcontract this job—not to me directly, but to a publishing company whom you trust (for whatever reasons) to then sub-subcontract the job to someone whom they trust (or more like believe you'll trust [for whatever reasons]) not to be insane or capricious or overtly "biased" in his Decidering.

"Biased" is, of course, the really front-loaded term here, the one that I expect Houghton Mifflin winces at and would prefer not to see uttered in the editor's intro even in the most reassuring context, since the rhetoric of such reassurances can be self-nullifying (as in, say, running a classified ad for oneself as a babysitter and putting "DON'T WORRY—NOT A PEDOPHILE!" at the bottom of the ad). I suspect that part of why

puts the Decider in exactly the position of Maxwell's Demon or any other kind of entropy-reducing info processor, since the really expensive, energy-intensive part of such processing is always deleting/discarding/resetting.

"bias" is so loaded and dicey in U.S. culture right now—and why it's so much-invoked and potent in cultural disputes—is that we are starting to become more aware of just how much subcontracting and outsourcing and submitting to other Deciders we're all now forced to do, which is threatening (the inchoate awareness is) to our sense of ourselves as intelligent free agents. And yet there is no obvious alternative to this outsourcing and submission. It may possibly be that acuity and taste in choosing which Deciders one submits to is now the real measure of informed adulthood. Since I was raised with more traditional, Enlightenment-era criteria, this possibility strikes me as consumerist and scary...to which the counterargument would be, again, that the alternatives are literally abysmal.

Speaking of submission, there was a bad bit of oversimplification two paragraphs above, since your guest editor is not really even the main sub-subcontractor on this job. The real Decider, in terms of processing info and reducing entropy, is Mr. Robert Atwan, the BAE series editor. Think of it this way. My job is to choose the twenty-odd so-called Best from roughly 100 finalists the series editor sends me.[4] Mr. Atwan, though,

[4] It's true that I got to lobby for essays that weren't in his 100, but there ended up being only one such outside piece in the collection. A couple of others that I'd suggested were nixed by Mr. Atwan—well, not nixed so much as counseled against, for what emerged as good reasons. In general, though, you can see who had the real power. However much I strutted around in my aviator suit and codpiece calling myself the Decider for *BAE '07*, I knew that it was Mr. Atwan who delimited the field of possibilities from which I was choosing...in rather the same way that many Americans are

has distilled these finalists from a vast pool of '06 nonfiction—every issue of hundreds of periodicals, plus submissions from his network of trusted contacts all over the United States—meaning that he's really the one doing the full-time reading and culling that you and I can't do; and he's been doing it since 1986. I have never met Mr. Atwan, but I—probably like most fans of BAE—envision him as by now scarcely more than a vestigial support system for an eye-brain assembly, maybe like 5'8" and 100 lbs., living full-time in some kind of high-tech medical chair that automatically gimbals around at various angles to help prevent skin ulcers, nourishment and wastes ferried by tubes, surrounded by full-spectrum lamps and stacks of magazines and journals, a special emergency beeper Velcroed to his arm in case he falls out of the chair, etc.

Given the amount of quiet behind-the-scenes power he wields over these prize collections, you're entitled to ask about

worried that what appears to be the reality we're experiencing and making choices about is maybe actually just a small, skewed section of reality that's been pre-chosen for us by shadowy entities and forces, whether these be left-leaning media, corporate cabals, government disinformers, our own unconscious prejudices, etc. At least Mr. Atwan was explicit about the whole pre-selection thing, though, and appeared to be fair and balanced, and of course he'd had years of hard experience on the front lines of Decidering; and in general I found myself trusting him and his judgments more and more throughout the whole long process, and there were finally only maybe about 10 percent of his forwarded choices where I just had no idea what he might have been seeing or thinking when he picked them.

Mr. Atwan's standards for inclusion and forwarding[5]; but he's far too experienced and cagey to encourage these sorts of questions. If his foreword to this edition is like those of recent years, he'll describe what he's looking for so generally—"essays of literary achievement that show an awareness of craft and forcefulness of thought"—that his criteria look reasonable while at the same time being vague and bland enough that we aren't induced to stop and think about what they might actually mean, or to ask just what principles Mr. Atwan uses to determine "achievement" and "awareness" and "forcefulness" (not to mention "literary"). He is wise to avoid this, since such specific questions would entail specific answers that then would raise more questions, and so on; and if this process is allowed to go on long enough, a point will be reached at which any Decider is going to look either (a) arrogant and arbitrary ("It's literary because I say so") or else (b) weak and incoherent (as he thrashes around in endless little definitions and exceptions and qualifications and apparent flip-flops). It's true. Press either R. Atwan or D. Wallace hard enough on any of our criteria or reasons—what they mean or where they come from—and you'll eventually get either paralyzed silence or the abysmal, Legionish babble of every last perceived fact and value. And Mr. Atwan cannot afford this; he's permanent BAE staff.

[5] I believe this is what is known in the nonfiction industry as a transition. We are now starting to poke tentatively at "Best," which is the most obviously fraught and bias-prone word on the cover.

I, on the other hand, have a strict term limit. After this, I go forever back to being an ordinary civilian and BAE reader (except for the introductions). I therefore feel free here to try for at least partial transparency about my Decidering criteria, some of which are obviously—let's be grown-ups and just admit it—subjective, and therefore in some ways biased.[6] Plus I have no real problem, emotionally or politically, with stopping at any given point in any theoretical Q & A & Q and simply shrugging and saying that I hear the caviling voices but am, this year, for whatever reasons (possibly including divine will—who knows?), the Decider, and that this year I get to define and decide what's Best, at least within the limited purview of Mr. Atwan's 104 finalists, and that if you don't like it then basically tough titty.

Because of the fact that my Decidering function is anentropic and therefore mostly exclusionary, I first owe some account of why certain types of essays were maybe easier for me to exclude than others. I'll try to combine candor with maximum tact. Memoirs, for example. With a few big exceptions, I don't much care for abreactive or confessional mem-

[6] Can I assume that some readers are as tired as I am of this word as a kneejerk derogative? Or, rather, tired of the legerdemain of collapsing the word's neutral meaning—"preference, inclination"—into the pejorative one of "unfairness stemming from prejudice"? It's the same thing that's happened with "discrimination," which started as a good and valuable word, but now no one can even hear it without seeming to lose their mind.

oirs. I'm not sure how to explain this. There is probably a sound, serious argument to be made about the popularity of confessional memoirs as a symptom of something especially sick and narcissistic/voyeuristic about U.S. culture right now. About certain deep connections between narcissism and voyeurism in the mediated psyche. But this isn't it. I think the real reason is that I just don't trust them. Memoirs/confessions, I mean. Not so much their factual truth as their agenda. The sense I get from a lot of contemporary memoirs is that they have an unconscious and unacknowledged project, which is to make the memoirists seem as endlessly fascinating and important to the reader as they are to themselves. I find most of them sad in a way that I don't think their authors intend. There are, to be sure, some memoirish-type pieces in this year's BAE—although these tend either to be about hair-raisingly unusual circumstances or else to use the confessional stuff as part of a larger and (to me) much richer scheme or story.

Another acknowledged prejudice: no celebrity profiles. Some sort of personal quota was exceeded at around age thirty-five. I now actually want to know less than I know about most celebrities.

The only other intrinsic bias I'm aware of is one that a clinician would probably find easy to diagnose in terms of projection or displacement. As someone who has a lot of felt trouble being clear, concise, and/or cogent, I tend to be allergic to academic writing, most of which seems to me willfully opaque and pretentious. There are, again, some notable exceptions, and by "academic writing" I mean a particular cloistered dialect and mode; I do not just mean any piece written by somebody who teaches college.[7]

The other side to this bias is that I tend, as a reader, to prize and admire clarity, precision, plainness, lucidity, and the sort of magical compression that enriches instead of vitiates. Some-

[7] Example: Roger Scruton is an academic, and his "A Carnivore's Credo" is a model of limpid and all-business compression, which is actually one reason why his argument is so valuable and prizeworthy, even though parts of that argument strike me as either odd or just plain wrong (e.g., just how much humane and bucolic "traditional livestock farming" does he believe still goes on in this country?). Out on the other end of the ethicopolitical spectrum, there's a weirdly similar example in Prof. Peter Singer's "What Should a Billionaire Give?," which is not exactly belletristic but certainly isn't written in aureate academese, and is salient and unforgettable and unexcludable not despite but in some ways *because* of the questions and criticisms it invites. May I assume that you've already read it? If not, please return to the main text. If you have, though, do some of Singer's summaries and obligation-formulas seem unrealistically simple? What if a person in the top 10 percent of U.S. earners already gives 10 percent of his income to different, non-UN-type charities—does this reduce his moral obligation, for Singer? Should it? Exactly which charities and forms of giving have the most efficacy and/or moral value—and how does one find out which these are? Should a family of nine making $132,000 a year really have the same 10 percent moral obligation as the childless bachelor making $132K a year? What about a $132K family where one family member has cancer and their health insurance has a 20 percent deductible—is this family's failure to cough up 10 percent after spending $40,000 on medical bills really still the moral equivalent of valuing one's new shoes over the life of a drowning child? Is Singer's whole analogy of the drowning kid(s) too simple, or at least too simple in some cases? Umm, might my own case be one of the ones where the analogy and giving-formula are too simple or inflexible? Is it OK that I think it might be, or am I just trying to rationalize my way out of discomfort and obligation as so many of us (according to Singer) are wont to do? And so on...but of course you'll notice how hard the reader's induced to think about all this. Can you see why a Decider might regard Singer's essay as brilliant and valuable precisely *because* its prose is so

one's ability to write this way, especially in nonfiction, fills me with envy and awe. This might help explain why a fair number of *BAE '07*'s pieces tend to be short, terse, and informal in usage/syntax. Readers who enjoy noodling about genre might welcome the news that several of this year's Best Essays are arguably more like *causeries* or *propos* than like essays per se, although one could counterargue that these pieces tend, in their essential pithiness, to be closer to what's historically been meant by "essay." Personally, I find taxonomic arguments like this dull and irrelevant. What does seem relevant is to assure you that none of the shorter essays in the collection were included merely because they were short. Limpidity, compactness, and an absence of verbal methane were simply part of what made these pieces valuable; and I think I tried, as the Decider, to use overall value as the prime triage- and filtering mechanism in selecting this year's top essays.

...Which, yes, all right, entitles you to ask what "value" means here and whether it's any kind of improvement, in specificity and traction, over the cover's "Best." I'm not sure that it's finally better or less slippery than "Best," but I do know it's different. "Value" sidesteps some of the metaphysics that makes pure aesthetics such a headache, for one thing. It's also more openly,

mainstream and its formulas so (arguably) crude or harsh? Or is this kind of "value" a stupid, PC-ish criterion to use in Decidering about essays' literary worth? What exactly are the connections between literary aesthetics and moral value supposed to be? Whose moral values ought to get used in determining what those connections should be? Does anyone even read Tolstoy's "What Is Art?" anymore?

candidly subjective: since things have value only *to* people, the idea of some limited, subjective human doing the valuing is sort of built right into the term. That all seems tidy and uncontroversial so far—although there's still the question of just what this limited human actually means by "value" as a criterion.

One thing I'm sure it means is that this year's *BAE* does not necessarily comprise the twenty-two very best-written or most beautiful essays published in 2006. Some of the book's essays are quite beautiful indeed, and most are extremely well written and/or show a masterly awareness of craft (whatever exactly that is). But others aren't, don't, especially—but they have other virtues that make them valuable. And I know that some of these virtues and value have to do with the ways in which the pieces handle and respond to the tsunami of available fact, context, and perspective that constitutes Total Noise. This claim might itself look slippery, because of course any published essay is a burst of information and context that is by definition part of 2006's overall roar of info and context. But it is possible for something to be both a quantum of information and a vector of meaning. Think, for instance, of the two distinct but related senses of "informative." Several of this year's most valuable essays are informative in both senses; they are at once informational and instructive. That is, they serve as models and guides for how large or complex sets of facts can be sifted, culled, and arranged in meaningful ways—ways that yield and illuminate truth instead of just adding more noise to the overall roar.

That all may sound too abstract. Let's do a concrete example, which happens also to involve the term "American" on the front cover. In your 2007 guest editor's opinion, we are in a state of three-alarm emergency—"we" basically meaning America as a polity and culture. Only part of this emergency has to do with what is currently called partisan politics, but it's a significant part. Don't worry that I'm preparing to make any kind of specific argument about the Bush administration or the disastrous harm I believe it's done in almost every area of federal law, policy, and governance. Such an argument would be just noise here—redundant for those readers who feel and believe as I do, biased crap for those who believe differently. Who's right is not the point. The point is to try to explain part of what I mean by "valuable." It is totally possible that, prior to 2004—when the reelection of George W. Bush rendered me, as part of the U.S. electorate, historically complicit in his administration's policies and conduct—this BAE Decider would have selected more memoirs or descriptive pieces on ferns and geese, some of which were quite lovely and fine. In the current emergency, though, such essays simply didn't seem as valuable to me as pieces like, say, Mark Danner's "Iraq: The War of the Imagination" or Elaine Scarry's "Rules of Engagement."

Here is an overt premise. There is just no way that 2004's reelection could have taken place—not to mention extraordinary renditions, legalized torture, FISA-flouting, or the passage of the Military Commissions Act—if we had been paying attention and handling information in a competent grown-up way. "We" meaning as a polity and culture. The premise does not entail specific blame; or rather the problems here are too entangled and systemic for good old-fashioned finger-pointing. It is, for one example, simplistic and wrong to blame the for-profit media for somehow failing to make clear to us the moral and practical hazards of trashing the Geneva Conventions. The for-profit media is exquisitely attuned to what we want and the amount of detail we'll sit still for. And a ninety-second news piece on the question of whether and how the Geneva Conventions ought to apply in an era of asymmetrical warfare is not going to explain anything; the relevant questions are too numerous and complicated, too fraught with contexts in everything from civil law and military history to ethics and game theory. One could spend a hard month just learning the history of the Conventions' translation into actual codes of conduct for the U.S. military...and that's not counting the dramatic changes in those codes since 2002, or the question of just what practices violate (or don't) just which Geneva provisions, and according to whom. Or let's not even mention the amount of research, background, cross-checking, corroboration, and rhetorical parsing required to understand the cataclysm of Iraq, the collapse of congressional oversight, the ideology of neoconservatism, the legal status of presidential signing statements, the political marriage of evangelical Protestantism and corporatist laissez-faire.... There's no way. You'd simply drown. We all would. It's amazing to me that no one much talks about this—about the fact that whatever our founders and framers thought of as a literate, informed citizenry can no longer exist, at least not without a whole new modern degree of subcontracting and dependence packed into what we mean by "informed."[8]

In the context of our Total Noise, a piece like Mark Danner's "Iraq: . . . Imagination" exemplifies a special subgenre I've come to think of as the service essay, with "service" here referring to both professionalism and virtue. In what is loosely framed as a group book review, Danner has processed and arranged an immense quantity of fact, opinion, confirmation, testimony, and on-site experience in order to offer an explanation of the Iraq debacle that is clear without being simplistic, comprehensive without being overwhelming, and critical without being shrill. It is a brilliant, disciplined, pricelessly informative piece.

There are several other such service essays among this year's proffered Best. Some, like Danner's, are literary journalism; others are more classically argumentative, or editorial, or personal. Some are quite short. All are smart and well written, but what renders them most valuable for me is a special kind of integrity in their handling of fact. An absence of dogmatic

[8] Hence, by the way, the seduction of partisan dogma. You can drown in dogmatism now, too—radio, Internet, cable, commercial and scholarly print—but this kind of drowning is more like sweet release. Whether hard right or new left or whatever, the seduction and mentality are the same. You don't have to feel confused or inundated or ignorant. You don't even have to think, for you already Know, and whatever you choose to learn confirms what you Know. This dogmatic lockstep is not the kind of inevitable dependence I'm talking about—or rather it's only the most extreme and frightened form of that dependence.

cant. Not that service essayists don't have opinions or make arguments. But you (I) never sense, from this year's Best, that facts are being specially cherry-picked or arranged in order to advance a pre-set agenda. They are utterly different from the party-line pundits and propagandists who now are in such vogue, for whom writing is not thinking or service but more like the silky courtier's manipulation of an enfeebled king.

...In which scenario we, like diminished kings or rigidly insecure presidents, are reduced to being overwhelmed by info and interpretation, or else paralyzed by cynicism and anomie, or else—worst—seduced by some particular set of dogmatic talking-points, whether these be PC or NRA, rationalist or evangelical, "Cut and Run" or "No Blood for Oil." The whole thing is (once again) way too complicated to do justice to in a guest intro, but one last, unabashed bias/preference in *BAE '07* is for pieces that undercut reflexive dogma, that essay to do their own Decidering in good faith and full measure, that eschew the deletion of all parts of reality that do not fit the narrow aperture of, say for instance, those cretinous fundamentalists who insist that creationism should be taught alongside science in public schools, or those sneering materialists who insist that all serious Christians are just as cretinous as the fundamentalists.

Part of our emergency is that it's so awfully tempting to do this sort of thing now, to retreat to narrow arrogance, preformed positions, rigid filters, the "moral clarity" of the immature. The alternative is dealing with massive, high-entropy amounts of info and ambiguity and conflict and flux; it's continually discovering new vistas of personal ignorance and delusion. In sum, to really try to be informed and literate today is to feel stupid nearly all the time, and to need help. That's about as clearly as I can put it. I'm aware that some of the collection's writers could spell all this out better and in much less space. At any rate, the service part of what I mean by "value" refers to all this stuff, and extends as well to essays that have nothing to do with politics or wedge issues. Many are valuable simply as exhibits of what a first-rate artistic mind can make of particular fact-sets—whether these involve the 17-kHz ring tones of some kids' cell phones, the language of movement as parsed by dogs, the near-infinity of ways to experience and describe an earthquake, the existential synecdoche of stagefright, or the revelation that most of what you've believed and revered turns out to be self-indulgent crap.

That last one's[9] of especial value, I think. As exquisite verbal art, yes, but also as a model for what free, informed adulthood might look like in the context of Total Noise: not just the intelligence to discern one's own error or stupidity, but the humility to address it, absorb it, and move on and out therefrom, bravely, toward the next revealed error. This is probably the sincerest, most biased account of "Best" your Decider can give: these pieces are models—not templates, but models—of ways I wish I could think and live in what seems to me this world.

—2007

[9] You probably know which essay I'm referring to, assuming you're reading this guest intro last as is SOP. If you're not, and so don't, then you have a brutal little treat in store.

trichome—hairlike or bristlelike outgrowth **Trimurti**—Hindu trinity

Hindu version of the trinity: sits in chair w/ three faces facing three

a common center (exotic sex resembling a triskelion) **triturate**—to

medicated or flavored tablet **truckle** (v.)—to be servile or submis

projection on which (e.g.) a cannon pivots; also fans, PC monitor **try**

roof panels **Tu enim Caesar civitatem dare potes hominibus, verbis**

to words" **uncus**—a hook-shaped part (biology); nose? toe? **uvuli**

(adj.)—relating to water that's above the groundwater table but in

valetudinarian—sickly, weak, morbidly health-conscious person

to hunting **venery**—pursuit or indulgence of sexual appetite; sexual

wormlike marks or carvings as on masonry **vermiferous**—wormy,

peratures to speed up plant development **vernation**—the arrange

before art exhibition opens **verso**—left-hand page of book **ves**

vidette—mounted sentinel stationed in advance of an outpost **vitu**

spiral scroll-like ornament as on Ionic column **welt**—raised seam be

whinstone—hard, dark kinds of stone like basalt and chert **widder**

wiggan—stiff fabric used for stiffening **windrow**—long row of cut hay

snow or leaves heaped up by wind **wonky**—shaky, feeble; wrong,

damage from devastation, violence/ruin **WYSIWYG** (adj.)—desktop-

will look like **wyvern**—(heraldry): a two-legged dragon w/ wings and

to talk coarsely or loudly **yean**—to bear young **yenta**—person/woman

the huge ash tree that holds together earth, heaven, and hell by its

of Brahma the creator, Vishnu the preserver, and Shiva the destroyer; different ways **triskelion**—figure w/ three arms or legs coming out of rub, crush, or grind into fine powder: to pulverize **troche**—small sive; (n.) bed w/ casters for rolling stuff **trunnion**—pin or cylindrical **square**—carpenter's right-angled ruler **T-top**—auto w/ removable **non potes**—saying: "Caesar, you can grant citizenship to men but not **tis**—inflammation of the uvula; special kind of sore throat **vadose** the ground **vail** (v.)—to doff cap; to lower your flag in submission **vaunt**—brag, boast; "an air of vaunt around him" **venatic**—of or related act **vermiculate**—wormish **vermiculation**—wormlike movements; worm-riddled **vernalization**—subjecting seeds or seedlings to low tem-ment of young leaves within a bud **vernissage**—private showing held **tal**—chaste, pure **videogenic**—like photogenic or telegenic but w/ video **perations**—angry remarks **volute**—spiral formation as in whelk shell; tween sole and upper of shoe **whelm**—to cover with water, submerge **shins/withershins**—in a counterclockwise or contrary direction or grain left to dry after harvest before bundling **windrow**—row of awry **woodbine**—climbing vine with yellowish flowers **wrack** (n.)—pub./computer term for screen showing exactly what the printed page a barbed tail **yashmak**—veil worn by Muslim women **yawp** (v.)—into gossip, meddling (Yiddish) **Yggdrasil**—in Norse mythology, roots and branches **ylang-ylang**—oil from Asian tree used in perfume

JUST ASKING

Q: Are some things worth dying for? Is the American idea[1] one such thing? Who's ready for a thought experiment? What if we chose to regard the 2,973 innocents killed in the terrorist attacks of 9/11 as heroes and martyrs, "sacrifices on the altar of freedom"?[2] That is, what if we decided that a certain minimum baseline vulnerability to terrorist attack is part of the price of the American idea? That ours is a generation of Americans called to make great sacrifices in order to preserve our way of life—not just of our soldiers and money on foreign soil, but

[1] Given the Gramm-Rudmanesque space limit here, let's all just agree that we generally know what this term connotes—open society, consent of the governed, enumerated powers, *Federalist* 10, pluralism, due process, transparency...the whole messy democratic roil.

[2] (The phrase is Lincoln's, more or less.)

the sacrifice of our personal safety and comfort? Maybe even of more civilians' lives?

What if we chose to accept the fact that every few years, despite everyone's best efforts, some hundreds or thousands of us may die in the sort of terrible suicidal attack that a democratic republic cannot 100 percent protect itself from without subverting the very principles that make it worth protecting?

Is this thought experiment monstrous? Would it be monstrous to refer to the 40,000-plus domestic highway deaths we accept each year because the mobility and autonomy of the car are worth the price? Is monstrousness why no serious public figure now will speak of the delusory trade-off of liberty for safety that Ben Franklin warned of more than 200 years ago? What exactly has changed between Franklin's time and ours? Why now can we not have a serious national conversation about sacrifice, the inevitability of sacrifice—either of (a) some safety or (b) some portion of the rights and liberties that make the American idea so precious?

Q: In the absence of such a conversation, do we trust our current leaders to revere and safeguard the American idea as they seek to "secure the homeland"? What are the effects on the American idea of Guantánamo, Abu Ghraib, PATRIOT Acts I and II, warrantless surveillance, Executive Order 13233, corporate contractors performing military functions, the Military Commissions Act, NSPD 51, etc., etc.? Assume for the moment that some of these really have helped make our persons and property safer—are they worth it? Where and when was the public debate on whether they're worth it? Was there no such debate because we're not capable of having or demanding one? Why not? Have we become so selfish and frightened that we don't even want to think about whether some things trump safety? What kind of future does that augur?

—2007

ACKNOWLEDGMENTS

The David Wallace Literary Trust and the publisher wish to thank Sam Freilich, Vanessa Kehren, Victoria Matsui, Steve Kleinedler, Margaret Anne Miles, and Joseph Pickett for their invaluable help.

COPYRIGHT ACKNOWLEDGMENTS

The following pieces were originally published in slightly different form in the following books and periodicals:

"Federer Both Flesh and Not," originally published as "Federer as Religious Experience" in the *New York Times,* 2006.

"Fictional Futures and the Conspicuously Young" in *The Review of Contemporary Fiction,* 1988. Some of the ideas and language in this essay appear in "E Unibus Pluram," *A Supposedly Fun Thing I'll Never Do Again,* Little, Brown, 1997.

"The Empty Plenum: David Markson's *Wittgenstein's Mistress*" in *The Review of Contemporary Fiction,* 1990.

"Mr. Cogito" in *Spin,* 1994.

"Democracy and Commerce at the U.S. Open" in *Tennis,* 1996.

"Back in New Fire," originally published as "Impediments to Passion" in *Might Magazine,* 1996.

"The (As It Were) Seminal Importance of *Terminator 2,*" originally published as "F/X Porn" in *Waterstone's Magazine,* 1998.

"The Nature of the Fun" in *Fiction Writer,* 1998.

"Overlooked: Five direly underappreciated U.S. novels > 1960" at Salon.com, 1999.

"Rhetoric and the Math Melodrama" in *Science.*

"*The Best of the Prose Poem: An International Journal,* ed. Peter Johnson" in *Rain Taxi,* 2001.

"Twenty-Four Word Notes," reprinted from the *Oxford American Writer's Thesaurus* with permission from Oxford University Press. Copyright © 2004, 2008, 2012 by Oxford University Press.

"Borges on the Couch" in the *New York Times Book Review,* 2004.

"Deciderization 2007—A Special Report," originally published as the introduction to *The Best American Essays 2007,* 2007.

"Just Asking" in *The Atlantic,* 2007.

ABOUT THE AUTHOR

David Foster Wallace was born in Ithaca, New York, in 1962 and raised in Illinois, where he was a regionally ranked junior tennis player. He received bachelor of arts degrees in philosophy and English from Amherst College; his senior English thesis, the novel *The Broom of the System*, was published in 1987, and his senior philosophy thesis was published as *Fate, Time, and Language* in 2010. He earned a master of fine arts at the University of Arizona. His second novel, *Infinite Jest*, was published in 1996. He also published the story collections *Girl with Curious Hair*, *Brief Interviews with Hideous Men*, and *Oblivion;* the essay collections *A Supposedly Fun Thing I'll Never Do Again* and *Consider the Lobster;* a book about hip-hop, written with his friend Mark Costello, *Signifying Rappers;* and a book about infinity, *Everything and More.* Over the years, Wallace taught at Emerson College, Illinois State University, and Pomona College. He was awarded the MacArthur Fellowship, a Lannan Literary Award, and the Whiting Writers' Award and served on the Usage Panel for *The American Heritage Dictionary of the English Language.* He died in 2008. His last novel, *The Pale King*, was published in 2011 and was a finalist for the Pulitzer Prize.